Divine Film Comedies

Divine Film Comedies creates a meaningful dialogue between stories in the Hebrew Bible and New Testament and comedies spanning the history of film. The text lies at the intersection of three disciplines: humor/comedy studies, film studies, and theology. Drawing on films from the silent era to the twenty-first century, the book highlights parallels between comedic sub-genres and sacred narratives, parables, and proverbs, illuminating a path to seeing and understanding both scripture and film through a comic lens. The book will be of interest to students and scholars of theology and film, media, and communications.

Terry Lindvall occupies the C. S. Lewis Chair of Communication and Christian Thought at Virginia Wesleyan College. He has authored ten books, including *God Mocks: A History of Religious Satire from the Hebrew Prophets to Stephen Colbert* (2015), *Surprised by Laughter: The Comic World of C. S. Lewis* (2012), and *Sanctuary Cinema: The Origins of the Christian Film Industry* (2011).

J. Dennis Bounds teaches courses in cinema and video at Virginia Wesleyan College and Christopher Newport University. He has presented workshops both nationally and internationally on screenwriting. Bounds has authored various articles and book chapters, and is the author of *Perry Mason: The Authorship and Reproduction of a Popular Hero* (1996).

Chris Lindvall is a graduate of the University of Virginia and received his MFA in Comedy Screenwriting from the Savannah College of Art and Design. He is presently an associate writer for Disney Studios in Southern California.

Routledge Studies in Religion and Film
Edited by Robert Johnston and Jolyon Mitchell

Available:

American Theology, Superhero Comics, and Cinema
Anthony Mills

Divine Film Comedies
Terry Lindvall, J. Dennis Bounds, and Chris Lindvall

Religion in Contemporary European Cinema
Edited by Costica Bradatan and Camil Ungureanu

The Silents of Jesus in the Early Cinema
Edited by David Shepherd

Transnational Cinema and Ideology
Milja Radovic

World Cinema, Theology, and the Human
Antonio Sison

Forthcoming:

Hermeneutic Humility and the Political Theology of Cinema
Sean Desilets

The Holy Fool in European Cinema
Alina Birzache

Theology and the Films of Terrence Malick
Edited by Christopher B. Barnett and Clark J. Elliston

Divine Film Comedies

Biblical Narratives, Film Sub-Genres, and the Comic Spirit

Terry Lindvall, J. Dennis Bounds, and Chris Lindvall

Routledge
Taylor & Francis Group

NEW YORK AND LONDON

First published 2016
by Routledge
711 Third Avenue, New York, NY 10017

and by Routledge
2 Park Square, Milton Park, Abingdon, Oxon, OX14 4RN

Routledge is an imprint of the Taylor & Francis Group, an informa business

© 2016 Taylor & Francis

The right of Terry Lindvall, J. Dennis Bounds, and Chris Lindvall to be identified as authors of this work has been asserted by them in accordance with sections 77 and 78 of the Copyright, Designs and Patents Act 1988.

Library of Congress Cataloging in Publication Data
Names: Lindvall, Terry, author. | Bounds, J. Dennis, author. |
Lindvall, Chris, author.
Title: Divine film comedies : biblical narratives, film sub-genres, and the comic spirit / Terry Lindvall, J. Dennis Bounds, and Chris Lindvall.
Description: New York : Routledge, 2016. |
Series: Routledge studies in religion and film
Identifiers: LCCN 2015035486
Subjects: LCSH: Motion pictures–Religious aspects. |
Comedy films–History and criticism. | Religion in motion pictures.
Classification: LCC PN1995.9.R4 L555 2016 |
DDC 791.43/682–dc23LC record available at
http://lccn.loc.gov/2015035486

ISBN: 978-1-138-95612-4 (hbk)
ISBN: 978-1-138-95613-1 (pbk)
ISBN: 978-1-315-66587-0 (ebk)

Typeset in Sabon
by Out of House Publishing

Dedicated to the inspired guidance of Robert Johnston and Fuller Theological Seminary in bridging the worlds of film and Christian faith and to Tensch Philips and Tom Vourlas for their committed and delightful service as the visionary proprietors of the NARO theatre in Norfolk, Virginia, for creating programs that explore faith and film.

Contents

Acknowledgments

One line of eulogy in Anglican minister Laurence Sterne's wildly digressive *Tristram Shandy* aptly captures the carefreeness of the authors. Describing the cheerful character of Parson Yorick, Sterne extolled him thus: "[H]e had but too many temptations in life, of scattering his wit and his humor, – his gibes and his jests about him." Alas, poor Yorick, we know him well, even in the mirror. If we become too insouciant or jocular in this text, it is not because of the good editors, but because the merry spirit of Yorick dwells too well in our bones (two Anglicans and a Baptist).

Terry Lindvall would like to acknowledge and thank the Louisville Institute, whose generous support of a research grant made this project (and one to follow) possible. J. Dennis Bounds would like to acknowledge the Virginia Beach Writers Group for reviewing early drafts of the research. Chris Lindvall thanks his funny family, his former writing adviser at Savannah College of Art and Design, the inimitable Chris Auer, and all his friends who have made him chuckle, titter, or chortle, and gives thanks especially to God, who gave the gift of mirth in the first place. And, of course, Dennis and Terry must thank their wives (Margaret and Karen, respectively) and daughters (Jamie, Anna, Kristen and Rachel, and then Caroline Lindvall), who keep them fully grateful for the joy and support they bring into their lives. We also thank Rob Johnston and Jolyon Mitchell for trusting imps to enter the hallowed world of Routledge and our quite witty editor, Christopher Feeney, who astutely corrected our egregious mistakes, saving us from some public folly.

We would also like to thank all the old mocking men with whom we have shared our indefensible opinions for over a score of years: Ben Fraser, Bill Brown, Gil Elvgren, George Selig, John Lawing, and Andrew Quicke.

Introduction

In Umberto Eco's medieval novel *The Name of the Rose*, a conspiracy of monks hides the existence of a second volume of Aristotle's *Poetics*, an apocryphal text that outlines the Greek philosopher's view of comedy.[1] The Venerable Jorge of Burgos, blind head librarian, tries to squelch the idea of comedy, even killing those who would betray the book's secrets. To prevent publication, the corners of its pages are laced with poison. Those who seek laughter are killed in the name of religion.

The cleric's argument is that the Church's authority rests on maintaining reverence and fear. Comedy, by its very mischievous nature, seeks to undermine that authority, enabling people to see from a different perspective.[2] Franciscan monk William of Baskerville (the rational Sherlock Holmes of the novel, following the scholastic tradition of St. Thomas Aquinas, who integrated Aristotle into theology) counter-argues for the book's necessary publication, even proposing that Jesus laughed and that the saints used ridicule to mock their enemies. The cloistered Benedictines and the Inquisition are not convinced by this argument, especially as it comes from one of the followers of the merry St. Francis of Assisi, *un jongleur de Dieu*, one of God's jesters. St. Francis once admonished his followers, "Let us leave sadness to the devil and his angels. As for us, what can we be but rejoicing and glad?"[3]

The problem of comedy in the academy or in the cloister or in the pulpit persists. It is unpredictable and subversive. But it can, as Eco points out, open the "operations of the belly" and then open those of the mind. Laughter can be a wholesome medicine for thought, an enema for ideas.

The notions that comedy can provide a corrective remedy to what ills us and that it can be a means by which grace comes into our lives underlie this quest of blending the life of Christian faith and laughter as they are communicated through films. Most works on theology and film focus upon more solemn works, from the heavy existential films of Ingmar Bergman (e.g. *The Seventh Seal*, 1957), the Roman Catholic suffering of Robert Bresson (e.g. *Diary of a Country Priest*, 1951), or the transcendental style of Bruce Beresford (e.g. *Tender Mercies*, 1983), not to mention all the overwrought biblical epics that privilege spectacle over

substance. Even *film noir*, horror, and Western films have garnered significant attention.[4] We have been encouraged to examine our faith in
genres apart from these, most of which are too frequently taken too solemnly (as if cinema held the primary myths that revealed ultimate meanings – we recall what Hitchcock told Ingrid Bergman, "Remember, it's
only a movie"). All films that entertain and challenge and signify tend to
puff themselves up as oracles at Delphi, somehow enabling a gnome like
"know thyself" to take flesh through pondering film images. But we are
forewarned not to chew whipped cream as if it were beef jerky.

Only film comedy, the lowest and most vulgar of the genres, the true
whipped cream of cinema, has been neglected, and that to our detri-
ment. According to Aristotle's *Poetics*, comedy suffered neglect for the
reason that it was not "at first, taken seriously."[5] Thus, seeing that comedy films are overlooked when it comes to thinking of faith, we throw
them out like banana peels to make us aware of how they celebrate
the falls and vicissitudes of our lives. The fictional Hollywood director
John L. Sullivan waxes eloquently in Preston Sturges' *Sullivan's Travels*
(1941), "There's a lot to be said for making people laugh. Did you
know that that's all some people have? It isn't much, but it's better than
nothing in this cockeyed caravan." Sturges' success is due in part to the
special humanity he gives to those people in the cockeyed caravan, his
"loony bevy of street folk, complete with their dialects, malapropisms,
and puppet-show like movements that inhabit his films."[6] Yet such characters are not puppets, but derive the fullness of their humanity from
being made in the very image of God, *imago Dei*. Out of God's essence
come His comic facsimiles.

Funny wears various costumes. From the motley cap to the wedding
gown, comedy dresses up in numerous sartorial forms. It also wears the
cowl and clerical collar. Under the general rubric of comic masks reside
at least 12 sub-genres, categories that emphasize peculiar aspects of the
entire wardrobe. Such scholars as Gerald Mast, Wes Gehring, Michael
Tueth, and others have capably classified these mini-offshoots of the
genre and we have borrowed merrily from them.

Our list covers the following: slapstick, adventure comedy, romantic/
screwball comedy, musical comedy, parody, character (*picaro*) comedy,
film blanc, *reductio ad absurdum*, anarchic comedy (including farce or
animal comedy), satire/black comedy, and mockumentary.[7] These categories overlap and co-mingle, but what else would we expect of a genre
that includes tricksters and clowns and whose *raison d'être* is, as Donald
O'Connor sang in *Singin' in the Rain*, "make 'em laugh; make 'em laugh;
make 'em laugh!"

As we hope to make evident, we see parallels among these sub-genres
with various sacred narratives, parables, and proverbs. We believe the
holy texts hold comic bits that expand our understanding of the religious

life and that a comic vision enables us to gain a heavenly perspective on the texts themselves. As far as religious comedies go, we found these types quite convenient for our reflections. The definition of religion which usually includes beliefs, myths, rituals, and morals derives from *religare*, namely to bind together, to re-connect. Referring to the communion of man and God (or the gods), the term will be, as long as the human is part of the relationship, potentially comic; for the human, although crowned in glory, will always fall short and be bathed in folly. Thus we find each of our sub-genres addressing issues of this relationship with the sacred and divine. Each one allows us to tease out some old understanding of our lives in the light of eternity.

Our perspective is rooted in theories of the comic, finding patterns, conventions, and concepts that unite biblical stories and film comedy sub-genres. However, what biblical scholars Mark Biddle and Doug Adams have done with humor in biblical stories is to open them up to fresh interpretive lenses, showing how certain texts invite laughter or a sense of irony in their telling. Herein we combine two aspects of the academic wedding the populist, showing how comedy is more closely connected to the tone of sacred writings and how film comedies communicate theological concerns that may well be ultimate.

Essentially they illumine each other and do so by way of humor. One does not expect to find laughter in holy places or to find theological truths in profane places; yet we argue that an understanding of comedy joins these two narrative disciplines. We think that as theologians rarely take their field (or themselves) lightly, and as critics rarely take film comedy seriously, we argue that both can be cross-fertilized. The comic brings together alternative but plausible readings of Bible stories and finds embedded theological truths in film comedies. Our case studies of particular cinematic texts find parallels in biblical forms and thus inform comic ways of seeing in both.[8] Of course, we also attend to Oscar Wilde's quip that "if you want to tell people the truth, make them laugh; otherwise they'll kill you."

Comedy, along with its companion laughter, was frequently castigated by religious leaders. The golden-tongued preacher St. John Chrysostom warned that it was the devil who gave us the chance to play. The strict Rule of St. Benedict commanded, "as for coarse jests and idle words or words that lead to laughter, these we condemn with a perpetual ban." Yet Evagrius listed *hilaritas* as one of the great virtues of the Church, one that countered the deadly sin of sadness. Pope Gregory the Great (who would reduce the deadly sins to vices) called the laughter of God at mockers, a "just laughter." He condemned the laughter of unbelief, against those who laughed sardonically when Jesus said a ruler's daughter was only sleeping. In his *Moralia*, he wrote that the laughter of the elect will radiate from the heart and not from the belly. However, by the

Middle Ages, the belly began to shake with laughter. Christian preaching emphasized a homiletic strategy of *ridendo dicere verum* (speaking the truth laughingly).[9] Some preachers, however, were comically described as roosters: they rise early, ascend a perch, crow loudly, take the best grain, and lay the hens.

But comedy became more integrated into the life of the saint, with poet William Dunbar calling for a celebration: "Man, please thy Maker, and be merry, And give not for this world a cherry." Christian humanist Erasmus sang *In Praise of Folly*, basing his work on St. Paul's text in I Corinthians: "God has made foolish the wisdom of this world." Erasmus warned of inviting a dull professor to a feast, as he will "mar the good cheer either by a morose silence or by conducting a quiz. Invite him to a ball and you learn how a camel dances." He knew that "fools furnish the one kind of thing that rulers are glad to get from any quarter and in any shape – jests, japes, laughter." His fellow cleric Rabelais daftly proposed that "to laugh is proper to man" while introducing his giant laughter makers and leading the Church in what Mikhail Bakhtin called "carnival," in celebration of the body, with all its grotesque, universal, ambivalent, and mostly vulgar bits.[10]

This is not to say that religious leaders trusted the Church to comedy. The inadvertent founder of Methodism, John Wesley, disciplined one of his preachers on the charges of adultery, heresy, and the man's tendency to "break a jest, and laugh at it heartily." Holiness and outbursts of humor were not seen as compatible, as one sought to have one's heart "strangely warmed" and not delightfully tickled.

Committed Christian and Englishman Lord Shaftesbury wrote an *Essay on the Freedom of Wit and Humor* (1709), where he championed: "Truth may bear all lights, [even] ridicule itself." "For what ridicule can lie against reason?" For Shaftesbury, the comic could expose immorality and imposture. After writing his name, he offered (in capital letters) three mischievous propositions as the religious basis of comedy.

First, he argued that wit and humor are corroborative of religion and promote true faith. He next pointed to how these rhetorical strategies were used by the holy founders of religion. Finally, he concluded, "notwithstanding the dark complexion and sour humors of some religious teachers, we may be justly said to have in the main a witty and good-humored religion." His insights were corroborated by a Holland House wit, clergyman Sydney Smith, who saw comedy as logic in masquerade. ("As the French say, there are three sexes – men, women and clergymen." He mentioned one female parishioner who "looked as if she had walked straight out of the ark.") So too author George Macdonald gently reminded his readers that it is "a heart that is not sure of its God that is afraid to laugh in His presence." Anything that is serious is worthy of humorous consideration and everything must be enjoyed in the presence of God.

By the 20th century, when the nickelodeon brought millions into the dream factory of the movies, wits like the Roman Catholic journalist G. K. Chesterton would extol the numerous virtues of laughter, quipping, "A good joke is the one ultimate and sacred thing which cannot be criticized. Our relations with a good joke are direct and even divine relations." It was this same risible saint who gave us our permission to interrogate our religion through the lens of film comedy when he reminded his readers that "It is the test of a good religion whether you can joke about it." We believe our faith to be not only true, but worthy of a good joke.

However, in approaching sacred writings, one does not force jokes into texts. One can easily twist Scriptures like Leviticus 3:16 (all fat is the Lord's) or Psalm 50:9 (where the Lord says "I will accept no bull from your house") for cheap laughs. But such Procrustean tactics are not needed. Biblical scholar J. William Whedbee identifies four interrelated characteristics of literary comedy structures appropriate for the Bible.[11] First, a comic perspective can be examined according to a plot line. If it ends with an integrated, mostly harmonious, happy ending, no matter what conflicts or difficulties occur at the beginning or throughout, it should be considered comic. Northrop Frye called the structure of harmony/disorder/happy ending a U-shaped plot, moving down into the depths before making everything right and good and blessed. Often the plot aims at transforming or redeeming the characters. Thus, comedies almost always end in marriages, births, or celebrations of some kind. For example, Roberto Rossellini's hagiographic *The Flowers of Saint Francis* (1950) celebrates the legends of St. Francis as God's Jester. At the end of the film, as he and his simple followers seek God's directions for their various ministries, Francis directs all his friars to turn around in circles until they are very woozy and wobbly. Whatever direction they giddily fall toward, that is God's direction for them to begin their journey. It is an innocent but dizzying bit of providence showing through the falls of men.

Second, characterizations of basic comic types appear. Conventional characters like clowns, fools, tricksters, rogues, and buffoons represent the human types in their various follies. Even animals (e.g. the sly serpent in the Garden or Balaam's simple but perceptive ass) can take on these roles. The key character here is Jacob, whose name means deceiver, trickster or *picaro*. Obtuse foreign rulers, like Nebuchadnezzar, are also shown to be very stupid, more so than the donkey.

Third, one finds linguistic games and jests that delight the reader. Hyperbole, word-play, puns (especially on names like Malachi, which means "my messenger"), discrepancy, incongruity, reversal, and surprise open up various experiences of laughter. Some are sardonic and mocking, in which the laughter is at someone else's expense. The foolish man who seeks to escape the lion and is then mauled by a bear or bitten by a snake in his own home is a ripe candidate for satire. The meaning of satire as something thrown at one's enemies (as Goliath satirizing David) is a linguistic strategy of throwing a demoralizing word before slashing with a decapitating sword. Yet even here, laughing at someone mostly seeks to restore that person back into the community, or celebrates the virtues against the folly of the vices.

While in Freud's estimation puns are the lowest form of verbal humor, puns on Hebrew names are ubiquitous. Everywhere you look, you will bump into a pun. For example, Adam (*adamah*) means soil; Cain (Genesis 4:9–14) is divinely ordained to become a wanderer and nomad, and travels to the land of Nod, which means Land of Wandering. Multiple plays on Noah appear as rest and *naham* as comfort/relief for this man of the soil who floats on water and plants a vineyard (what relief). The Tower of Babel parodies the act of creation, and of course refers to those who sought to become like God, but ended up "babbling" or confused. Most comic are the sons of Shem (i.e. "name") who want to make a *name* for themselves.

Finally, Whedbee calls readers to recognize multiple comic functions and intentions. Comedy both subverts the status quo and conserves social norms. It knocks down and builds up. Weapons of satire are used for comedies of deliverance, as foreign and false gods are mocked so that God's people can be seen as vindicated (e.g. Exodus 10:2).

Our task is to discern the comic patterns in these biblical narratives and to fathom the biblical meanings in comedy films. We confess that we enjoy these movies wholeheartedly. We might even say enthusiastically, derived from the idea of being enthused, *en theos*, in God. When we laugh with God, we find we confess our miserable humanity and receive the mercy which is given freely. Some of these films remind us of our co-authors' depravity. Most of these films inspire us to live better lives, to practice prayer and charity, to seek God, and to enjoy Him forever. "Life is a tragedy to those who feel," quipped British writer and innovative architect Horace Walpole, "but a comedy to those who think." We hope by our thoughts on Scriptures and films to encourage a vision of the world that is more comic than that usually espoused by authors on religion and film.

Notes

1 Umberto Eco, *The Name of the Rose* (Warner Books, 1980), 152. When the venerable Jorge asserts that Jesus did not laugh, the Franciscan Brother William of Baskerville counters with several examples of the Savior's wit.
2 See "Christian Laughter," in Andrew Stott, *Comedy* (Routledge, 2005), 121–124.
3 William Morrice, *Joy in the New Testament* (Eerdmans, 1984), 154.
4 Christopher Deacy, *Screening the Afterlife: Theology, Eschatology and Film* (Routledge, 2012); Douglas E. Cowan, *Sacred Terror: Religion and Horror on the Silver Screen* (Baylor University Press, 2008); Douglas Brode, *Dream West: Politics and Religion in Cowboy Movies* (University of Texas Press, 2013).
5 Aristotle, *Poetics*, in *Basic Works of Aristotle* (ed. Richard McKeon) (Random House, 1941).

6 Andrew Horton (ed.), *Comedy/Cinema/Theory* (University of California Press, 1991), 14.
7 Key sources dealing with typologies of comedy are Andrew Horton and Joanna E. Rapf (eds.), *A Companion to Film Comedy* (Wiley-Blackwell, 2013); Gerald Mast, *The Comic Mind: Comedy and the Movies* (Bobbs-Merrill Company, 1973), 4–9; Michael V. Tueth, *Reeling with Laughter: American Film Comedies from Anarchy to Mockumentary* (Scarecrow, 2012); and Terry Lindvall, "History of Film Comedy" and "Types of Film Comedy," in *Encyclopedia of Humor Studies* (ed. Salvatore Attardo) (Sage Publications, 2014), 520–522 and 522–528.
8 Amos N. Wilder, *Early Christian Rhetoric: The Language of the Gospel* (Harvard University Press, 1964).
9 See Terry Lindvall, *God Mocks: A History of Religious Satire from the Hebrew Prophets to Stephen Colbert* (New York University Press, 2015).
10 Mikhail Bakhtin, *Rabelais and His World* (ed. Helen Iswolsky) (Indiana University Press, 1984).
11 J. William Whedbee, *The Bible and Comic Vision* (Fortress Press, 2009).

1 Theological Assumptions of Religious Film Comedies

When the Lord told Moses to tell Aaron how to bless Israel, He laid down the format of the grand Hebrew blessing: "The Lord bless you and keep you; the Lord make his face shine on you and be gracious to you; the Lord turn his face toward you and give you peace" (Numbers 6:24–26). Central in this consecration of His people, God underscored this joyous nonverbal sign of the shining face, the *Shekinah* glory grinning at His own people. He looks upon His broken and wayward and weak people with gladness. He does not turn His face in shame, but shines and smiles and accepts these creatures covered in mud. Professor Maurine Sabine of the University of Hong Kong suggested that the depiction of God in movies, especially comedies, is a part of humanity's desire to understand divinity. "One could also say that this reflects a touching and altogether human desire to see God face to face," particularly if that face is one marked by laughter.[1]

We propose seven principles that underlie our understanding of the meeting of God's shining face, for seeing the Christian faith translated into film comedy. We believe these films can serve as icons, enabling us to look through them and not just at them, to see the goodness and grace of a God who revealed Himself in words and in flesh.

As will be evident, we opt for incongruity as the best explanation of the nature of comedy. As a set of theoretical concepts, an incongruity approach offers what Noel Carroll called an "eminently serviceable method for discovering the secret to the humor one encounters daily in the form of jokes, comic asides, cartoons, sitcoms, and so on."[2] For us, the comic is defined as the enjoyment of perceived incongruity, which includes everything from Monty Python's "And now for something completely different" to the platypus and honest lawyers.

First, we argue that laughter is divine in origin. The incongruity of the Trinity, of three persons in one, opens the Godhead to a lively set of juxtapositions among Father, Son, and Holy Spirit. The creative play of creation invites the laughter of fun, a romping and frolicking with the stars, the seas, and the mountains. All creation sings out with praise, with hills dancing and rivers clapping, with the Psalms painting the glory of its rejoicing. The old, odd German mystic Meister Eckhart could see that what goes on in the heart of the Trinity is laughter, as the Father's laughter unites Son and Spirit, and "the whole Trinity laughs and gives birth to us."[3] Perhaps it is a harbinger of the need for community to enable laughter to reach its full potential. A contagious laughter expands when two or three are together in His name. Even Sarah, giving birth to Isaac at a ripe old age, surrenders to its communal blessing and declares that everyone who hears of this birth will laugh with her.[4]

Second, the humor of incongruity in human nature existed before the Fall. Two sets of juxtaposed odd elements create the potential (and likelihood) for laughter. In the creation of humanity itself, God takes the humus of the earth and breathes His Spirit into it, creating that oxymoron, a spiritual animal, on one side related to angels and on the other side cousin to hyenas. Then, surveying His creation, He calls everything good except for one condition. It is not good, He intones "that man should be alone." That's only half of a good joke. Thus, the other grand incongruity of creation is that God split His image into two genders, so divinely alike and so hilariously different.

To exploit Aristotle's definition of the human, man becomes the only animal that weeps and laughs and knows that he weeps and laughs. One becomes conscious of the incongruity in life, that something isn't what it is supposed to be.

Third, this awareness of the cosmic discrepancy comes as the comic sours and darkens with the disobedience of Adam and Even. A bent laughter even characterizes God, whose laughter in the Psalms is heard by His wayward people mostly in derisive ways. God mocks, especially the proud and pretentious unbelievers. Laughter is affected by the Fall just as every other human experience is. One finds a creature that is not quite at home with herself. C. S. Lewis found evidence of the comic in this miserable state of being depraved. In fact, he saw coarse humor springing from such a rotten condition. Humor was spoiled and ruined like the Fall, just as sexual desire or self-worth was bent for selfish designs. Yet, like all other aspects of the human experience, humor can be redeemed.[5] While Jesus pronounced a judgment of woe upon those who laugh now, those who do not recognize the grace among them or those who mock the poor, He also promised laughter to those who weep now, who humbly recognize their need and seek the face that shines.

Fourth, the comic is scattered throughout the sacred texts and sacred history.[6] One finds the laughter of humor, farce, irony, and satire. Establishing Israel upon a foundation of laughter, God miraculously uses two very old people and sexual activity to beget His chosen people. He rhetorically asks "Why did Sarai laugh?" when she heard that she would be pregnant at 90 years old, in the desert, from a man who might finally give her pleasure. He knew the punchline would be Isaac, which in Hebrew translates as laughter, for He gave the name to the baby of the laughing couple. God Himself blended comedy with sex and marriage and set a precedent for all who would follow.

Playful laughter erupts in the rabbinical tradition over Moses' chutzpah in challenging God's inconsistent use of pronouns regarding Israel, much like a husband and wife arguing over their children. Yahweh called the Israelites His people when He sent Moses to deal with Pharaoh: "Come, I will send you to Pharaoh that you may bring forth *My* people, the Israelites, out of Egypt" (Exodus 3:10). But when Israel disobeys God, and worships the golden calf, God yells at Moses, "Go down, for *your* people, whom you have brought out of the land of Egypt, have corrupted themselves" (Exodus 32:7). Then Moses argues back: "Hey, God. You can't call them your people when they're good and my people when they're bad. Whether they're good or bad, they're still *Your* people!" Tradition has it that God laughed at the bold wit of Moses.[7]

When Rabbi Aryeh Kaplan was asked if there were any jokes in the Talmud, he replied drolly, "Yes, but they're all old."

The celebration of the Psalms and the wisdom of the Proverbs increased the laughter. In Israel's joyful return from captivity back to Zion, the Psalmist shouts that "we were like those who dream; then our mouth was filled with laughter and our tongue with singing" for all the great things God had done for them. They were glad with liquid laughter (Psalm 126:1–2). Proverbs reminds its young men that "a glad heart makes a cheerful countenance" (15:13); "a cheerful heart has a continual feast" (15:15); and "a cheerful heart is a good medicine" (17:22). The Hebrew life exudes the joy of living, robustness, a hearty, zesty comedy.

Humorous aphorisms, proverbs, and parables dot the pages of the Hebrew and Christian Scriptures, eliciting thoughtful laughter and amused insight. Many serve as Jonathan Swift's mirror for those who have eyes to see themselves, exposing folly in those who have ears to hear. While Bildad the Shuhite may not be the most dependable witness, he still observes rightly that God does not reject a blameless man, reminding Job that God would "yet fill your mouth with laughter and your lips with shouting" (Job 8:21).

Fifth, the redemption of laughter is connected to the redemption of every human experience. Its redemption comes in part through the incarnation, in the Word of God taking on flesh. In fact, the comic is more apparent in the incarnate Christ than in the Father: the Son's use of puns, paradox, riddles, slapstick behaviors (spitting in mud for a blind eye), satire (mocking the whitewashed sepulchers of the religious leaders), and the sheer pleasure that people receive in listening to his comic parables about goats, sheep, virgins, and wine. His rabbinic mode of answering questions with questions often seems mischievous and even offensive to those in authority. Yet people enjoyed His parables and women and little children were not only attracted to His presence, but took pleasure in His attention. There was something playful in this Man of Sorrows.

As it has been recorded, Jesus wept. But if Jesus could suffer and share in all our infirmities and weaknesses, could He not also laugh? Twice Jesus speaks of laughter. Those religious leaders and lawyers who laugh now will one day weep and gnash their teeth. However, the beatitude of Luke 6:21 blesses those that weep now: "for you shall laugh."

What is too often missing in Protestant circles is an appreciation of the oriental qualities of Semitic humor. Jesus played, albeit roughly, with religious leaders and rejected the dismal face (Matthew 6:16). Gaiety dances through the Gospel of Luke, so much so that little children wanted to be around Him.[8]

Religious wit and humor find their way into the film narratives of Sir Thomas More (*A Man for All Seasons*, Fred Zinnemann, 1966) and Martin Luther (*Luther*, Eric Till, 2003). In the former, the Cardinal Wolsey attempts to justify King Henry VIII's divorce from Catherine, arguing that "she's barren as a brick; are you going to pray for a miracle?" To which More responds, "There are precedents." In the latter, Luther gives a lecture to his students which turns into a stand-up routine:

> When I became a monk I believed the monk's cowl would make me holy. Was I an arrogant fool? Now they have made me a doctor of divinity and I am tempted to believe that this scholar's robe will make me wise [laughter]. Well, God once spoke through the mouth of an ass, and … [laughter], perhaps he is about to do so again. Eighteen out of twelve apostles are buried in Spain [laughter]. And yet here in Wittenberg we have the bread from the last supper, milk from the Virgin's breast, a thorn that pierced Christ's brow on Calvary and nineteen thousand other bits of sacred bone.

Sixth, comedy can help modern society rediscover the supernatural, or so at least sociologist Peter L. Berger has argued. In *A Rumor of Angels*, Berger outlines several "signals of transcendence," prototypical human experiences that point to a perception of a divine presence. Such gestures as "order" or "hope" or "damnation" provide arguments that we are not alone, that this material world is not all there is.

Two of his signals apply here: namely the gesture of "play" and the argument of "humor." Working from Dutch historian Johan Huizinga's studies on the ludic, i.e. the playful, Berger shows how the joyful activity of play enables us to step outside of time, giving us a taste of eternity, as one steps not only from "one chronology into another, but from time into eternity."[9] Even as one remains cognizant of death, and stumbling toward the inevitable grave, one recognizes that joy breaks out of time. As C. S. Lewis wrote eloquently in his sermon, "The Weight of Glory":

> [H]uman life has always been lived on the edge of a precipice. Men propound mathematical theorems in beleaguered cities, conduct metaphysical arguments in condemned cells, make jokes on scaffolds, discuss the last new poem while advancing to the walls of Quebec, and comb their hair at Thermopylae. This is not *panache*; it is our nature.

It is the nature of *homo ludens*, the creature that plays.[10] Time itself is suspended. In the midst of ordinary life, a dynamic moment of laughter stops the world in its spinning, and in this kairos of stasis, holds us enthralled.

For Berger and Lewis, the argument from humor departs from theoretical explanations offered by Sigmund Freud and Henri Bergson, who view and interpret the causes of laughter as, respectively, a discrepancy between superego and libido or between a living organism and non-organic mechanical behaviors. However, all agree that the comic is "fundamentally discrepancy, incongruity, incommensurability."[11] When Berger sees the great discrepancy between man and the universe, he recognizes the basic incongruity of the biblical person, in which "the comic reflects the imprisonment of the human spirit in the world." Comedy and tragedy are at root closely related. Commenting on Nazi concentration camps, David Rousett argued that the comic was "an objective fact that was *there* and could be perceived as such, no matter how great the inner terror and anguish of the mind perceiving it."[12]

Comedy thus "brackets" the tragedy of being human. What this implies is that this tragic or miserable imprisonment is not final, but will be overcome. "Humor mocks the 'serious' business of this world and those who try to carry it out." Particularly in the Christian realm, humor exposes the limits of power, as laughter points to something transcending reason, suffering, power, and death. As the old joke goes, "O Grave, where is thy victory? O Death, where is thy sting?" Rather than deify humanity, humor humbles it, showing it that it needs something beyond itself. And here, for Berger, erupts the truth that "the Fool is wiser than the Humanist."[13]

This implication leads, finally, to the promise of the comic, the coming of laughter in the eschaton. While the "four last things" augur death, judgment, hell, and heaven, it is the last of these that offers the end of the Christian experience. The spiritual journey of the Christian culminates in the comic expressions of a wedding and a feast. The world ends not in a bang or a whimper, but a celebration of laughter. In a rush of energy and love and jubilation, the bridegroom pursues the bride and brings her into

His tent. The Kingdom of God challenges the false idols of this world, and dents the perception of humor as sacrilegious.

In seeking to reclaim humor for the heart of theology, Doris Donnelly emphasizes how incongruity offers a holy site of intersection where it is possible to see Scripture and the Christian pilgrimage through a comedic lens. Humor is a gift that functions as a

> precondition to holiness; in order to be holy one much must get one-self out of the way and allow ourselves to see ourselves as we really are. Humility and humor must go hand in hand. Humor points us humbly toward the Holiness of God. God gives us gifts of balance, perspective and opportunities for creativity through the blessing of humor.[14]

Humor offers a fresh and vibrant hermeneutical key to understanding grace and holiness.

Following Donnelly, Roy Eckardt examines human laughter as a response of forgiveness and a means to reconciliation. Laughter, with eternity on its side, defies and protests the *telos* of Auschwitz.[15] It allows a person the opportunity to transcend the tragic and irrational bumps in life, providing perspective and balance. Fred Layman pointed out that those who have suffered and been oppressed find hints of self-preservation in and through humor. In the promise of liberation and in redemption, laughter offers an eschatological joy, laughter not of cynicism or despair, but one of hope and faith. In *One Flew Over the Cuckoo's Nest*, Ken Kesey has his irrepressible character McMurphy observe as he entered the insane asylum that the first thing that got him about that place was "There wasn't anybody laughing. I haven't heard a real laugh since I came through that door.... Man, when you lose your laugh, you lose your footing."[16]

Christian martyr Dietrich Bonhoeffer distinguished between ultimate and penultimate things in our lives. The one offense that the gods cannot endure is that mortals should forget that they are mortals. Laughter is thus related to the Christian virtue of humility, of not thinking too highly of ourselves, of not thinking of ourselves. Laughter can help save us from being pompous or pretentious or proud. There is constantly a need for this comic perspective, a point of view outside the self that pokes the self in the ribs. In all of Karl Barth's *Church Dogmatics*, there is only one page by the great Swiss theologian on the topic of humor; elsewhere, he humorously captures the place of humility:

> The angels laugh at old Karl. They laugh at him because he tries to grasp the truth about God in a book of *Dogmatics*. They laugh at the fact that volume follows volume and each is thicker than the previous one. As they laugh, they say to one another, "Look! Here he

comes now with his little pushcart full of volumes of the *Dogmatics*!" And they laugh about the men who write so much about Karl Barth instead of writing about the things he is trying to write about. Truly, the angels laugh.[17]

Earlier, Danish Christian writer Søren Kierkegaard employed the comic in his writings to break those illusions into which we immerse ourselves. If we feel good, look good, or appear good, we live under poetic illusions (those moods and feelings which indicate we are living a satisfactory life), practical illusions (that sense of achievement, hard work, virtue, respectability, success, or status that gives evidence that we have obtained the good life), or speculative illusions (the notion that if we read, think, and talk about ethical or religious matters, we are good). All three need to be subverted and laughter helps do that.

In one of his own parables, Kierkegaard speaks of being caught up into the seventh heaven.

> There sat all the gods in assembly. By special grace I was granted the privilege of making a wish. "Wilt thou," said Mercury, "have youth or beauty or power or a long life or the most beautiful maiden or any of the other glories we have in the chest? Choose, but only one thing." For a moment I was at a loss. Then I addressed myself to the gods as follows: "Most honorable contemporaries, I choose this one thing, that I may always have the laugh on my side." Not one of the gods said a word; on the contrary, they all began to laugh. From that I concluded that my wish was granted, and found that the gods knew how to express themselves with taste; for it would hardly have been suitable for them to have answered gravely: "Thy wish is granted."[18]

So, we too come before the gods in the gallery, the critics who sit in the cheap seats for whom peanuts are ambrosia and nectar, and set forth our show, our own spiritual journeys into the dark lands of movie comedies, hoping to find traces of God's presence in the midst of laughing voices.[19]

Notes

1 We are aware of a physiological progression to full bodily laughter, from the underwear muscle of the zygomatic major (which is the most insincere, employed, for example, in saying "nice sermon, pastor"), to the orbicularis oculi (that fine sheathe of muscles around the eyes which gives genuineness to our smiles), the frontal and platysma muscles (which open the face up and down so that one looks like a jolly lunatic), which is then followed by contractions of the intercostal, diaphragm and inter-laryngeal muscles, all preceded by microseconds with a slight tightening of the anal sphincter (which God built in; otherwise we would be laughing at both ends). The following

stages of kinesic, auditory, and communal actions lead to a grand upheaval of the body, with falling to the ground, slapping strangers, and often with some liquids passing indecorously out of the body or the nose.

2 Noel Carroll, *Humour: A Very Short Introduction* (Oxford University Press, 2014), 2.

3 Meister Eckhart, "Laughter and God," Society of the Sacred Heart of Jesus, online at www.societyofsacredheart.org/spirituality/laughter-and-god?start=1 (accessed January 3, 2014).

4 Terry Lindvall, *The Mother of All Laughter: Sarah and the Genesis of Comedy* (Broadman and Holman, 2003).

5 Peter L. Berger, *Redeeming Laughter: The Comic Dimension of Human Experience* (Walter de Gruyter, 1997).

6 Mark E. Biddle, *A Time to Laugh: Humor in the Bible* (Smyth and Helwys, 2013).

7 Belden C. Lane, "God Plays Rough for Love's Sake," *Christian Century* **104** (October 14, 1987), 880.

8 Elton Trueblood, *The Humor of Christ* (Harper & Row, 1964), 32.

9 Peter L. Berger, *A Rumor of Angels: Modern Society and the Rediscovery of the Supernatural* (Doubleday Anchor, 1970), 58.

10 C. S. Lewis, *The Weight of Glory* (HarperCollins, 1980), 46.

11 Bergson is closer to Berger and Lewis when he defines a situation as "invariably comic when it belongs simultaneously to two altogether independent series of events and is capable of being interpreted in two entirely different meanings at the same time." Berger, *Rumor of Angels*, 69–70; see Henri Bergson, *Laughter* [1900] (trans. Cloudesley Brereton and Kenneth Rothwell), repr. in *Comedy* (ed. Wylie Sypher) (Doubleday Anchor, 1956).

12 Berger, *Rumor of Angels*, 70.

13 Ibid., 73.

14 Doris Donnelly, "Divine Folly: Being Religious and the Exercise of Humor," *Theology Today* **48**:4 (January 1992), 1–14.

15 A. Roy Eckardt, "Divine Incongruity: Comedy and Tragedy in a Post-Holocaust World," *Theology Today* **48**:4 (January 1992), 399–412.

16 Ken Kesey, *One Flew Over the Cuckoo's Nest* (Signet, 1963), 65.

17 *Antwort: Karl Barth zum siebzigsten Geburtstag am 10. Mai 1956* (ed. E. Wolf, C. von Kirschbaum, and R. Frey) (Evangelischer Verlag, 1956), 895, cited in his own translation in R. M. Brown, *The Pseudonyms of God* (Westminster Press, 1972).

18 Søren Kierkegaard, "A," from *Either/Or*, in *A Kierkegaard Anthology* (ed. Robert Bretall) (Modern Library, 1946), 36.

19 "Gods in the Gallery," *Los Angeles Herald* **45**:37 (November 17, 1895), 20.

2 Slapstick Comedy

When God told Abraham that at the age of 100 he was going to be a father, the old geezer fell down on his face and laughed. It was a scene worthy of an early silent slapstick comedy. Buster Keaton couldn't have taken a better pratfall.

The cause of the fall was God's joke on Abraham, a joke that involved sex, surprise, and faith. Some opine that Abraham laughed out of disbelief, but whether it was from sheer incredulity or from the basic hilarity of the incongruous idea of Sarah breastfeeding in the geriatric ward, the joke of God caught him off guard and he fell over. Even more, Sarah laughed, with full earthiness, wondering if she was going to have the pleasure of Abraham in her nineties when she never had it in her thirties. As the old Yiddish joke goes, Abraham comes home and announces to Sarah: "We've waited so long and been so patient that God has promised us Super Sex tonight." Sarah looks at her drooping old man and says, "At your age, take the soup." What strikes the reader is that God both crowns Abraham and Sarah in glory and then bathes them in laughter, with a divine folly.

Falling down is funny. Chesterton observed that when a leaf falls, we do not laugh, but when a man falls down in the middle of the street, we laugh. Slapstick comedy, with its chases, pratfalls, and pies in the face, reminds one of the common denominator of human beings. Although made in the image of God, both male and female, we are made from earth, from the *humus* that gives rise to humor and humanity and humility. Slapstick comedy keeps us on our knees and our faces. It reminds us that we are creatures, prone to slip and fall and be picked up again. Harking back at least to the *commedia dell'arte*, slapstick devices create maximum noise with minimal striking force: "Two slats of wood are hinged at one end so that when its trajectory is halted on or near the victim's body, the back slat strikes the front slat, creating a loud smacking sound."[1]

Slapstick comedy offers broad physical mayhem, boisterous pranks, and exaggerated farce, mostly derived from *commedia dell'arte*. It involves a bit of clownish violence of slipping or tripping or colliding.

It is as subtle as landing on one's backside or spitting out a mouthful of water. It is the comedy of the body, roaring fun with 180-degree somersaults, rough and tumble pratfalls, silly walks, eye pokes, finger slams, and double takes. It is the falling of man and woman.

G. K. Chesterton explained it this way:

> We do not laugh at the mere fact of something falling down; there is nothing humorous about leaves falling or the sun going down. When our house falls down we do not laugh. All the birds of the air might drop around us in a perpetual shower like a hailstorm without arousing a smile. If you really ask yourself why we laugh at a man sitting down suddenly in the street you will discover that the reason is not only recondite, but ultimately religious. All the jokes about men sitting down on their hats are really theological jokes; they are concerned with the Dual Nature of Man. They refer to the primary paradox that man is superior to all the things around him and yet is at their mercy.[2]

Comedy is produced whenever a man acts like a machine, French philosopher Henri Bergson noted. The inelasticity of a divinely created human who falls like a tree, pops up like a toaster, or slaps like a stick shows what Bergson defined as the comic, namely when the mechanical is encrusted upon the living. It is in the incongruity of spirit and matter, of a human being who allows stimulus/response rather than thought to dictate his actions.

Such comic effect of a theological incongruity sneaks into the tramp films of Charlie Chaplin, the lowest of the lot. The Christian faith provides perspectives on his antics, particularly in adding pathos to the laughter. The spirit and body are wonderfully mixed.

Chaplin's life seems to have walked out of a Charles Dickens novel. The poverty, suffering, bouts of depression, and anguish of being abandoned by a drunken father and untended by a mother who was repeatedly institutionalized in the Cane Hill lunatic asylum, shaped his sympathy with the down and out.[3] Charles Spencer Chaplin was the Tramp, a child of the workhouse and a waif from the street. His antipathy for the cold cruelty of social welfare institutions and the bureaucrats who ran them would seep into his films.

While such tragedies of his personal life paralleled his artistic life, he also confessed to having a Christ fixation. Religion was anathema to him, but the love of the Galilean haunted him. His production of *The Circus* offered a Christocentric perspective on the Tramp, one who sacrificed for others.[4]

Chaplin's early films for Mack Sennett were rough, full of butt comedy (i.e. kicks in the posterior, later known as anal comedy), but previewed his talent for mixing heart with gags. By the time he directed *Easy Street* for Mutual in 1917, he had honed his character of baggy pants, derby, whirling cane, and toothbrush moustache into the loveable trickster.

Urban centers crowded with immigrants were rife with poverty, corruption, and moral degradation. They reflected the engraved images of William Hogarth's Beer Street and Gin Lane. Chaplin took such a crime-infested street and created a humorous romp, testifying to how it could be turned around for good with a little religion, justice, and American persistence. Three religious bits played for comedy reveal something of the efficacy of the social gospel of the time.

First, the film sympathizes with the poor and outsider. It is the least, the lost, and the last that Christ came to save. One might add the little, as the biblical tax collector Zacchaeus was a wee little man who was rescued from a tree and led by Jesus to his home "for tea." The Tramp represents such a marginal character that makes up the Kingdom of God.

Second, the film comically but kindly portrays the social gospel movement in action. In the midst of a suffering world, Progressive Protestants like Washington Gladden and Walter Rauschenbusch aimed at fulfilling the phrase of the Lord's Prayer, "may Your will be done on **earth** as it is in heaven." They sought to bring the justice and grace of God to this world, not only proclaiming the gospel for salvation, but promoting social righteousness, shelter, nurturing, and spiritual fellowship for the children of God. The goal was to establish the Kingdom of God on earth, here and now. In fiction, the works of Congregational minister Charles Sheldon shaped the vision of the social gospel, coining the phrase "What Would Jesus Do?" as a question in his novel *In His Steps* (1897).

Easy Street works out that question, as its Mission invites the alcoholic, the abused, and the aimless into a refuge for outcasts. (Another livelier Mission appears in Harold Lloyd's *For Heaven's Sake*, where the do-good millionaire not only rescues the financially strapped mission, but gathers a congregation of miscreants and thieves and gets them to sing hymns and donate their stolen goods on an offering plate. He enables the poor and criminal to escape arrest and remember their mothers.)

Third, the film illustrates the reformation of a useless character into a socially responsible citizen. Charlie will become not only the enforcer of the law, but a model of grace and civility.

The film opens with a derelict Charlie asleep on a stoop outside the Hope Mission. He "hears" angelic singing and enters the mission. His spiritual awakening comes as much from a beatific glance at the comely Mission worker (Edna Purviance) as from an incomprehensible sermon. Gags appear during Charlie's participation in the service. First, he must sit by a drunk who sings loudly, but smells horribly. Second, he is asked to hold a baby, and as he cradles the child, he holds its bottle upside-down and erroneously thinks it has wetted him. Finally he steals the offering box, only to humorously give it back once he is "saved." Humorous human elements keep the religious experience from becoming too pious or sappy.

Charlie is redeemed and reformed and decides to become a policeman in order to help clean up Easy Street. Joining a beleaguered police force, bullied by local thugs on Easy Street, Charlie finds that divine protection keeps him from being pulverized himself, as he deals with overpopulated rooms, doped fiends, feeding the hungry, and protecting women.

After several humorous battles with the tough guy (Eric Campbell), involving a gas lamppost to anesthetize and vanquish him, he brings order and security to the slum street. However, when the Bully breaks out of jail, he must contend again to restore safety, especially his own. At one point, he is accidentally hopped up with dope and in the resulting frenzy, overpowers the hoodlums. God works in mysterious ways. Being chased throughout the film, he finally subdues the Bully, finding a comic use for a cast-iron stove. The Bully is himself transformed into a model citizen, one that even walks on the outside of the sidewalk when taking his woman to church.

It is significant that the slapstick ends up in church. All the lowlife finds community not in violence, but in a new faith center. Charlie is eventually able to clean up the street and guide his fellow sinners into the New Hope Mission. The social gospel has been realized with remarkable success.

Film historians consider *Easy Street* (1917) to be the best of Chaplin's Mutual films.[5] Even the critics of the day found the film to be "furnished with hearty laughter" and filled with "diversions [which] make for a merry evening."[6] Julian Johnson of *Photoplay*, however, did find the "burlesquing of a rescue mission" at the beginning of the film in poor taste.[7] This critic was not tolerant of even the hint of condescension when directed at the Church. Mocking a rescue mission was still taboo at this time; within a few years that would change.

Comedy film historian Gerald Mast found the whole idea of the plot to be "strange" for Chaplin and did not consider him to be one to "promote beatific ideals and moral uplift" or assume the role of "social savior."[8] He felt that the whole film was ironic and the supposedly happy ending was nothing more than an ironic statement about "the hope and the reality [that the film portrayed] [being] permanently irreconcilable." For Mast, Chaplin was pulling a grand "Pollyannaish hoax." The present authors disagree and feel that the ending holds up and can be taken, not as ironic, but as another example of the social gospel's (and the Salvation Army's) influence on the creative efforts of filmmakers such as Chaplin and the expectations of the film audience. Chaplin was fascinated by Charles Dickens and parallels his happy turn of events for orphans and the destitute. There seems to be more wish fulfillment in the film than irony, as the film closes with an inspirational title card: "Love backed by force, forgiveness sweet, Brings hope and peace to Easy Street." It may be utopian,

Figure 2.1 An escaped convict, Charlie Chaplin, disguised as a minister, is called to improvise a pantomime sermon on David and Goliath in *The Pilgrim*, Charles Chaplin Productions, 1923. Author's screenshot.

but it consistently completes the opening of the Hope Mission with a New Hope Mission.[9]

Moving on to First National for more money and creative control, Chaplin did attack the hypocrisy of bourgeois church bureaucrats, even as he celebrated the simple gospel and its childlike reception in *The Pilgrim* (1923). The vagabond Charlie is an escaped convict, a wistful funny little figure, who steals the clothes of a clergyman and is mistaken for a new pastor in town. As such, he expected to give his first sermon in the church of Devil's Gulch.[10]

Chaplin trying to act as a chaplain to a staid congregation offers several very funny bits. Among a bevy of vigilant Carrie Nation prohibitionists, a "large Deacon" (Mack Swain), with a whiskey bottle hidden in his back pocket, picks up the masquerading minister on Sunday morning and takes him directly to the church. When he enters he sees 12 members in the choir loft, which he misinterprets as his courtroom jury. When a Bible is presented to him, he raises his right hand as if promising to tell the truth before questioning. Several jigs with a collection box and Charlie's naïve pleasure as an audience member in the choir's singing are preludes to a delightful biblical pantomime on David and Goliath.

At first, Charlie does not realize that he is the main "performer" for the Sunday service.[11] He shows sheer delight in putting his foot on the altar/bar rail of the church and sitting with the rest of the congregation to see what is about to happen. Informed that it is his time to preach, he engages a bored young boy whose imagination is fired by Charlie's tour de force miming of the biblical battle of the small Jewish boy and his

Philistine nemesis. As such, it stands as a trope for all of Chaplin's comedies of the underdog fighting against seemingly insurmountable odds. With large gestures, he pantomimes how big Goliath, his moustache and his sword were. David is little and with his sling-shot (windmill, wind-up gestures) brings down the mighty giant. Cutting off the Philistine's head, he tosses it over his shoulder, and back kicks it away. Then he bows to his stunned music hall congregation.

The Pilgrim offers an ambiguous ending of grace, as Charlie is revealed as a jailbird, but showing redemptive potential, is taken to the Rio Grande to escape to Mexico. However, as violence erupts on the other side, he straddles the law and anarchy, never finding the world in which he fits. He is a stranger in a strange land, a pilgrim on his way.

Chaplin's relationship to religion was complex and ambiguous. Scholar Constance Brown Kuriyama sees a fusion of tragedy and comedy as the key to survival.[12] The idea of comedy rooted in suffering Chaplin credited to Max Eastman's *The Enjoyment of Laughter*. Kuriyama identifies the roots of Chaplin comedy as twofold: severe bouts of depression stemming from his childhood and a Christ fixation. Chaplin himself maintained that "comedy was based on conflict and pain, and was therefore a transformation of pain into pleasure." The little Tramp was a means to rid himself of his demons. He was, in Flannery O'Connor's words, "haunted by Christ."[13]

The haunting is most evident in his first feature film, bleeding with autobiographical elements, *The Kid* (1921). Chaplin and his young wife Mildred Harris had just lost their three-day-old son. Feeling estranged from his young wife and finding his creative instincts frozen, he yet proceeded to write and direct this pathos-saturated film. Comedy often begins with tragedy, with Roman rhetorician Cicero advising that if you want your audience to end up laughing, you first get them to cry or feel sorrow. A theology of tears precedes one of rejoicing even as the sounds of celestial laughter ring after a journey through suffering and pain.

The Kid is rooted in Chaplin's own impoverished background, when he had been sent to an orphanage because of the instability of his family and the insanity of his mother. The film offers a tribute to his mother (and all mothers), evoking his customary pathos with its opening title announcing, "A comedy with a smile – and perhaps a tear." Edna Purviance stars as the Mother, framed by a stained-glass window that sanctifies her with a halo (a likely homage to the Madonna).[14] She leaves a charity hospital, a venal social institution run by heartless people, with her newly born son, realizing she is unable to provide for him. After an inter-title describing the Mother "whose only sin is motherhood," she is associated with Christ through a superimposed image of the suffering Lord carrying his cross up to Calvary.[15] Dejected, Edna passes a wedding at St. Stephen's Church and then smuggles her baby into a limousine, with a note entreating the owner to "please love and care for this orphan child."[16] The limo is stolen by thieves who dump the baby beside a garbage can.

Charlie the Tramp forages for food in the same alley, as people toss garbage from their windows. When he finds the baby among the refuse, he looks up in wonder. Nevertheless, after trying to rid himself of this bundle, the man without anything takes the orphan and makes a home for him in his humble hovel.

Interdependent bonds grow between Charlie and the kid (Jackie Coogan) as they share hotcakes and pray grace over them. The two conspire to break and fix windows until a copper sees what they are doing.

Edna has by this time become an opera star who does charity work in the slums, diligently seeking her own lost child. Charity, which is a duty to some, is a "joy" to her. Edna gives generously and hilariously. At one point she sits on a doorstep holding another woman's baby, when her Kid shows up sitting behind her. In an evocatively moving scene, she gives him a toy dog and an apple.

Coming upon Charlie and a ruffian fighting, with Charlie saying a quick prayer to be rescued, she admonishes them to heed the words of Jesus and remember "if he smites you on one cheek, offer him the other." As the Bully offers Charlie his other cheek, Charlie beans him with a brick, over and over again.

Discovering a note that had been left with the Kid, authorities come to take him to the orphan asylum. When Social Services arrive to take the boy away from Charlie a knock-down fight occurs, with the Kid thrown in the back of a truck, clasping his hands in desperate prayer for help. Charlie is able to thwart the bureaucrats and rescues the boy. As they escape to a flophouse, Charlie sneaks the boy in. The suspicious supervisor investigates just as the Kid kneels beside their single bed to say his prayers. When the overseer looks for him, he hides under the bed, then under the covers, but is finally found out and Charlie must pay the extra penny. The mixture of piety and slapstick is quite engaging, eliciting both sympathy and hilarity.

Ironically, a sign in the flophouse warns "MANAGEMENT NOT RESPONSIBLE FOR VALUABLES STOLEN." When the proprietor reads of a thousand-dollar reward for the lost child, he steals Charlie's most valuable belonging.

Charlie wakes and panics. Exhausted, he slips off to Dreamland, where everyone in the same slum neighborhood wears wings, plays harps, and dances about. Even a dog has wings and flies. The Kid with wings tickles Charlie's nose with a feather. Charlie goes shopping to a Jewish merchant for his own set of angelic wings with which he can soar and spin about. However, "sin sneaks in" as St. Peter sleeps by the gate. Three devils enter in and tempt Lita Grey, a lovely 12-year-old angel, to "vamp" Charlie. While her boyfriend is away, she shows Charlie a little leg. Another devil whispers into Charlie's ear and he goes on to be naughty with her. When

Figure 2.2 Even in Chaplin's dreamworld of heaven, the devil inveigles his way into paradise to tempt the Tramp with a little bit of lust for Lita Grey. *The Kid*, Charles Chaplin Productions, 1921. Author's screenshot.

her boyfriend returns, he is serene at first, until another devil incites jealousy. A huge fight ensues, with feathers flying everywhere and when Charlie tries to escape, he is shot down by the law. The dream sequence portrays Charlie's separation from his beloved child and there being no peace even in paradise.

The Kid by this time has been reunited with his mother, finding his true home. When a policeman wakes Charlie from his dream, he takes him to the home, where he is also welcomed in through the front door. The loss of his own child, the "little Mouse," inspired him to make a film entitled *The Waif* which became *The Kid*, with Charlie as a surrogate father for an abandoned child. Chaplin gave himself a Christ-like image – of one who would sacrificially give up "his son" for another.

Chaplin once declared himself to be an atheist, daring "God to strike him dead," yet *Easy Street*, *The Pilgrim*, and *The Kid* are replete with biblical imagery. Chaplin had also considered playing the role of Christ in Papini's *Life of Christ* or Hartmann's *The Last Thirty Days of Christ* – which would have caused an uproar in the religious community.

In 1915 poet Vachel Lindsay excluded Charlie Chaplin from his Museum of the Photoplay Art, even though it was rumored that Chaplin had a soul. Lindsay did not like his vulgar work, but admitted his enviable laurels; he might invite him in as a "tentative adviser, if not a chastened performer … and make sure he has eaten of the mystic Amaranth Apples of Johnny Appleseed." Charlie was frequently attacked for both his vulgarity and immorality.

An adoring sketch of Chaplin's mother, Mrs. Charles Hill Chaplin, Hannah, emerges from his autobiography. Separated from Chaplin's father, impoverished, and losing her voice (she had been a variety stage soubrette), she "turned to religion, in the hope, I suppose, that it would restore her voice"[17] and her fortunes. Chaplin remembered her faith with fondness as a model of the heart's perseverance in the face of tremendous odds. In her weakness, her faith yet affirmed the religious virtue of Christ in His compassion and loving kindness.

Chaplin remembers her reading to him one afternoon as he lay in bed with a fever.

> It was late afternoon, and she sat with her back to the window reading, acting and explaining in her inimitable way the New Testament and Christ's love and pity for little children. Perhaps her emotion was due to my illness, but she gave the most luminous and appealing interpretation of Christ that I have ever heard or seen. She spoke of His tolerant understanding; of the woman who had sinned and was to be stoned by the mob, and of His words to them: "He that is without sin among you, let him cast a stone at her."
>
> She read into the dusk, stopping only to light the lamp, then told of the faith that Jesus inspired in the sick, that they had only to touch the hem of His garment to be healed.
>
> She told of the hate and jealousy of the High Priests and Pharisees, and described Jesus and His arrest and His calm dignity before Pontius Pilate. ... And from the cross looking down at His mother, saying: "Woman, behold thy son." And in His last dying agony crying out: "My God, why hast Thou forsaken me?" And we both wept.
>
> "Don't you see," said Mother, "how human He was; like all of us, He too suffered doubt."
>
> Mother had so carried me away that I wanted to die that very night and meet Jesus. ... In that dark room in the basement at Oakley Street, Mother illuminated to me the kindliest light this world has ever known, which had endowed literature and the theatre with their greatest and richest themes: love, pity and humanity.[18]

She also detested religion without compassion. Chaplin recounts her indignation at one Reverend John McNeil, an evangelist, who had gone to visit Chaplin's father, then in hospital dying from alcoholism. The Reverend said, "Well, Charlie [Sr.], when I look at you, I can only think of the old proverb: 'Whatsoever a man soweth, that shall he also reap.'"[19] Chaplin sums up his mother's religion as such, "Although religious, she loved sinners and always identified herself with them. Not an atom of vulgarity was in her nature. Whatever Rabelaisian expression she used, it was always rhetorically appropriate."[20] He saw her as a sincere, dignified woman with a sense of tasteful earthiness.

"I cannot believe that our existence is meaningless or accidental, as some scientists tell us." As he grew older he became more preoccupied with faith, particularly as a precursor of all our ideas: "To deny faith is to refute oneself and the spirit that generates all our creative forces."[21] His faith was "in the unknown, in all that we do not understand by reason." Chaplin believed that in that unknown existed an infinite power for good. While he did not believe in religion or Christianity, he remained fascinated by Christ and the New Testament (although he thought the Hebrew Bible too full of "horrific cruelty degrading to the human spirit").[22]

Chaplin's religion, like his mother's, included love and pity for the poor and weak and for children. What struck him deeply was Christ's forgiveness of the adulterous woman, His healing of the sick, and His hatred of hypocrisy. But as Hannah lost touch with reality, losing her mind due to malnourishment when Chaplin was only seven, she went to Cane Hill lunatic asylum and he was sent to a workhouse. It seemed that only a loving God would visit her in her distress.

For Chaplin, God and women would be intertwined. In *Easy Street* when the Tramp first sees Edna, the preacher's daughter, she is playing the organ, hair backlit in a nimbus glow. He repents and prays. Edna is the Madonna of Easy Street. *The Kid* opens with Edna the nameless woman, whose sin was motherhood, standing before the charity hospital: the sudden frozen image of Christ bearing a cross in hazy counterpoint to the woman and her infant burden.[23] Three images meshed from Chaplin's memory: Madonna and child, the crucifixion scene with Christ speaking to his mother, and the adulterous woman whom Christ forgave, all meshed together.

Ruth Perlmutter described Chaplin as the wandering Jew, "forever condemned to wandering in alien cultures."[24] He was the pilgrim Everyman who could squeeze a tear from a mother and a laugh into a sermon.[25] He could turn the slapstick of a tumble or a kick in the behind into a confession of one's fall into comedy, where someone waited to pick him up and redeem him through loving laughter.

When Chaplin produced *The Circus* (1928), he thought of calling it *The Clown* and compared it to a film on the life of Christ:

> If I could produce a film on the story of Christ, I would show him welcomed with delirious joy by men, women, and children; they would throng round him in order to feel his magnetism. Not at all a sad, pious, and stiff person, but a lonely man who has been the most misunderstood of all time.[26]

Theologian Ronald Holloway argues for the importance of Chaplin, whose facility with music hall slapstick, horseplay and miming, sudden action, quick turn of events, and something unexpected revived the importance of play and humility in the presence of God. Even his costume captured the essence of the sinful publican who comes to God without any pretense or arrogance, expressing Chaplin's conception of the average man, of almost any man, of myself. The derby, too small, is a striving for dignity. The moustache is vanity. ... He is trying to meet the world bravely, to put up a bluff, and he knows that too. He knows it so well that he can laugh at himself and pity himself a little.[27]

So, too, slapstick allows one to fall in the presence of God and know that in the final iris out, the road will be toward God's feast of fools, where God uses the foolish things of the world to confound and humble the wise.[28]

Anarchy and farce do not seem to offer the kind of raw material that a biblical comedy would include. Farce flouts tradition, reason, sanity, and good taste. It laughs at others, particularly characters who are stupid and foolish, which means men. Sometimes, these men even dress in drag (Euripides' *Bacchae* or Billy Wilder's *Some Like It Hot*, 1959). Farce is mostly negative – cruel, nightmarish, and brutal, with slapstick cudgels whacking the protagonist. Violence is funny, as funny as a man digging a pit and falling into it. The irony compounds the farce of it all. The word farce comes from *farsa*, meaning stuffed, a means of throwing in everything including the kitchen sink to expose how ridiculous the world and its inhabitants are.

Slapstick does not only dwell in silent films. In one brutally funny and wonderfully implausible film released in 1990, Chris Columbus' *Home Alone*, the roughhouse play, destructive mayhem, and bodily humiliation reach a peak, or nadir, in exploiting various aspects of slapstick comedy. While Jeanne Cooper of the *Washington Post* found the funny film from John Hughes' script "too crass, too loud and too violent to be added blithely to Christmas viewing traditions," we, in our humble opinion, believe the film functions as one of the most religious films in the film comedy genre. More than merely a film in which an old man and a boy offer each other a redeeming lesson on the importance of family, in *Home Alone* we find God in the midst of the world's trouble.

At first sight, the slapstick comedy plays havoc with a headstrong child, Kevin McCallister (Macaulay Culkin), whose family leaves him behind as they take a Christmas trip and he becomes the "man of the house" who could make his "family disappear." Home alone and frightened even of his basement, he must battle two inept burglars, the "Wet Bandits" Harry and Marv (Joe Pesci and Daniel Stern). The theme of David versus two clumsy Goliaths suggests itself, but we see a *sensus plenior*, a fuller meaning in the story. We see the Christmas story of Immanuel, of God with us, as the core theme unified by numerous scenes, the least of which is the crèche in which Kevin first hides.

Kevin is resilient and precocious, like a "human ninja turtle."[29] Sitting at the dining-room table, he crosses himself and gives thanks for his "highly nutritious micro-waved macaroni dinner and the people that put

Figure 2.3 Kevin (Macaulay Culkin) meets a Father/God figure in Old Man Marley (Roberts Blossom) in the refuge of Trinity United Methodist Church. *Home Alone*, Hughes Entertainment, 1990. Author's screenshot.

it on sale." As the burglars plan to break in on Christmas Eve, a gleefully resourceful Kevin sets up a series of Rube Goldberg booby traps, ready to sabotage the dimwitted intruders. He devises icy stairs and sidewalks, tar, tacks, Christmas bulbs, swinging paint cans, and an iron, all arranged so that the incompetent bad guys receive somersault falls, Brodie tumbles, double-take tortures, singed scalps, nails in the feet, and all manner of biblical afflictions, torments, and pratfalls.[30]

However, when he sneaks into the warm but nearly empty church, with the children's choir singing "O Holy Night," he slowly walks the aisle, takes off his cap, and examines stained-glass images of Jesus and his disciples. Then he spies his neighbor, Old Man Marley (Roberts Blossom), the gruff individual rumored to be the "South Bend Shovel Slayer" who did away with his family, and Kevin gasps out loud. This is not the first time Kevin has encountered him. The first meeting occurs in the drug store when the boy is attempting to buy a dentist-approved toothbrush. Marley trudges in wearing heavy boots and slams his hand on the glass counter. Director Columbus gives us a close-up of the bleeding palm of his hand. The mark of the stigmata stands out. It will not be the only time we see the wounded hand, as it will heal in stages throughout the film. Yet the sign of divinity interrupted the daily life of the boy and now confronts him in the church.

The God figure in the film is Old Man Marley, the seemingly brusque and distant neighbor who has trouble with his own children. Seeing the boy, Marley rises from his pew and comes over, hovering at a low angle like Rudolph Otto's *tremendum mysterium*. He opens his mouth and says, quietly, "Merry Christmas." The effect is both funny and strangely holy.

The ensuing conversation is quite telling. As the *real* Old Man Marley asks if he may sit, he joins Kevin as the music supplies the Christmas spirit. Adolphe Adam's 1847 Christmas hymn not only celebrates the birth of Jesus, but the redemption of humanity. Kevin will need to be redeemed before the night is over. But now, the stars are brightly shining as the song celebrates the night of the Savior's birth. Then it acknowledges, "Long lay the world in sin and error pining, 'til He appear'd and the soul felt its worth."

"You can say hello when you see me; you don't have to be afraid," whispers the comforting Stranger." There are a lot of things going around about me but none of it's true." The appearance of the Old Man beside the besieged boy leads to a fresh understanding of God, a history of God's gracious and humbling way with His children who do not accept him, a confession of sins, and a thrill of hope for a weary world that wishes to rejoice.

Old Man Marley first tells the boy that all the rumors he has heard about him are not to be trusted. He is not a terrible executor of judgment. When he acknowledges that he is not welcome, Kevin responds, "In church?" "No," he says gently, "everyone is welcome in church." Then he asks Kevin if he's been a good boy this year. "I think so, er, no," comes the answer. And thus begins Kevin's honest confession in church, for which he receives absolution. "This is a good place to be if you're feeling bad about yourself." "I've been a pain lately. I said some things I shouldn't have said." He then confesses Romans 7, saying that he loves his family even as he doesn't act like it. "Deep down, you always love them."

Old Man Marley explains the complicated relationship he has with his own people. He couldn't come to hear his granddaughter that Christmas Eve because he was not welcome with his son. "Years back," he confides, "I had an argument with my son. He's grown up. We lost our tempers and said we didn't want to see each other again. I'm afraid he won't talk to me." The distance between the Father and his children is painfully set forth.

He acknowledges that he fears his own people will not respond to him; he weeps over Jerusalem; he cares for his estranged children, as he sneaks in to hear his granddaughter sing "He knows our need; our weakness is no stranger." God empties Himself and bends to being human, to care with all human hopes and fears.

Kevin asks, "Aren't you a little old to be afraid?" And when Marley asks him, "What's your point?" the boy replies, "You should call your son." Also, he says that he's sure the granddaughter misses him "and the presents."

When Kevin stands up to depart, Marley says, "We'll see what happens. Nice talking to you." He takes the boy's hand and we see that his hand is healing. A Band-Aid indicates that the restoration of the world has begun.

We notice the diegetic sounds of "One seems to hear words of good cheer." As Kevin leaves the refuge of the church with "The Carol of the Bells" being sung in the background, he goes out into a troubled, dangerous world, ominous bells clanging and foretelling the tribulation that is to come. However, Kevin does not realize that even as he leaves the sanctuary, the Old Man is with him. Christmas lights seem to magically illumine the darkness as he walks home. Immanuel, God with us, will keep him company, unbeknownst, in the midst of Kevin's busy scheme of sabotage. Of course, in this "O Holy Night," the burglars will not only fall on their knees, but on their faces and butts as well.

New York Times reviewer Caryn James perceives that this human ninja turtle became the hero of his own adventure.[31] Actually Kevin doesn't become the hero. He needs rescue from peril. The two burglars catch him and hang him up on a nail. That is when the mighty right hand of God, swinging his shovel, flattens the enemy with a final resolve. *Dextera Domini.*

The prophets and the Psalms attest to the mighty right hand and arm of the Lord, being "glorious in power" and dashing "in pieces the enemy" (Ezekiel 15:6). "Neither did their own arm save them: but Thy right hand, and Thy arm and the light of Thy countenance, because Thou had favor unto them" (Psalm 44:3). The hand of action and power, the arm of salvation and rescue, deliver the vulnerable boy from the hands of the two bungling Philistines. "O sing unto the lord a new song; for He has done marvelous things. His right hand and his holy arm have gotten him the victory" (Psalm 98:1). "Come on," says Old Man Marley, "let's get you home." Then the police come to sort out the makers of mayhem.

Slapstick at Christmas in *Home Alone* puts us on our knees, with every tongue confessing Immanuel, that God is with us. And the families are reunited in a new and glorious morn. As Marley hugs his family, we see in the third close-up that his hand has completely healed. The lessons and the carols punctuate the final words of "O Holy Night":

> Truly He taught us to love one another;
> His law is love and His gospel is peace.
> Chains shall He break for the slave is our brother;
> And in His name all oppression shall cease.
> Sweet hymns of joy in grateful chorus raise we,
> Let all within us praise His holy name.
>
> Christ is the Lord! O praise His Name forever,
> His power and glory evermore proclaim.
> His power and glory evermore proclaim.

All this is not to deny that the movie is first and foremost a brutally funny film. Slapstick reminds spectators of the violence of life, of a war on earth and in heaven. The slapstick rod is applied to the backs of all fools, and if a man cannot really make a fool of himself, Chesterton observed, we "may be quite certain the effort is superfluous."[32] Yet slapstick is not mere cruelty and sadism, but a blessed farce that reminds us that the tumbles, blows, stings, and arrows of this life will pass away and end in laughter. All will fall down, even into the earth, but there will be a rising up. For as in *Home Alone*, Someone is there, quietly tucked away in the manger and able to bring new life: Immanuel, God with us. In his little Kevin, Hughes found the same vehicle as Chaplin's Little Tramp – both being the individual enveloped in the divine.

Notes

1 From "Physical Comedy," Wikipedia, online at https://en.wikipedia.org/wiki/Talk%3APhysical_comedy (accessed October 10, 2015).
2 G.K. Chesterton, "On Humour," *Encyclopedia Britannica*, 14th edn. (New York, 1929), 883–885.
3 Stefan Kanfer, "Exit the Tramp, Smiling," *Time* (January 2, 1978), 63.
4 Ronald Holloway, *Beyond the Image: Approaches to the Religious Dimension in the Cinema* (Film Oikoumene, 1977).
5 Gerald Mast, *The Comic Mind: Comedy and the Movies* (Bobbs-Merrill Company, 1973), 82.
6 Gerald D. McDonald, Michael Conway, and Mark Ricci, *The Films of Charlie Chaplin* (Citadel Press, 1965), 142.
7 Ibid.
8 Mast, *Comic Mind*, 82.
9 Charlie Chaplin, "What People Laugh At," *American Magazine* **86** (November 1918), 34, 134–137; see James Agee, "Comedy's Greatest Era," *Life* (September 3, 1949).
10 Alison Smith, "The Film in Review," *Picture Play Magazine* 18:2 (April 1923), 53; Louis E. Bisch, "What Makes You Laugh," *Photoplay* (January 1928), 34. According to Smith, the film is partially a burlesque of the "Turn to the Right" plot in which a crook arrives at a small town, meets a beautiful girl, is converted, and turns right.
11 This same gimmick is used in *The Circus* in that the little Tramp stumbles into the circus tent attempting to escape capture by the cops – inadvertently becoming "the funny man," and superseding the role of the traditional clowns. This gimmick of the clueless performer – the inadvertent expert – provides an excellent position from which to introduce a little disequilibrium into the equilibrium.
12 Constance Brown Kuriyama, "Chaplin's Impure Comedy: The Art of Survival," *Film Quarterly* 45:3 (Spring 1992), 26–37.
13 When stumped by his script, Chaplin would go to his dressing room: "I have to go to Gethsemane." And when he returned, he'd moan, "It's back to Golgotha for another grueling round of retakes."
14 Out of her Christian family upbringing, Edna Purviance sought to persuade Chaplin into faith.
15 Charles J. Maland, *Chaplin and American Culture* (Princeton University Press, 1989), 57.
16 A scene edited out shows an old man marrying a young, distraught woman, an ironic insert considering that Chaplin would soon court and marry Lita Grey, who at the age of 12 had played the teen angel.

17 Charles Chaplin, *My Autobiography* (Simon & Schuster, 1964), 20.

18 Ibid., 22–23. She hated hypocrisy as well and in an altercation with a Miss Taylor, Mrs. Chaplin reacted to the young woman's arrogance by shouting: "'Who do you think you are? Lady Shit?' 'Oh!' shouted the daughter. 'That's nice language coming from a Christian.' 'Don't worry,' said Mother quickly. 'It's in the Bible, my dear: Deuteronomy, twenty-eighth chapter, thirty-seventh verse, only there's another word for it. However, shit will suit you'" (57–58).

19 Ibid., 58.

20 Ibid., 289.

21 Ibid., 290.

22 Ibid., 134.

23 Julian Smith, *Chaplin* (Twayne, 1984), 49.

24 Ruth Perlmutter, "The Melting Plot and the Humoring of America: Hollywood and the Jew," *Film Reader* 5 (1982), 251.

25 Maland, *Chaplin and American Culture*, 57.

26 Holloway, *Beyond the Image*, 72.

27 Ibid., 66–67.

28 Harvey Cox, *The Feast of Fools: A Theological Essay on Festivity and Fantasy* (Harper and Row, 1969).

29 Caryn James, "*Home Alone*: Holiday Black Comedy for Modern Children," *New York Times* (November 16, 1990).

30 Peter Rainer of the *Los Angeles Times* opined that the movie should have stayed a Road Runner-style cartoon, with the characters colliding and caroming off the walls. Instead it became a sentimental John Hughes vehicle with a mischievous Tiny Tim. He completely misses any theological significance. "Kid Plays It for Laughs in *Home Alone*," *Los Angeles Times* (November 16, 1990).

31 James, "Holiday Black Comedy."

32 Proverbs 26:3.

3   Adventure Comedy

The romance of an adventure comedy calls for the completion of a task, a challenge, or a quest. It successfully navigates through various dangers, toils, cares, and troubles, keeping the spectators on the edge of their chairs and then releasing them in howls of laughter. Adventure comedies offer roller-coaster rides, providing suspense or thrills that set us up before the comic relief. Unlike thrillers or horror films, we know the outcome. The ending is never in doubt. We know it will unleash comic energy and a trick on us. From Buster Keaton and Harold Lloyd comedies such as *Steamboat Bill Jr.* (1928) or *Safety Last* (1923), we race and ride and climb and hang by the edge of our imaginations.

Several characteristics distinguish the adventure comedy from other sub-genres. First, the narrative (the chase) is predominant over the gags (the pies).[1] Second, the thrust of the story is toward a particular goal, a *telos* that has a particular significance for the protagonist. Third, there is the ever-present danger or threat that offers obstacles to the adventure. Fourth, the plot involves the arousal not only of thrills but also of concern for key characters. Fifth, we often find complication of romance during the adventure, and finally we arrive at a happy ending and the satisfaction of the *telos*.

The roller-coaster thrills of adventure comedy borrow much of their energy from the wild stories of Moses challenging Pharaoh or Samson battling the Philistines (with a little Delilah thrown in for arousal). It is a comedy of someone in trouble and needing help. The daring deeds of the protagonist take on risks of a challenge, a quest, a task that others have neglected. In the classic Hollywood narrative, a man (and it almost always is a man) assumes the responsibility of attaining a goal, whether to depose a wicked prince or to rescue a girl. So, the Bible watches as Joshua marches around Jericho or St. Michael wields a sword against the prince of the air.

The comic adventures of Jonah provide one of the best topsy-turvy stories in all of Scripture. The reluctant prophet vainly tries to escape a divine calling, only to be caught up in a storm and the belly of a great whale. Vomited up upon a beach, he makes his way to the wicked city of Nineveh, preaches a hell and brimstone sermon, and angrily watches as the city repents. The *telos* of his adventure is satisfied and, at least for the people and cows of Nineveh, a happy ending is had by all. However, having done his business, Jonah still doesn't get the comic lesson of grace.

The vicissitudes of a comic adventurer can carry religious overtones for the viewer. The great swashbuckler of the silent film era, Douglas Fairbanks, found his popularity resting on his adventure films, from *The Thief of Bagdad* (Raoul Walsh, 1924) to *Robin Hood* (Allan Dwan, 1922). His celebrity was so global that over 300,000 fans mobbed him and his wife Mary Pickford in Moscow, two renowned capitalists in a Communist country.

American preoccupation with motion, with the train, the automobile, proliferating chain stores, numerous magazines, and the movies, spilled over into the speed, energy and athletic prowess of Fairbanks the movie star, with whom everything happened immediately. The restless person, constantly in motion, with dashing and reckless bravado, was almost a parody of himself. With a sweep of his hat, the swaggering Fairbanks would bow, with his hands on his hips, and then throw his head back in laughter. Alistair Cooke called him a "popular philosopher" and "gymnastic evangelist." If there were such a thing as Bergson's *élan vital* or Shaw's life force, it was incarnated in Douglas Fairbanks. For those collecting dust in a stuffy and monotonous rut, he offered a delightful, enthusiastic way to enjoy life; he invited passive spectators to join his Coney Island way of life. He was called a "living embodiment of the principle of the persistence of vision" as a human: even motionless, he twitches and flickers. Director D. W. Griffith found trying to control the prankster akin to "trying to catch quicksilver in a sieve." Under the governance of Triangle Film Corporation, and with director (and seminarian) John Emerson, a former ministerial student who wrote his scripts with his witty wife Anita Loos, he scintillated onto the screen, like a June bug in heat.[2] Fast was funny.

Billy Sunday, baseball evangelist and crusader, hit the sawdust trail in the same way he had run bases for the Chicago Whitestockings. With his pep, he was akin to Fairbanks on his stage, a speedy first-base runner, circling the bases in under 15 seconds. He could slide with the best of them. His platform antics, like any good reform-minded showman, appealed to a broad, good-humored Protestant audience, the middle-class suburban family (virtually the same as Fairbanks fans): "I am burning up to do you good and keep you out of hell." His sermons aimed at conversions as he believed that social reform first required personal transformation; the fundamental problem was human sin. Even William McLaughlin, Sunday's authorized biographer, compared his style to Fairbanks', "displaying as much energy, determination and virtuous enthusiasm." Billy Sunday was referenced in *The Wrong Mr. Fox*, where an actor is dropped off at a church instead of his theatrical engagement and whips up a Sunday sermon with acrobatics and cheerleading.[3] Fairbanks and Sunday preached to the same crowd, and religion, comedy, and adventure inhered in both men.[4] As John Tibbetts put it, Fairbanks was characterized by "natural exuberance, unlimited energy, a seemingly naïve faith in those old American virtues that seem to have all but evaporated." He was Billy Sunday on celluloid.

In *Double Trouble* (Christy Cabanne, 1915), Fairbanks played the dual roles of Eugene Brassfield, a cigar-smoking playboy, and Florian Amidon, the foppish President of the Sabbath Day Society, with "fluttery gestures, the limp handshake and nervous smile." The film's sly and silly attack on the nervous and fluttery reformer is a mere prologue for Fairbanks' assault on the limp weaklings who hide behind morality. The next year he would articulate his hearty sermon on health, vigorous exercise, and the good life in *The Habit of Happiness* (Allan Dwan, 1916), where he champions the idea that "any sickness can be cured by and through and with laughter!"[5] Playing Sunny Wiggins, he exorcizes the demons of gloom and depression as he teaches a dyspeptic millionaire (who spends his time listening to Chopin's Funeral March) how to laugh. Laughter and a sunny pragmatic faith are wedded together in the Fairbanks philosophy. Wiggins forms the "Happiness Society" in the Bowery as a counter-reformation to the solemn moral evangelism of the social gospel.

His films have bits of comic religion inserted throughout.[6] Augy Holliday, his suicidal character in *Flirting with Fate* (Christy Cabanne, 1916), contracts an unknown thug to do him in. However, he is saved from this killer's bullet when the assassin is converted in a rescue mission. As an inter-title informs us, "Even professionals have hearts and mothers" who wanted their sons to amend their lives. Poster banners declare that "Jesus is our Saviour"; "Though your Sins be as Scarlet"; and "God is Love." The assassin threatens the congregation until the minister reminds him of his mother, with the note that it "takes longer to save assassins than other sinners." Although the film ends like all good comedies with a wedding, when Holliday and his bride head off to their honeymoon, the killer, whom the groom does not know has reformed, chases him up a tree and asks; "My young friend, are you prepared to meet your God?" When he discovers that the sinner has been transformed, Holliday rejoices as a bridegroom entering his chamber.

However, in his penultimate silent film, *The Gaucho* (F. Richard Jones, 1927), Christian faith plays a major role in dictating the arc of the story. Written under his pseudonym, Elton Thomas, Fairbanks scripted a dashing adventure plot that spun on a miracle of faith healing, in part a testament to the southern Roman Catholic faith of his mother, Ella Fairbanks. Divorced himself, Fairbanks married the divorced Mary Pickford, America's Sweetheart, to become Hollywood's first celebrity couple, residing at Pickfair, their Beverly Hills estate. They would become the first to place foot- and handprints into the wet cement of the forecourt of Grauman's Chinese Theatre in Hollywood.

The story of "How the Gaucho and Ruiz the Usurper Came together at the City of the Miracle" begins with a prologue. In the picturesque country of the Andes of Argentina, a sweet young shepherdess tends her sheep with her crook and staff. When she sees one lamb caught on a rock over a cliff, she seeks help from other boys and tries to retrieve the lost lamb. As she reaches for it, she falls down into a ravine near a stream. Hitting her head on a rock, she seems unconscious, even dead, when the Madonna appears, a double exposure of Mary Pickford in a radiant cameo with glistening sparklers as a halo, against the screen of the rock cliff.

The Madonna's hands stretch out and heal the little girl. The Virgin Mary then transfers healing power to the Girl of the Shrine. Other poor villagers gather, kneel, and take off their hats, their shining faces beaming with joy, as they offer prayers and genuflect. A sick little child is brought to the mediating shepherdess by a pleading mother. A prayer is said and water from the pool poured on the infant brings health (and fatness) to the baby, with the camera panning across the glad faces of devout worshipers. Upon this holy spot a shrine was then built.

Ten years later, a modest virgin, with her head covered, lays her hands on the sick, restoring them to health. With many cures, the coffers of the church are filled with grateful offerings of gold. However, a discordant note resounds with the presence of a leper, a "victim of the Black Doom," who haunts the shrine in his rags and dark shroud, and "makes his living out of his affliction and refuses help."

Into this legendary place comes the outlaw Gaucho (Douglas Fairbanks) with his posse of 100 horsemen. Followed by a spitfire mountain girl (Lupe Vélez), the jaunty South American cowboy enters the city of miracles, singing his refrain "Yesterday was yesterday. Today is today. There is no tomorrow until it is today."

In the city, the usurper Ruiz has set up his kingdom, displaying his own idolatrous posters, proclaiming "RUIZ is supreme" and "Taxes shall be levied on Christ ... enings," a play on his anti-religious bigotry. Soldiers accost the priest, wanting the gold, and demand "What will you do with all your wealth?"

The humble padre shows them the true treasures of the church, the poor, to whom he distributes according to their needs. Ruiz's lieutenant declares that it belongs to him, stealing it from the church and putting the poor (and the leper) in prison. Soldiers proceed to demand taxes for marriages and burials and all religious activities.

The Gaucho and his men arrive and climb the steps of the church, where the priest stands before a tapestry of Mary and the Unicorn. One of his henchmen strikes the priest. The Gaucho knocks his own man down, shouting, "You strike an old man?" Turning to the priest, he says, "See Padre, I get what I want without the help of God and his Holy Book." The Gaucho then asks the priest what he wants done to the man who struck him.

The priest answers quietly, "Forgive him; forgive him, he doesn't know what he does." At which the Gaucho first looks puzzled over this generous act of forgiveness and then laughs loudly, poking his deputy, "Do you see that, you don't know what you do?"

Addressing the priest again, the Gaucho says, "Strange words – where did you learn them?" The priest points to his Holy Book with the Ten Commandments. "I get what I want – without the help of God and His Holy Book," brags the Gaucho.

The priest asks, "Do you mock God and His Holy Book?" "I neither mock nor pay homage," he retorts and then calls for a feast. The white-haired priest smiles as the Gaucho merrily orders, "Bring Padre to the feast!" Looking directly into the eyes of the virgin, who stares him down with grace and tender boldness, he tells his henchman to also bring her to the feast.

The deputy who had been reprimanded for striking the priest conspires with Ruiz to betray the Gaucho, described as a "vainglorious man swept on to dizzy heights, [who] heeds not the depths below." Betrayal tends to make a victim more sympathetic, even religious. But the Gaucho remains cocky.

At the feast, the Gaucho calls for all the prisoners from the jail to be brought, as the priest would sit in judgment on them. While the Gaucho summons more food and more wine, demanding more merriment among his guests, the priest sits grieved. With beggars standing before him, he protests that it is not for him to judge. Gaucho commands it: "What does the Book say?" "Give to the poor," says the priest, smiling.

The final case was the victim of the Black Doom, brought in with sticks. Disgusted and repulsed, the Gaucho passes sentence on him: "You poison the very air we breathe. Go to a lonely spot and kill yourself." When the priest protests, the Gaucho heartlessly retorts, "It's what I would do to myself. Hola, more wine."

A drunken Gaucho seeks to enjoy the Girl of the Shrine, who stands in a window; yet he is arrested by her piety. Madonna-like, she looks at him. He is struck with religious awe. Stabbed by his girlfriend, for seemingly being unfaithful, the leper grabs his bloody hand and infects him. The leper mockingly says, "Now you find some lonely spot and kill yourself. When you can do this [puts hand over a candle] and feel no pain, you'll be like me."

Confronted by his mortality, the Gaucho confesses to his Señorita, "Something has happened to change my life; I now go on a new adventure. Adios." He decides to kill himself. Then in a quiet grove, the Girl of the Shrine comes to him, "All things whatsoever, ye shall ask in prayer, believing, you shall receive." "Even this?" "Do you believe?" "I do not know. I do not understand. I do not understand you. You're like a beautiful sunset – like one night on the pampas – a bird song. I believe in you."

Figure 3.1 The swashbuckler Gaucho (Douglas Fairbanks, Sr.), cigarette dangling from his insouciant lips, hosts a banquet for the judgment of sinners, unaware of his own spiritual destiny. *The Gaucho*, Elton Corporation, 1927. Author's screenshot.

She responds, "If ye have faith ... nothing will be impossible." Stubbornly, he repeats, "I have faith in you." She points upward, turns away, and he follows into the chapel shrine itself. Simultaneously Ruiz arrives at the City of Miracles with his troops. Misled by the traitorous lieutenant, Gaucho's men go to Cañon Diablo (canyon of the devil).

In the chapel, she kneels and prays. The Gaucho moved, bowed, humbled, kneels on the outskirts of a rock altar. "Teach me to pray," he asks. With his hand on his heart, he bows his head, his hand dangling in the pool of water. The leper approaches and watches from the shadows. As she prays, the beatific vision of the Virgin Mary once again appears, radiant and glistening. Healing comes to the Gaucho and he jumps up, thanking the girl. "Don't thank me, thank God!" In the almost insouciant and carefree fashion of the early Gaucho, he energetically leaps and praises God. He continually puts his hand over the votive candles, which burn him and hurt. He rejoices in being able to feel pain. The girl quotes the Gospel, "Freely you have received; freely give."

Ruiz captures the Gaucho and arrests him and the girl (and the priest too) and calls for a scaffold to be built in the square to give the people "a show!" The Gaucho is oblivious of his predicament and impending execution, still full of wonder and amazement at his healing. Placed in a prison holding cell, he hops about, still thanking God and then devises a plan to escape the guards.

As Ruiz prepared to lash the bare-backed priest and the Girl of the Shrine, the Gaucho has been able to rally his men and invade the fortified town with a cattle stampede, running long-horned cattle before his merry band of men. Having rescued all and restored order, the Gaucho proclaims that the doors of the Shrine should "be open for all time." His men tear down Ruiz's notices (which are eaten by a goat) and post the Ten Commandments. The Gaucho calls all to "Live by these. You need no others."

He looks again at the Girl of the Shrine and acknowledges, "You're not of the earth. Your spirit will live through the ages." His own mountain girl now commands the Gaucho to marry her, but he demurs, saying "Tomorrow." It is then that she echoes his words, "Yesterday was yesterday. Today is today. There is no tomorrow until it is today." He agrees to start a new adventure.

What marks the adventure comedy of Fairbanks is an often forgotten virtue called *eutrapelia*, one celebrated by St. Thomas Aquinas (and borrowed from Aristotle's *Nicomachean Ethics*) as cheerfulness. Essentially *eutrapelia* means a "good or well-turning," a balanced mean between the clownish *bomolochos* (buffoons and fools who increase the fun, derived from those hungry wretches who sought to snatch a bit of the sacrifice at the altars of the gods, one ever ready to make jokes for food) and the *agroikos*, the solemn boors and priggish churls whose inability to laugh enjoins them to quench laughter rather than make it.

Fairbanks plays the *eiron*, the self-deprecating hero who is as benevolent as he is mischievous. He is the hero who schemes to hatch a happy ending and fulfills the incarnation of *eutrapelia*, a contagious celebration of recreational play and joking, what C. S. Lewis called the laughter of play. But as the Gaucho discovers, such merriment is not enough to sustain life. Disease and death mar the adventure and it takes One beyond death to bring the happy ending.

For theologian Hugo Rahner, the well-turned persons who jest with good taste are "called witty or versatile, that is to say, full of good turns, for such sallies seem to spring from the character, and we judge men's characters, like their bodies, by their movements."[7] For Aristotle and then for Aquinas, this *eutrapelia* offered a form of rest, providing a respite from the toil and moil of life. Playfulness, of the kind Jesus shared with children that came unto Him and with those who had heavy burdens and yokes, became recreation of both sorts.[8] Thomistic tradition came to honor the virtue of *eutrapelia*, which in Latin is known as *jucunditas* or sheer enjoyment.

As for comedy adventure, one could find no better personality than Fairbanks, with his incredible ebullience, a character that was brisk, breezy, and full of gusto. His acrobatic energy translated into a humbled enthusiasm, literally being "in God." His own habits, publicized in his 1917 self-help book *Laugh and Live*, celebrate his resourcefulness and daring. Such positive thinking would lead to American civil religion with virtues of fun, the cinematic incarnation of Norman Vincent Peale's philosophy. However, the derring-do and snappy dynamism of the Gaucho's adventures come up against divorce, sin, and death, enemies that sheer grit cannot overcome.[9]

The grand adventure is a comic faith, a hope built on the belief that one is called by God for a particular purpose in life. *Simon Birch* (1998) is one of the few films that capture the sentiment. "Simon Birch is the reason I believe in God," intones narrator Joe Wenteworth (Jim Carrey) in Mark Steven Johnson's liberal adaptation of John Irving's *A Prayer for Owen Meany*. Against a backdrop of stained-glass windows and a church graveyard, the church bell rings. In a Sunday school class a dour, smoke-sneaking, sourpuss Sunday school teacher holds court. Joe continues, "He was the instrument of my mother's death, but because he is the reason, I believe in God. What faith I have, I owe to Simon Birch, the boy I grew up with in Gravestown, Maine."

The diminutive stature of Simon Birch (Ian Michael Smith) opens up the heart-wrenching and poignant "comedy" of a young boy who unswervingly believes that God made him for a purpose: "I'm a miracle, you know?" His best friend Joe (Joseph Mazzello), born illegitimately, lives with his beautiful mother Rebecca (Ashley Judd), who refused to name the boy's father when she got pregnant in her senior year of high school. The two boys swim at the quarry together, talk about girls, compare their testicles to prunes and raisins, and play baseball.

The boys are befriended by Ben Goodrich (Oliver Platt) and attend church. Simon directly challenges Reverend Russell (David Straithairn) in the midst of his announcements after the Reverend has called Ben out for talking. Simon declares that there are more important things than coffee and donuts after the service. They're merely refreshments so people can socialize and talk about upcoming events. "Who ever said church needs a continental breakfast? If God's made the church bake sale a priority, we're in a lot of trouble."

Later, the Reverend finds the elfin hero sitting in a corner and asks what he's doing. "Thinking about God," he responds. "In a corner?" scoffs the minister. To which Simon responds, "Faith is not in a floor plan." He tells the humorless religious leaders that "things will be different when God makes me a hero."

Seeking to discipline him, the minister and Miss Leavey (Jan Hooks), the repressed Sunday school teacher, berate him for believing that God has called him to be a hero. Rebecca rescues him and admonishes the religious leaders.

Figure 3.2 Interrupting the pastor during the service, Simon Birch (Ian Michael Smith) challenges the priorities of the church. *Simon Birch*, Hollywood Pictures, 1998. Author's screenshot.

Then, in a freak accident, Simon actually hits a baseball that beans Rebecca and kills her. Simon weeps to the heavens and cries "I'm sorry" over and over again. The boys split for a brief season of mourning but reunite in their shared loss. They begin a quest to find Joe's father, even stumbling into delinquency, after which they are told they have to "do time" in community service at the Christmas pageant and church trip.

The Christmas pageant becomes the comic center of a boy seeking divine guidance. Miss Leavey continually shouts at her cast, "The Star of Bethlehem is not a piñata! The Virgin Mary does not chew gum." Because of his diminutive size, Simon is selected to play the baby Jesus in the manger. However, his crush Marjorie plays Mary, and, leaning over him, gives him a vision of her budding breasts. A larger boy plays the angel, whose fear of heights leads him to upchuck just when Simon grabs her breasts. After the comic disaster, the Reverend exiles Simon from church, needing a break. When Simon shares that God has providentially called him, the minister denies it, exposing his own faithlessness.

Events lead to Reverend Russell's confession that he is Joe's father. Simon ends up on the school bus returning from the winter church trip. As the bus driver swerves to avoid hitting a deer, he crashes the bus into an icy lake. Joe and Simon save the other children, with the small one sacrificing his life for the others. Simon dies in the hospital grateful that God's plan for him had been fulfilled.

In the epilogue, an adult Joe Wenteworth speaks in a gentle voice-over: "Ben Goodrich legally adopted me just two days before my 13th birthday. Not a day that goes by that I don't thank God for bringing him into my life. With Simon's help, I had finally found my real father." Joe stands over Simon's grave and recites the same prayer that Simon whispered over Rebecca's grave: "Into paradise … may the angels lead you." A young boy in a baseball uniform shouts for him: "Dad, come on, we're going to be late for the game." The son's name? Simon, of course.

Joe's adventure of seeking an absent father carries him through a vale of tears, but with the victory of finding another spiritual father (the son of a good, rich one) and his heavenly Father. The comedy is not of this world, however. It is a future hope, as evidenced in a son named Simon.

Like *Simon Birch*, *Millions* (Danny Boyle, 2004) highlights the story of two boys, this time brothers Damian (Alex Etel) and Anthony (Lewis McGibbon). Since the death of their mother, the elder, Anthony, seeks his own desires, while his younger sibling Damian is filled with faith, yearning to do good works for others. He also talks with dead saints.

As they move into a new house in a new community with their father, they begin a different school. When the teacher asks her pupils whom they most admire, most children name famous soccer players, but Damian names St. Roch, the patron saint of invalids who distributed all his worldly goods among the poor, like Francis of Assisi. Damian then proceeds to speak of other saints, like St. Agatha, "who ripped her own eyes out so she wouldn't have to marry a man," and St. Catherine of Alexandria of fireworks fame. His deepest desire, however, is to talk to his mother, who he believes is also a saint somewhere in heaven.

While Damian's brother learns how to exploit people with the poignant story of their mom dying, Damian retreats to a small cardboard fort he builds near the railroad tracks. He enjoys the shaking when a train passes by and the delight of various saints stopping by to chat with him. When a cigarette-smoking St. Clare of Assisi visits (Damian collects the saints like baseball cards, knowing all their statistics), Damian asks her if she is allowed to smoke and she answers, "You can do what you like up there, son. It's down here you have to make the effort." The film's Chestertonian sense of heaven as the playground and earth as a battleground is starkly contrasted.[10]

The spiritual isolation and quest of a child (as in M. Night Shyamalan's *Wide Awake*, 1998) is given comic tone when a duffel bag-load of British pounds is thrown from a train and lands on Damian's fort, seemingly dropped directly from heaven. He becomes responsible for distributing it to the poor as the gospel would have him do, even as his brother wants to spend it selfishly. The plot invents a pressure deadline in that euros are replacing pounds as the currency (a historical muff from this side of the decision), so something must be done quickly, even if it means buying pizza for homeless people and donating to Mormons to buy a microwave.

When Dorothy, a social worker, visits his school and speaks about the need for water in sub-Saharan Africa, Damian donates a thousand pounds. Everything gets complicated when the robber arrives. With his

Figure 3.3 St. Clare of Assisi (Kathryn Pogson) makes her smoking cameo and imparts wisdom to the kind-hearted Damian (Alex Etel), whose recitation of various saints' biographies amazes even her. *Millions*, Pathé Pictures International, 2004. Author's screenshot.

home ransacked, Dorothy becoming romantically involved with his father, and mobs of people lining up for handouts, Damian goes back to the railroad tracks and burns the rest of the money. As he does so, he notices a figure on the other side of the tracks. It is his mom, a saint.

The adventures of comedy take one through rough patches, through valleys of shadows of death and even death itself, but like Frye's U-shaped curve of archetypal comedy, bring one up to a joyous, even laughing, place. Br'er Rabbit found his laughing place to be a place of safety and delight, even if the villains suffered bee stings for their dastardly motives. So, too, the comedy of life's journey slouches through the inferno and purgatory until it brings one into the fresh, bright, laughing paradise of God.

What strikes one most forcibly in the adventure comedy is its sense of fun, of unbridled play throughout the dangers and tribulations of life. One laughs after the crisis has passed. The mother laughs after the child is born. Joy comes in the morning, after the dark night of the soul. Life's adventures, even through the inferno and purgatory of the journey, reach the gates of paradise, where the first sound that Dante heard was the celestial laughter of the heavens. He had made it home.

The medieval mind envisioned life as an adventure, as in the French genre known as "romance" in which knights defended the virtue of their damsels, squeaked through narrow escapes, and took on all the perils of exploring unknown lands. In seeking the adventure, knights (of the

Arthurian Round Table, for example) actively embarked on some holy or selfless quest. Like the Gospel of Mark, everything happened "suddenly" in both the literary stories of Aristo and the adventures of St. Paul through the Book of Acts: a scourging, a possessed pythonic girl, an earthquake – and all of that just in Philippi. Poisonous snakes come later. Saints, from Francis to the Irish monks, sought adventure, as Jacobus de Voragine's volumes of *The Golden Legend* show. And they sought the completion of the adventure's *telos*, even when it meant death, with humor and panache. But it was only the beginning of comic adventures.

In his final Narnian chronicle, *The Last Battle*, after many characters had passed from death to a new life, C. S. Lewis announced:

> All their life in this world and all their adventures had only been the cover and the title page: now at last they were beginning Chapter One of the Great Story which no one on earth has read: which goes on forever: in which every chapter is better than the one before.

And, Lewis added, they revived old jokes, and "You've no idea how good an old joke sounds when you take it out again after a rest of five or six hundred years."

Notes

1 Donald Crafton, "The Pie and the Chase: Gag, Spectacle and Narrative in Slapstick," in *Classical Hollywood Comedy* (ed. Kristine Brunovska Karnick and Henry Jenkins) (Routledge, 1995), 106–119.

2 John C. Tibbetts, *His Majesty the American: The Films of Douglas Fairbanks, Sr.* (A. S. Barnes, 1977), 35.

3 William Gerald McLaughlin, *Billy Sunday Was His Real Name* (University of Chicago Press, 1955). Sinclair Lewis' *Elmer Gantry* as a Man of God was an extension of Sunday and Fairbanks. Lewis' fictional evangelist would "give 'em a good helpful sermon, with some jokes sprinkled in to make it interesting and some stuff about the theatre or something that'll startle 'em and wake 'em up."

4 William T. Ellis, *Billy Sunday, the Man and His Message* (F. W. Mead Publishing Co., 1936), 26.

5 Norman Cousins, *Anatomy of an Illness As Perceived by the Patient: Reflections on Healing and Regeneration* (Norton, 2005).

6 In *The Nut* (Theodore Reed, 1921), a little angel with curls cries and laughs as she operates a switchboard in heaven in contrast to a little devil in hell. Tibbetts, *His Majesty the American.*

7 Hugo Rahner, *Man at Play* (Herder and Herder, 1972).

8 By Cicero's time, *eutrapelia* had become synonymous with buffoonery, a smart but garrulous windbag. Such was the warning of St. Paul in his Epistle to the Ephesians, cautioning against both ribaldry (*morologia*) and *eutrapelia* (now a twisting of the good, in smug smartness in speech). What Paul saw in the pejorative sense of this word was the chatter of fools, *scurrilitas*, stemming from the vice of the *scurra*, the clown, the raucously rude windbag. St. Clement warned against using jocose and unbecoming words at social gatherings, while St. Ambrose advised against being too nimble in joking. Baylor University

professor Robert Darden in his book *Jesus Laughed: The Redemptive Power of Humor* (Abingdon Press, 2008) notes that "the context [of this verse] is something a little deeper. Ephesians 5:3 and 5:5 refer specifically to sexual impurity. New Testament scholar David Garland tells me that the Greek noun *eutrapelia* (particularly in this context) refers not so much to jesting (as the KJV translates it) but 'coarse joking, suggestive overtones, double entendres' – generally about sex." Our understanding of this is that it twists the good for licentious purposes.

9 Two worthy sports films, *Angels in the Outfield* (Clarence Brown, 1951) and *Hoosiers* (David Anspaugh, 1986), bounce onto the screen as religious adventure comedies. See Ken Gire's "Reflections on *Hoosiers*," in *Reflecting on the Movies: Hearing God in the Unlikeliest of Places* (Victor Cook Communication, 2000), 127–136, for a celebration of life and the gracious God of second chances.

10 Roy M. Anker, *Of Pilgrims and Fire: When God Shows Up at the Movies* (Eerdmans, 2010), 178–188.

4   Romantic Comedy

The classic pattern of "boy meets girl, boy loses girl, and boy gets girl back" not only parallels the divine romance of Christ the bridegroom pursuing his runaway bride, but of ordinary, obtuse men chasing after Grace, Joy, Faith, and other aptly named women.

Even with the familiar formula, various wrinkles occur in the basic plot line. Twists and surprises alter the trajectory of the romance, even with one or both of the couple not realizing that they are *the* girl and *the* boy. So, too, one may find that beauty is not in the eye of the beholder, but, as in *A Midsummer Night's Dream*, our perceptions of love can be quite askew.

Romantic comedy begins with a conflict, a crisis, an obstacle to true love. Right after the vivacious Moabite Ruth marries a Hebrew boy, he dies. Girl meets boy; girl loses boy. The husband of her mother-in-law, Naomi, dies as well. What looks like a soap opera directed by George Cukor, gathering a flock of females, turns on the devotion of one woman to her in-law. Naomi tells Ruth to get on with her life, go out dancing and meet young Moabite bucks. But Ruth responds with one of the most memorable lines for traditional wedding ceremonies, "Your people will be my people and your God my God."

Promising "where you go, I will go," she travels with Naomi back to Bethlehem, the city of bread, where a distant relative of Naomi, Boaz, took notice of the loyal, and remarkably comely, caretaker. He gave her a job in his fields and instructed his foremen to make certain she prospered. Ruth and Boaz formed an unlikely couple. She was young, vibrant, and recently widowed; he was a successful farmer, an old bachelor, and his mother, Rahab, had not been the most reputable of women. In fact, she was known for welcoming spies into her bedroom.

Naomi instructed her on the way to win a man, this man. Go warm up his feet when he is sleeping. Such a daring and provocative move might have shocked him had not his mother persuaded her way into the geneology of Abraham through Salmon. Now the girl who got one Jewish boy, and then lost him to the great enemy of romance, ended up with a Jewish man. But what is more astounding is the fruit of this union; for this May/December couple give birth to Obed, the father of Jesse, the root of the family tree of David and the Messiah. The salvation of all mankind rests on one very improbable romantic comedy.

Romantic comedy differs from screwball in that it tends toward a sentimental closure. In romcom, love plays the primary role. Cupid's arrows are aimed at the heart rather than the funny bone or bum. The flavor of its laughter is much gentler, and at its extreme may become the *comédie larmoyante*, the tearful sentimental comedy.[1] The coupling of the couple takes precedence over the doubling of the laughter.

The divine romantic comedy centers on that volatile dance that happens between potential lovers of any age. Film historian David Bordwell identifies the romantic plot – lovers searching for each other, finding each other, battling each other, but ultimately finding love with each other – as either the major plotline or at least a subplot of most film narratives from the start of classic Hollywood cinema.[2] The romantic plot can manifest as either dramatic or comedic or a combination of the two (with one usually gaining purchase over the other as the film is marketed to its potential audience).

In romantic comedy, laughter is the result not of the expressing of emotion, but of the responding to the emotion. There is a bouncing – an echo effect – present in comedies. As a character responds to an emotion, the response is echoed by the audience. Or at least it should be, if the dynamics and temperature of the scene were designed correctly.

The basic structure of the romantic comedy film is made up of four acts. First, the story begins with the proto-lovers meeting; then the narrative struggles through the proto-lovers either hating each other or at least one hating the other; then to something of a near-miss as the proto-lovers almost connect but instead seem to be driven farther apart; and finally to the resolution that transforms the proto-lovers into lovers who are then united in time for the end credits.

Beyond this basic structure, when we examine the romantic comedy genre itself, we soon discover that these films tend to fall into three distinct but occasionally overlapping categories. First, there is the triangle. This occurs, for example, when two males pursuing one female (*The Philadelphia Story*, George Cukor, 1940).

The second type of romantic comedy highlights mismatched lovers. This is the largest category, in which the two proto-lovers discover their characters are binary opposites. That is, if one is rich, the other is poor or middle class. If one is from the city, the other is from the country. And to play upon a relationship book popular in the 1990s, if one is from Mars, the other is from Venus.

Examples of the mismatched lovers can be found from the earliest films of the studio era to contemporary titles. The film *Bringing up*

Baby (Howard Hawks, 1938) involved a wealthy scatterbrained woman (Katharine Hepburn) who falls for an uptight archeologist (Cary Grant). In *It Happened One Night* (Frank Capra, 1934) the world-weary reporter (Clark Gable) links up with a spoiled heiress (Claudette Colbert). In *As Good As it Gets* (James L. Brooks, 1997), a wealthy, misogynist writer of romance novels (Jack Nicholson) falls in love with a down-to-earth waitress (Helen Hunt).

The third type of romantic comedy is the sort of story where the proto-lovers do not become physical lovers. They may carry on a platonic relationship because of job or position in society. This includes the unrequited love story. In *Mrs. Doubtfire* (Chris Columbus, 1993), the male proto-lover (Robin Williams), a divorced father, wants more time with his kids and wants to reunite with his ex-wife (Sally Fields). So, in some sense this makes both the male and female the post-lovers. To do this, he transforms into "Mrs. Doubtfire" in an effort to become the nanny to his own children. He does what he can to undermine his ex-wife's efforts at romance with another man. In the end, he doesn't get back with his wife, but he does get more time with his kids.

In a two guys and a girl formation, *Keeping the Faith* (2000), the director Edward Norton casts himself as the young priest, Father Bryan Finn, and Ben Stiller as Rabbi Jake Schram. The film begins with Finn offering a "confession" to a bartender about his love for a childhood friend, Anna Riley (Jenna Elfman), who just came back into his life. The film flashes back to their teenage years with Schram, Riley, and Finn as best friends. In the short scenes given to us we see all three presented in an asexual relationship. The teenage Riley is presented as somewhat of a tomboy as a way to establish that the friendship supersedes any romantic teenage angst.

Flash forward to the present. Schram and Finn are both adults and both religious leaders in their own faiths. Finn is a Roman Catholic priest while Schram is a rabbi. Both are seen in an opening montage as bumbling through certain rites of passage for their respective positions: Finn loses control of the censer and whacks one of the parishioners on the head; Schram faints at a bris.

Yet, at by the end of the montage, each is seen as a competent, modern, and progressive example of both faiths. Finn, still narrating the film as a part of his confession to the bartender (who identifies as Muslim), notes the camaraderie between him and Schram. They are even working on a venue to combine the congregations of his church and Schram's synagogue.

And then, she comes back into town and into their lives.

At first, Finn, being the good Roman Catholic priest he is, has no problem in defining his affection for Riley. Platonic. *Philia*. Non-sexual. Good, solid adult friendship with absolutely no "benefits." He even

Figure 4.1 Cutting a contemporary vibe, Rabbi Schram (Ben Stiller, flashing what is either a Vulcan hand gesture or a Hebrew good luck sign) and his best friend, Father Finn (Edward Norton), hit the town. *Keeping the Faith*, Spyglass Entertainment, 2000. Author's screenshot.

impresses her with his boasting of his strength of will in having had no sexual intercourse ever and he's just fine about that. This forms a moment that any viewer paying attention would label as Finn's "famous last words."

At the same time, Schram is under pressure to tone down his progressive ways. It hits a watershed moment when he invites an African-American choir from Harlem to sing a traditional Jewish song – the *Ein Keloheinu* – a joyous song, a prayer about praising the Lord. This upsets the older, more set-in-their-ways synagogue members and leadership. One of the ways that the leadership – particularly head rabbi Ben Lewis (Eli Walach) – reacts is to advocate that Schram must seek out a suitable bride. This begins a series of blind dates with good Jewish girls. Yet, Schram is becoming attracted in a very non-platonic way to Riley.

When Finn and Riley learn of the pressure Schram is under to marry, they offer to go on a double date with Schram and a very promising Jewish woman – a network reporter who combines beauty and smarts named Rachel Rose (Rena Sofer). In having to pretend to be childhood friends who became a romantic couple, Finn finds his resolve collapsing under Riley's romantic, albeit fake, affection during the date. As in Max Beerbohm's "The Happy Hypocrite," he becomes what he pretends to be: in love.

To raise the stakes for this triangle even higher, Schram and Riley begin a torrid love affair without telling anyone – certainly not the people in the synagogue and especially not Finn. The weight of the affair is compounded in that Schram's mother (Anne Bancroft) is estranged from Schram's brother because he married a *shiksa* (a young, non-Jewish woman). Schram loves his mother and doesn't want a repeat of that alienation. This is the film's most pointed aspect – particularly as it relates to romantic theology and tradition. Intermarriage between Jew and non-Jew is prohibited in tradition as it is handed down in culture. The writer of the film is Jewish and from the evidence of the script the focus is on Judaism and Jewish tradition, with a nod to the Christian faith as it is filtered through Catholic tradition.

And the aspect of Roman Catholic tradition that the movie spends the most time with is celibacy. (And as old Samuel Johnson once quipped, "marriage has many pains, but celibacy has no pleasures.") It fits, considering that the film is a romantic comedy and the hallmark of this genre is romance. Ultimately, Finn confesses his love for Riley, which causes her much self-loathing dialogue. She now feels that she has torn a loyal priest away from his faith. What they get to as a way of solution for Finn is in the form of some sage advice from Father Havel (Milos Forman), who serves as Finn's mentor. When Finn confesses his growing feelings for Riley to Father Havel, the older priest makes his own confession.

Finn: I keep thinking about what you said in seminary, that the life of a priest is hard and if you can see yourself being happy doing anything else you should do that.

Father Havel: That was my recruitment pitch, which is not bad when you're starting out because it makes you feel like a marine. The truth is you can never tell yourself there is only one thing you could be. If you are a priest or if you marry a woman it's the same challenge. You cannot make a real commitment unless you accept that it's a choice that you keep making again and again and again.

Havel continues to tell Finn that every ten years since becoming a priest, he had fallen in love with a woman and considered leaving the priesthood. Yet each time he stayed faithful to his calling. Just having the feeling is not evidence that he is not meant to be a priest – just evidence that he is a man with the emotions of a man. It will make him better as a priest.

This may be a way to deal with a plot twist in a romantic film, but it is even more interesting as it is used to settle the conflict. The stakes were established: Finn was a celibate priest who now loves a woman. Why not leave the Church and pursue her? First, the stakes are not truly weighty stakes at all. Riley doesn't love Finn in a romantic way. Finn misinter-preted her affectation of affection during the double date. A truer test of this priest would be for Riley to actually love Finn and want to marry him if only. ... However, the love she actually has is meant for Schram – a rabbi who is at risk of losing his job but not his faith if he brings his affair out into the open.

At the end, Schram admits to his mentor and – even more importantly to his mother – that he is in love with Riley and they plan on marrying. He doesn't face any blowback from either admission. It seems that the synagogue members and elders vote to keep Schram and his progres-sive ways. And Schram's mother admits that her shunning of Schram's brother was a mistake and she has grown enough – progressed enough – to accept this violation of Jewish tradition.

The denouement of the film occurs at the opening of the interfaith club that Finn and Schram had been working on by way of subplot throughout the film. The truly divine romance is a bromance between Jew and Gentile, arm in arm, dancing the night away to some crazy karaoke.

The film doesn't leave the audience with any real sense of a high-stakes testing of Finn, Schram, and Riley. Yes, their faith is tested. Schram has to consider being rejected by his synagogue and his mother. Finn has to consider for the first time leaving the position that he had felt a clear calling to. However, their faith is not tested at the level that Daniel and Julia are tested in *Defending Your Life* (Albert Brooks, 1991). Instead we are given a taste of indecision. If Schram's mother had held to her earlier belief that a rabbi – especially her son, the rabbi – should never marry outside the Jewish community, then Schram would be tested. If Riley had returned Finn's romantic overture in kind, then Finn would have a real choice to make – to remain a priest or to renounce his collar and marry Riley. But the film gives us a momentary drive-by view of a calamity that nearly happened. Cars on the road that nearly miss are never as interest-ing as ones that crash.

A number of films present romance as something that is out of reach for the characters.

In *Big* (Penny Marshall, 1988), Tom Hanks plays a young boy who has his wish granted: he becomes "big" – that is, an adult. Yet he is still at the emotional age of eight. In the body of an adult he falls in love with a woman played by Elizabeth Perkins. The film concludes with Hanks returning to being a kid and his love for Perkins remains unfulfilled as she watches the man disappear and the young boy manifested.

The unrequited romantic comedy takes a religious turn in the film *Nacho Libre* (Jared Hess, 2006). Ostensibly, the film focuses on the Franciscan or Jesuit (the filmmakers are not quite clear on the type of

Catholic missionary organization he is a part of) brother Ignacio and his efforts to become a Mexican masked wrestler – a "luchador." Ignacio (Jack Black) is introduced as a young boy who lives in a rather sad orphanage in Mexico. As he confesses later, his father was a Mexican deacon and his mother was a Lutheran missionary. Each tried to convert the other but instead they fell in love. But they died leaving young Ignacio to grow up in an orphanage. So early on in the story we see Ignacio torn between two denominations – interpretations – of faith in God in conflict. It is no wonder that Ignacio should grow up torn between two impulses: his role as a brother ministering to the orphans in his care and the lure of the life of the luchador.

He becomes a cook but complains that he doesn't have enough money to buy fresh supplies for the recipes. We do get to see his system of getting some day-old chips to put on the soup he makes for the orphanage. These come in bags labeled "orphan chips" and are set out behind a restaurant in town. This is also where he meets Steven (Héctor Jiménez), a wiry, skeletal man in shorts who is more nimble than Ignacio and gets away with the chips.

After seeing a poster that offers amateurs the chance of becoming luchadores by wrestling in a sort of open-ring night, he becomes excited about the chance of wrestling until he meets Sister Encarnación (Ana de la Reguera) – an attractive young woman of whom Ignacio – along with other brothers of the orphanage – becomes very enamored. Ignacio makes his first move by inviting the sister to have toast with him in her quarters.

As they sit eating toast in her room, they become acquainted. He tries to make her see that he is a man of faith, even though the other brothers don't respect him.

Ignacio: And they don't think I know a butt-load of crap about the Gospel, but I do! Okay?

Later as he broaches the subject of wrestling, he gets Sister Encarnación's attitude toward the sport:

Sister Encarnación: You went to watch a wrestling match?
Ignacio: [after a pause] Kind of.
Sister Encarnación: You are a man of the cloth. Lucha Libre, it's a sin.
Ignacio: But, why?
Sister Encarnación: Because those men fight for vanity, for money, for false pride.
Ignacio: Yes it's terrible, terrible. But is it always a sin to fight?
Sister Encarnación: No. If you fight for something noble, or for someone who needs your help, only then will God bless you in battle.

And this becomes the struggle for Ignacio. He wants to impress/win the love/respect of Sister Encarnación but she is a nun and he is a brother of the orphanage. This raises the stakes for Ignacio because he wants both: the woman and to be a luchador. And her last words give him a way to bring both dreams together. Fighting for wealth and fame is one thing, but fighting "for something noble" is worthy of God's (and, by extension, Encarnación's) blessing.

Ignacio enlists the wiry fellow who took his orphan chips in the alley and enlists Steven (whose luchador name is Esqueleto, meaning "The Skeleton") to become tag-team wrestlers. Their training montage shows their preparation for the battles. One thing that Ignacio does is smear cow dung across Steven's eyes – much like Jesus put mud in the eyes of the blind man as a way of giving him sight – although Ignacio's actions are more played for laughs.

They lose their first fight, but even losing brings money. They begin to realize that just showing up is a win–win for them. If they win, they get the bigger prize, but if they lose, they still get to go away with money. Plus, with the mask on, no one can recognize him as Ignacio. Instead, he is the champion of the poor: Nacho the luchador.

This works for a while, but maintaining a dual identity is a constant struggle. He works to change the sister's mind about wrestling. He sets up a fake battle in her honor in town. That doesn't go well as he is defeated in front of her. This only shows that she is pretty much correct about how fighting is a sin.

As Ignacio speaks to the orphans, he tries to reflect what he feels is the point of view that Sister Encarnación would approve of:

Ignacio: OK. Orphans! Listen to Ignacio. I know it is fun to wrestle. A nice pile-drive to the face … or a punch to the face … but you cannot do it. Because, it is in the Bible not to wrestle your neighbor.

Chancho (one of the orphans): So you've never wrestled?

Ignacio: Me? No. Come on. Don't be crazy. I know the wrestlers get all the fancy ladies, and the clothes, and the fancy creams and lotions. But my life is good! Really good! I get to wake up every morning, at 5a.m., and make some soup! It's the best. I love it. I get to lay in a bed, all by myself, all of my life! That's fantastic! Go. Go away! Read some books!

Yet, later in the film, Ignacio reveals that he still has desire for her as he sings in front of Steven:

When the fantasy has ended/and all the children are gone/Something good inside me/helps me to carry on/I ate some bugs/I ate some

Figure 4.2 Brother Ignacio (Jack Black) and Steven (Héctor Jiménez) pose as the luchadores Nacho and Esqueleto, in an attempt to astonish the crowd with their amazing costumes and stunning physiques. *Nacho Libre*, Paramount Pictures, 2006. Author's screenshot.

grass/I used my hand to wipe my tears/To kiss your mouth/I break my vows/no no no no no no way Jose/Unless you want to/Then we break our vows together.

Much like Father Brian Finn in *Keeping the Faith*, Ignacio toys with the idea of breaking his vow of celibacy in the face of an attractive woman. This raises the question of what is the tendency of filmmakers who deal with the role of the priest or brother within the Catholic Church. Sex between the priest/brother and the woman/nun is implied as an after-effect of their love for each other. But unlike the way it is explored in such narratives as *The Thorn Birds* (Daryl Duke, 1983) or *The Runner Stumbles* (Stanley Kramer, 1979), which explore the reasons and conflicts that result from a religious leader breaking his vow, such comedies as *Keeping the Faith* and *Nacho Libre* can look at this under a comic light.

For the bulk of the film, Ignacio balances his role as a cook and minister to the orphans and community and the lure of the wrestling ring. Yet, he gradually gets frustrated with what the more senior brothers at the orphanage mandate as his regular duties. As Ignacio puts it, "Maybe I'm not cut out for these duties. Cooking duty. Dead-guy duty. Maybe it's time to get another duty."

As he and his wrestling partner continue to make money losing to the more established wrestlers, they wrangle their way into a party being given in honor of Ignacio's idol, Ramses (played by the professional luchador "Silver King," Cesar Gonzalez), Ramses is shown as a mean, prideful, but successful luchador. The more Ignacio interacts with Ramses, the more he discovers these negative aspects – which are the same ones listed by Sister Encarnación in her admonition to Ignacio.

Once Ignacio is outed as a luchador during one of his fights (his mask is ripped off mid-wrestle), he is admonished back at the orphanage and even finds the sister has turned her back on him. He reaches out beyond his Christian faith (remember, he does know a "butt-load" about the Gospel) and seeks out a gypsy mystic known as "The Emperor" (Peter Stormare). After climbing up a steep cliff and eating a raw eagle egg (and subsequently falling from the perch), Ignacio banishes himself to the wilderness. He leaves a note for Sister Encarnación that proclaims his undying love for her.

An opportunity arises for Ignacio and Steven to challenge Ramses for top luchador. All they have to do is to defeat a series of luchadores, many of whom they have already fought. They almost make it but are stopped at number two. This is something that almost destroys Ignacio's resolve. Suddenly there is a change in their fortunes. The top team is disqualified when one of their wrestlers is injured in a drive-by (Steven runs over his foot with Ignacio's motor-cart).

To prepare for the final battle, Ignacio needs prayer from Steven – a show of faith and belief from his partner. Earlier in the film, Steven defies Ignacio's faith. Faced with seemingly insurmountable opponents, Ignacio urges Steven to fight the larger wrestler by using his gazelle-like reflexes.

Ignacio: Pray to the Lord for strength.
Steven: I don't believe in God, I believe in science.
Ignacio: You have not been baptized?

By proclaiming "I don't believe in God, I believe in science" Steven provides an intermediate goal for Ignacio. He must bring Steven into the faith. Ignacio sneaks up behind Steven, places a bowl of water under his chin, grabs Steven by the hair and dunks him into the bowl. Ignacio declares his partner baptized.

The final trial comes as Ignacio and Ramses face off for the title. Ramses is a formidable wrestler and all Ignacio's training seems to be coming up short. We see Steven praying (most likely not to "science") for Ignacio to succeed. It is when he is pinned down by Ramses' foot and the count has started that Ignacio turns to see the face of Sister Encarnación and

Figure 4.3 Unmasked by his opponent, Ramses (Cesar Gonzalez), Ignacio is energized by the presence of Sister Encarnación and the orphans and finds the strength – and the wings – to win the fight. *Nacho Libre*, Paramount Pictures, 2006. Author's screenshot.

several of the orphans sitting in the audience looking on with approval in their eyes.

Of course Ignacio is empowered by this and defeats Ramses – even to the point of sending Ramses running for his life through the crowd. This is when Ignacio leaps after him – defying gravity as he flies over the crowd – and tackles Ramses, thus winning the match.

The film concludes with Ignacio using his winnings to buy a nice bus for the orphanage, a new light-blue cassock to wear as he and Sister Encarnación take the orphans on a field trip. The implication is that the two will raise the orphans as if "in loco parentis" (emphasis on the "loco") – not breaking their vows, but in essence fulfilling them. They act as partners in raising the orphans. This gets at the heart of the vow itself. In vowing celibacy as either brother or nun, one takes on the role of parent without the connection of sexual relations. The connection is made as each is betrothed, in a way, to Christ.

In romantic comedy we can see how including the Christian faith shapes each film to be more than the sum of various plot points. It's the divine aspect that enables each character to attain a sense of verisimilitude with the audience. Anyone viewing one of these films will experience a connection of the traditional genre pattern with the option of consideration through a theological lens.

Temptation is very real. As Oscar Wilde once penned, "The only way to get rid of temptation is to yield to it … I can resist everything except temptation." To make a vow to God is to invite temptation to break that vow. In *Keeping the Faith* the audience is encouraged to think seriously about making and keeping vows in the face of real-world temptations. It's easy to keep a vow in the face of abstract temptation, as when Father Havel compares the job of the priest to the job of a marine. Keeping that vow in the face of real temptation in the form of Anna Riley – the one woman Finn had true feelings for – becomes the true test. In much the same way Ignacio keeps his vow to care for the orphans and resist the temptations of the glory that is Nacho Libre – the way of the luchador – until he is truly tested with two things: he meets Sister Encarnación and finds a passageway into the wrestling world through an advertisement posted on a wall.

With its mix of contemporary spirituality with Christian theology, romantic films present a telling criticism of contemporary America and its "me-centric" view of life. This isn't far from the biblical injunction to avoid making any vow: "Simply let your 'Yes' be 'Yes,' and your 'No,' 'No'; anything beyond this comes from the evil one" (Matthew 5:37).

In Father Finn's sermon to his congregation that is presented early in the film, he notes that God is a lot like Blanche DuBois (in Tennessee Williams' play *A Streetcar Named Desire*), in that "He's always depended on the kindness of strangers." As such we are admonished like his congregation to consider that one of the key functions of faith in God is our kindness. Even Ignacio, as he faces exile for being Nacho Libre, exclaims "There is no place for me in this world. I don't belong out there, and I don't belong in here. So I'm going out into the Wilderness. Probably, to die." Certainly it is meant to elicit sympathy from the nun, brothers, and orphans. Yet, implicit in his words is his need to be kind to both his listeners and himself.

Ultimately, love is the key emotion present in all romance comedies – divine or not – and from out of love comes the evidence of kindness. Many romantic comedies play off of kindness – and a lack of kindness – as evidence or absence of true love. In other romantic comedies the word "love" is thrown around at the various weddings that are featured. In the Adam Sandler vehicle *The Wedding Singer* (Frank Coraci, 1998), many characters comment on the concept of love. As her mother soothes her bride-to-be daughter, she makes it clear that love is optional. Money and evidence of monetary success are what women should seek first. And although her fiancé claims to love his bride-to-be, he is unkind to her. Kindness to himself and the orphans becomes the driving force for Ignacio to try to find success as a luchador.

In each film, the way of Christ is evidenced in kindness – kindness to self and to others. As Ignacio – Nacho Libre himself – might say about kindness, "It's the best. I love it."

Notes

1 Jessica Milner Davis, "Romantic and Sentimental Comedy," in *Encyclopedia of Humor Studies* (ed. Salvatore Attardo) (Sage Publications, 2014), 265.
2 David Bordwell, "The Classical Hollywood Style, 1917–60," in David Bordwell, Janet Staiger, and Kristen Thompson, *The Classical Hollywood Cinema: Film Style and Mode of Production to 1960* (Columbia University Press, 1985), 16–17.

5   Screwball Comedy

In creation, God continually critiqued His own work. After making light or shrubs or guppies or geckos, He would pronounce: "It is good." The one declaration in creation that God did *not* pronounce "good," the one joke that was not yet good enough or ready to deliver, was that man should be alone. He needed a mate. So began the simple pattern of a young man wanting a young woman. Adam needed Eve.

The screwball comedy extends beyond the typical romantic comedy of boy meets girl/boy loses girl/boy gets girl back. While Northrop Frye's archetypal mythos of spring may invite the green world of young love and the transfer of a new couple into a new society (usually by a wedding), screwball comedies attend to the wackiness of the two genders, marked by rapid verbal wit and almost silly slapstick, a frantic pace, a madcap equality of the sexes, some destruction of property, and an inclusive (and conservative) comedy of remarriage.[1]

Scholar Wes Gehring calls screwball comedy the old "boy meets girl" formula gone topsy-turvy. The primary characters, often from more affluent classes, are blissfully eccentric. Romance goes madcap with unlikely pairs coming together. Where the romantic comedy brings in the bridegroom to woo and win his bride, even as Jesus loved the Church, the screwball comedy traces the uneven trajectory of love between peculiar people.

The mythos of spring still calls out the idea of fertility rites and yearning desires in the characters, even with the hero's desire resisted by some opposition (usually paternal) and complicated by some obstacle and numerous twists in the plot. As Shakespeare sent his lovers into forests, escaping into the green world of fresh beginnings, the Bible portrays men and women meeting at wells, the bar or the watering hole of biblical times. Take, for instance, the story of Jacob and his wild romances at a well in a field (Genesis 29).

First, Jacob, the trickster son of Laughter (Isaac in Hebrew means laughter) cheats his hungry brother Esau out of his birthright, even masquerading himself to his own father Isaac. Then, the Mother's Boy flees and takes to the road. He comes upon the tavern or bar of his day, the watering hole or well, where one met women and got into bar-room fights. (See Exodus 2 for Moses meeting Zipporah at the well, when he gets into a fight with some unsavory characters; Genesis 24 for Eliezer picking up the beautiful virgin Rebekah for Isaac just because she offered him a drink; or the sowing and reaping wild oats in Ruth 2.) Jacob finds the beauty Rachel at the well, gives her a kiss, and goes home to meet the parents. He's the first Jewish courtier, more like Ben Stiller and Woody Allen, who gets so drunk at the wedding that he ends up in bed with Rachel's weak-eyed older sister, Leah. Yet, all turns out well as he gets both sisters, their handmaidens, and lots of sheep and livestock. Yet who would want to live in the Red Tent with such a company?

The comedy transports the lovers from one kind of world to another, from the world of an obstructing father-in-law Laban to a new promised land of the hero and heroine. The characters go into a Green World, a world of magic, transformation, and discovery, where even the victimized Esau forgives and welcomes them back.

The primary differences between the romantic and screwball comedies are at least fivefold. First, the former emphasizes realistic human lovers while the screwball focuses upon slapstick lunatics, ones whose physical antics make them look crazy or drunk or both. Second, the screwball spoofs the romance, with Jacob's excessive inebriation on his honeymoon a source of many jokes. The screwball eschews the sentiment and mocks the romantic process, with dueling men and women playing games over melodrama. Third, one finds quirky and odd characters rather than your typical boy and girl next door. Fourth, screwballs often insert a third party into the mating rituals, a Leah to surprise the amorous, drunken Jacob. (As our vicar, Father Andy Buchanan, once quipped, "You think you go to bed with Rachel, but you wake up with Leah." Life throws you curve balls as well as screwballs.) Finally, the pacing in screwball comedies escalates quickly versus a slower *anagnorisis* and a gradually evolving attraction between two polar opposites.

The *anagnorisis* is that moment when crystallization occurs, a point of resolution in the action called the time of comic discovery or comic awareness or recognition. All of this ends like the romantic comedy, with a party or festive ritual, the most common being the wedding. As poet e. e. cummings penned, "springtime is my time, is your time, is love-time and viva sweet love." But the wedding in the Christian faith is far closer to Cana than to the love-times of the Greek god of wine, Dionysus, and his bacchanalian origins of comedy. That does not mean, however, that it is without its earthy laughter.

Take, for instance, the mix of traditional ritual and liberating novelty in the cross-class comedy of *Jumping the Broom* (Salim Akil, 2011), where one seemingly sweeps away the old and leaps into the new, but actually holds on to the blessed past. Learning that she has been sexually exploited once again, Sabrina Watson (Paula Patton) barters with God, promising never again to show her "boobies" to any man except the man she would marry.

> Oh God, I did it again. I gave up the cookie for a cute face, nice body, and some mediocre conversation. I don't even think he can spell mediocre. I promise God, again, that if you get me out of this situation with some dignity … [she sees the guy laughing on his iPhone with someone else while she dresses]. Okay, Just get me out of here. I promise to only share my cookies with my future husband. No more of this.

Driving away, she continues her prayer, "And, God, because it's obvious I don't know how to spot a human being, could you please make it clear who you want me to be with. I mean clear! Clear! The kind of clear …" Not watching where she is driving, she hits a pedestrian, Jason Taylor (Laz Alonso), not realizing that she has just run over her future husband. "Oh my God," she exclaims, "Are you okay?" It will prove to be an immediate answer to a heartfelt prayer. Later, she confesses, "God, did I say how much I love your sense of humor?"

The religious film comedy includes kissing and sex. The Song of Solomon invites one to scan a catalogue of lovemaking tips and that eccentric Danish Christian bachelor, Søren "The Crazy" Kierkegaard, pens paragraphs on the art of kissing, categorizing kisses according to length, participants, onomatopoeia (all the sounds one could make from smacking to hissing), etc. He concludes that only one kiss is qualitatively different from all other kisses and that is the first kiss. One never forgets one's first kiss.

As humorist Mike Yaconelli once wrote, the purpose of the Church is to kiss frogs, to bring about transformation through love. Of course one can also find the travails of the frog that went to a fortune teller and was told that he would meet a beautiful and intelligent woman in his future who would want to discover everything about him she could.

"Where?" asked the frog excitedly, "At a party, in church, at a restaurant?"

"No," said the fortune teller, "in a biology lab."

The comic disasters of romance have been recorded by us all, from a date falling off a horse in a muddy field and carried back to the house, only to be dropped in a mud puddle by one of the present authors just before arriving, to a date who brought out a puppet at a restaurant and spoke through the damn thing throughout the meal. Until we meet the true one, we all suffer the indignities of romance. Love teaches us humility.

If one wanted to trip into the Elysian Fields of comic romance, one need travel no further than one of the grand masters of screwball comedies, writer/director Preston Sturges. Sturges' golden rules for successful comedy start with how "a pretty girl is better than a plain one" and "a leg is better than an arm." It continues with "a birth is better than a death," and "a chase is better than a chat," but then like Hebraic climactic parallelism, it builds: "A dog is better than a landscape; a kitten is better than a dog; a baby is better than a kitten; a kiss is better than a baby; and a pratfall is better than anything."[2] That formula is put to good test in his *The Lady Eve* (1941), a playful screwball in which Jean Harrington, a.k.a. "Eve" (Barbara Stanwyck), tempts and hoodwinks her "Adam," Charles Pike (Henry Fonda), ophiologist, scholar of snakes. No protection is given this vulnerable, naïve "Hopsie," the herpetologist, when the female of the species decides to take him down. Gender inversion creates a series of loud pratfalls. Yet, it is the "age-old tale of Eve snagging Adam."[3]

In his research to understand snakes, Pike has brought a pet snake, "Emma," that he found in the Amazon with him as he joins a cruise back home to the United States. Not only a bachelor, Pike is also heir to the family brewery business, Pike Ale. On the ship he is pursued by all manner of the fairer sex, including a lady wrestler and a plump lady who drops her handkerchief. Harrington shines with her comic portrayal of a shady Eve, who with her card-sharp father trolls for an easy mark and sucker in Pike.

Harrington first gains Pike's attention by dropping a literal apple on his head, harbinger of his own fall. In fact, Adam falls quite a bit. Adam falls, and falls again and again. Often because he is tripped by Jean, with her dainty foot stuck out. The theme of falling leads to the medieval notion of *felix culpa*, the happy, blessed or fortunate fall. Both Augustine and Aquinas celebrated this *exsultet* of the Easter Vigil: "O felix culpa quae talem et tantum meruit habere redemptorem" (O happy fall that merited such and so great a Redeemer). Unfortunate things happen, like the Fall of man, that God then works for good, even in the incarnation exploding out of the disobedience of original sin. The misery of Hopsie's falls will eventuate into his blessed state.

When his snake Emma gets loose in her stateroom, Jean is afraid that it will crawl into her cabin bed. Scholar Theresa Sanders points out the connection between sex and snakes, bringing Freud and St. Aquinas into the discussion of the Garden of Eden and *The Lady Eve*. She notes that the "power of witches is more apparent in serpents" because it is through the "means of a serpent the devil tempted woman."[4] A phallic reading of the film is easily evinced in a book Pike reads, *Are Snakes Necessary?* Sturges slyly alludes to a popular publication of 1929 written by humorists James Thurber and E. B. White, a classic entitled *Is Sex Necessary?*

Yet Jean falls for Pike too, but when she and her shyster father are unmasked and sent packing, she vows revenge and reappears as "Lady Eve Sidwich." She plans a sweet comeuppance for having been jilted for being honest. She explains her new relationship with Pike as "I've got some unfinished business with him – I need him like the ax needs the turkey."

Figure 5.1 Even without her apple, the con woman Eve (Barbara Stanwyck) has her way with the guileless and hapless Charles Pike (Henry Fonda). *The Lady Eve*, Paramount Pictures, 1941. Author's screenshot.

Amid her schemes, Pike's valet/assistant looks on warily. Mugsy Murgatroyd (William Demarest) remains unconvinced: "You trying to tell me this ain't the same *rib* was on the boat?" Pike sees no relation, but Mugsy persists: "It's the same dame, I tell you." Pike may have that scientific knowledge of snakes, but lacks that personal knowledge of taste and discernment. As the French offer two verbs to know, *savoir* and *connaître*, intellectual knowledge and intimate knowing, Pike remains stuck in the former. The screwball comedy answers the question raised in the Wife of Bath's Tale (the same woman who sent five husbands on to Jesus quite early), namely "What do women want?" And Pike understands neither a woman nor the question.

As they marry, the film fits Stanley Cavell's term, a comedy of remarriage, of couples providentially intended to be together, being screwed with until they end up together. Eve bewilders and bewitches her Adam, and makes him "cockeyed," one of Sturges' favorite words. Confronted by the mystery that is woman, Adam is told "You don't know very much about girls. The best ones aren't as good as you probably think they are, and the bad ones aren't as bad. Not nearly as bad."

The quirkiness of the characters, the spoofing of love, romance, and marriage as a con game, the inversion of girl meets boy, loses boy, and gets boy back through duping and scamming, the slapstick falls, and the ultimate wedding consummation celebrate the full delight of screwball comedy.

Harry Cohn of Columbia Studios wanted to make a religious picture. DeMille was making millions off of his *Ten Commandments* (1923) and *King of Kings* (1927). So Harry argued with his brother Jack. Harry challenged Jack, claiming that he knew nothing about religion.

> "What the hell do you know about the Bible, Jack? I'll bet you fifty bucks you don't even know the Lord's Prayer," said Harry.
>
> "Oh, yes I do," boasted Jack.
>
> "Well then, let's hear it," prodded his brother.
>
> Jack started: "Now I lay me down to sleep …"
>
> "Okay, okay," conceded Harry. "You win," and handed over the fifty bucks.[5]

Hiring Frank Capra not only gave the brothers films with a religious slant, but romantic/screwball comedies as well. The Academy Award-winning *It Happened One Night* (1934) put opposite attractions on the road, dunking donuts and sharing carrots, culminating in the denial of one wedding and the promise of another. Even the walls of Jericho came tumbling down, all with the help of a phallic trumpet. The only thing missing was a baby.

And a baby does come in the most delightful of Columbia Studio screwball comedies, director Richard Boleslawski's *Theodora Goes Wild* (1936), where the scandal of screwball faith unleashes fresh laughter and sly fertility rites.[6]

Romantic and screwball comedies spin on an obstacle. The greater the initial conflicts between young lovers, the sweeter the reunion. Even when young lovers are separated, and then reunited and reconciled after social misunderstandings and connivances on their own part, the joy of reunion ushers in a season of laughter.

In one of her choicest and most delicious roles, Irene Dunne is the seemingly prim and proper, but assuredly not repressed, Theodora Lynn. In the scheme of comic narratives, names mean something. Take, for instance, the name Theodora, from the Greek meaning "gift from God," derived from "δῶρον" (*doron*, gift) and "θεός" (*theos*, god). The name refers to both a present or votive offering to a god or a gift given by God. The gift can be of honor or of personal charms. She who receives the name, be it Theodora or Dorothy, also receives the blessings of God.

The tale is almost a peculiar version of the country mouse meeting a city rat, and beating him at his own game. But more importantly, it is a film about the nature of the Fall, the heroine a mousy, cute church organist surreptitiously writing a scandalous novel entitled *Sinner* and then going to the Big Apple where temptation is written in neon lights and her male tempter the smooth, divorced, pushy, and inconsiderate illustrator of her own written script.

Premiering at Radio City Music Hall, the screwball antics were recognized by *Times* reviewer Frank Nugent, who proclaimed that Irene Dunne as Theodora goes silly.[7] (A Lynn may go wild, says her reprobate uncle, but never silly.) Complaining that director Boleslawski's frolicsome piece contains several moments of ingratiating comedy, Nugent still praises its merriment.[8] Adapting a Mary McCarthy story, Sidney Buchman (who also wrote *Holiday* (1939), *Mr. Smith Goes to Washington* (1939), and the Oscar-winning *Here Comes Mr. Jordan* (1941)) crafted a clever, fast-paced screenplay with a few twists, and tweaks the religious noses of the community while affirming the grace of God meddling in romantic affairs. The film exploits comedy dealing with divorce, suggested pre-marital sex, drinking, and an "illegitimate" baby; yet this "torrid" farce is mild rather than wild, but equally charming, with several satirical hits.

The film opens with church organist Theodora Lynn leading the worship in singing "Rock of Ages," in a town peopled with quaint and eccentric characters. The hymn's lyrics confess that Theodora Lynn wants to hide herself in God, petitioning the Lord for a hiding place in His presence from those who would pry into her life, from church hypocrites to city playboy. The hymn also confesses sin and entreats God to save her, for God alone can make her pure. Singing the hymn's refrain of "and make me pure," when she is pretending to be scandalous, makes sense.[9]

As the town's model saint, Theodora has secretly written a best-selling risqué novel under the *nom de plume* of Caroline Adams. Her spinster aunts and a bevy of prudish but titillated busybodies and "buzzards" called the Lynn Literary Society (with an over-the-top performance by Spring Byington as Rebecca Perry, the gossipy leader of the Ladies' Auxiliary Circle) rail against the scandalous immorality of the salacious book that the local newspaper editor Jed (Thomas Mitchell) gleefully publishes in serial form in the *Lynn Bugle*. "I want to apologize," he states scornfully, "for waking Lynnfield out of a twenty-year sleep." Meeting at the town hall, the Circle believes it their duty to keep Lynnfield "the one upstanding, God-fearing place left on earth" and passes a resolution to inform the newspaper that "this community condemns [this sexy trash] lock, stock, and barrel."

Pretending to go to meet her Uncle John, the black sheep of the Lynn family, and Rebecca Perry's niece, who is secretly married and pregnant, the sheltered Theodora sneaks off to New York City to meet her publisher. When she meets with Arthur Stevenson (Thurston Hall), dapper and authoritative, he mockingly reads a telegram from her hometown that describes her book as a "disgrace to American morals and a sin against American youth."

Theodora suddenly realizes that "I was a writer of wide reputation and most of it bad." She sees her *alter ego* Caroline Adams as immoral. The publisher laughs because the book is "sweeping the country." But, she

Figure 5.2 Theodora (Irene Dunne), the gift of God to Lynnfield, plays the organ and sings lustily, even while she pseudonymously publishes her scandalous novel, *The Sinner. Theodora Goes Wild*, Columbia Pictures Corporation, 1936. Author's screenshot.

meekly protests, "not clean." The impact of projecting her inner world, however fictional, makes her anxious.

Stevenson is nonplussed. Trying to explain herself, she asks him three questions: "Were you raised in a small town by two maiden aunts? Have you taught Sunday school for 15 years? Have you played the organ in church for ten years?" Tradition and a religious heritage make it difficult to confess one's sins, however imaginary, in public.

He remains amused, in a modern New Yorker way: "Nobody throws away a public in the millions and a tremendous career because of a conscience! It isn't done."

Then she is also pursued by the book's cover artist Michael Grant (a debonair but annoying Melvyn Douglas), a divorced sophisticate who recognizes that she is not the vamp or sinner she pretends to be. Michael takes a patronizing liking to her, promising to break her out of her "jail." At a dinner with her publisher, Theodora becomes irritated with his obnoxious presence as he smugly mocks her as a teetotaler. She brazenly orders a whiskey and gets drunk. When he playfully makes a pass at this "wild" woman, she panics and flees back to Lynnfield, Connecticut.

Following her back to Lynn, he inveigles his way into being hired as a gardener. Working around the yard he intends to shock the straight-laced and wholesome lady into a liberated state. Rumors proliferate among the town gossips. Yet Theodora finds herself enjoying this rascal. In a scene of going "green" into the woods from the gray of the city, they go berry-picking and fishing. However, when they return to town, they discover, to Theodora's chagrin, that it is Sunday and everyone is coming out of church. The scandal swells, but Theodora tells the disapproving prudes that she loves this man. He, however, gets nervous and escapes back to his urban fortress.

Impulsively she turns the tables. In a wild escapade, she invades his Park Avenue apartment, just as Michael's estranged wife arrives with his father, the Lieutenant Governor, who is campaigning to become Governor. Michael's loveless marriage is merely a convenient political front. Michael shows himself as just as stuffy and stifled and bourgeois as the ladies of Lynnfield. However, Theodora the redeemed sinner stands her ground, ready to cause a scandal if need be to declare her love. She will free Michael just as he tried to liberate her.

The aggressive woman of grace triumphs over the law, just as Sarah superseded Hagar as a woman of promise. Theodora comes to divorce him from the social decorum that has trapped him. A romance of joy interrupts the hypocrisy of Michael's political predicament. Providence, we see, ordains true love as opposed to pragmatic relations. This screwball is anchored in the apostle Paul's principle of grace over the constraining law of respectability. In his Letter to the Romans, St. Paul comments on Abraham's divorce from Hagar as symbolic of a sinner's liberation from the law of sin and death. The public propriety of decorum is challenged by a new freedom of love.

Theodora is engulfed in publicity as a scandalous "other woman," a co-respondent in two divorce cases. Her publisher's wife warns of Theodora going wild: "That adorable young thing is an unholy terror on wheels. There's nothing in the world more deadly than innocence on the manhunt!" She suspects, falsely, that her husband is fooling around as well.

Reporters hound Theodora for her racy confessions, as she dresses in feathers and explodes with mischief and cheek. As Michael pressed her to break loose from her laws, she now does so with pranks and chutzpah. When she crashes the Governor's ball, she makes certain that news photographers catch her kissing Michael. Notoriety reigns supreme. The bitchy separated wife Agnes demands an official divorce. Once free from the law, Michael is enabled to receive God's gift to him.

Back home, her spinster aunts, "the plaster saints," show backbone and stand up for their seemingly wayward niece. In a wonderfully comic scene, the two aunts march into the church while the congregation sings "Onward, Christian Soldiers." As the two oracles of the town arrive at their front pew, the singing stops the mouths of the hypocritical biddies gaping at them. Then, with all the boldness of martyrs, the two ladies triumphantly belt out "marching as to war, with the Cross of Jesus going on before!" The militant hymn punctuates their defense of one of God's sinners and saints, their niece Theodora.

As Theodora returns to her small provincial community, she is feted as a celebrity. However, she brings a newborn baby with her, an act which horrifies the now divorced Michael and causes Rebecca Perry to flutter and flap with judgmental posturing. However, when Theodora reveals that the baby actually belongs to Rebecca's own secretly married daughter, the disapproving and self-righteous hypocrite gets her comeuppance. "So help me," quips Theodora's supportive Aunt Elsie, "this town gets more narrow-minded every day." Theodora places the baby in the arms of a shocked grandmother, Rebecca.

The notion of disguise in love, as in Max Beerbohm's short story "The Happy Hypocrite," suggests that we become what we pretend to be. The real people beyond the facades are both wilder and tamer than we expected. The film's premise, a magical transformation of a protagonist, makes honest people out of embarrassed sinners.

The bourgeois belief regarding love and romance in Flaubert's *Madame Bovary* is built on the idea that "life should imitate art." It is Bovary's downfall, leading to a condition called Bovarism, "an unreal and imagined conception of the self and desire to be what one is not. Real joy is bypassed in exchange for an unattainable and impractical ideal." This unreal or romanticized vision of oneself leads to acting in socially sanctioned ways, but in denying one's heart. *Theodora Goes Wild* subverts both models of hiding one's true self and unleashing all one's basic instincts. Instead, it shows in the quaint and eccentric figures of New England and New York that one does best when one confesses one's sins and follows one's heart. In the presence of God, one can go wild and screwy.

The screwball comedy showcases odd ways in which God works in the lives of His children. It shows that whether we meet at a well or on eHarmony (conceived by my old Fuller Theological Seminary professor, Neil Clark Warren, since he looked out at so many desperate young bachelor students and thought he needed to do something practical – so wrote a pamphlet on "Selecting a Marriage Partner." It didn't bear fruit in this author's life until the 1980s when I met my wife Karen at a performance of *Messiah* where the song "For Unto Us a Child Is Born" lingered in my imagination), God works providentially to not only direct our paths, but to wind our paths in curving ways. Our call is to keep to the path and not stray. The Book of Proverbs offers enough guidance for young men and women not to deviate. Flee from the loose woman. Follow Wisdom. Seek Prudence. In one study session on the Book of Proverbs for a group of middle school boys, one of the present authors invited three beautiful and sexy high school girls to interrupt one session, rub the hair of these younger boys, and whisper in their ears, "I am Wisdom. I am Prudence. Follow me. Seek me." Those boys have never forgotten the enchantment of seeking wisdom.

The screwball comedy opens up romantic relationships and invites its participants to laugh with even more hilarity, even as the lovers get old and cranky. Clueless and irascible Adams will always need sassy Eves. And men will always chase women who have already decided to catch them. Chesterton, in another moment of utmost clarity, remarked that there is

> an idea that it is humiliating to run after one's hat; and when people say it is humiliating they mean that it is comic. It certainly is comic; but man is a very comic creature, and most of the things he does are comic – eating, for instance. And the most comic things of all are exactly the things that are most worth doing – such as making love. A man running after a hat is not half so ridiculous as a man running after a wife.[10]

In screwball comedies, nothing is simultaneously so comic, so humiliating, and so wonderful.

Notes

1 The French tale of Marcel Pagnol's *The Baker's Wife* (*La femme du boulanger*, 1938) squeezes a parable out of what happens when the bride of the baker Aimable (Raimu), who provides the living bread for the community, deserts him and runs away for an adulterous affair. Everyone must join in odd pairs to retrieve the wayward bride of the breadmaker (the bread of life cannot be shared until the bridegroom's wife is returned) and restore the blessed union so that they have bread to eat, even with a Communist teaming up with the priest to find Aurélie, the golden Gomer girl. Such is the allegory of God and Israel, who continually chased after false shepherds, to be pursued by prophets of every kind.
2 In his *Palm Beach Story* (1942) he crafted a line that stood as the essence of sex in screwball comedies: "You have no idea what a long-legged woman can do without doing anything at all." The Office of War Information blasted this film as un-American as it challenged old ways of marriage only to celebrate them in the end.
3 Staff, "Review: *The Lady Eve*," *Variety* (December 31, 1940).
4 Theresa Sanders, *Approaching Eden: Adam and Eve in Popular Culture* (Rowman and Littlefield, 2009), 47–51 (49).
5 Bob Thomas, *King Cohn: The Life and Times of Harry Cohn* (G. P. Putnam's Sons, 1967), 243.
6 Staff, "*Theodora Goes Wild*," *Variety* (December 31, 1935).
7 Frank S. Nugent, "The Screen: *Theodora Goes Wild*," *New York Times* (November 13, 1936).
8 This Polish director would also direct the overtly religious *Les misérables* (1935).
9 The hymn's historical composition also bears on the film's narrative. In 1776, Augustus M. Toplady, a staunch Calvinist, despised John Wesley's

Arminian theology of holiness. Toplady called the father of Methodism "a lurking, sly assassin" and so wrote "Rock of Ages" on God's forgiveness. It slapped Wesley's emphasis upon sanctification and free will. In this screwball comedy, the "sinner" is the best saint in Lynnfield, Connecticut, and the Providence of God as Toplady articulated it plays out with wacky sovereignty. One of the best-loved, best-known, and most widely used hymns attacks the hypocrisy of both the small-town gossips and the metropolitan sophisticates.

10 G. K. Chesterton, "On Running After One's Hat," in *All Things Considered* (Methuen & Co., 1915).

6 Musical Comedy

"Joy," says the devil Screwtape, spit spilling out in his rage, "is the music of heaven."[1] Disgusted at its sheer goodness, the denizens of hell protest this melodious joy as a most detestable source of laughter.

Unlike the angry hippie Jesus depicted in Norman Jewison's "rock opera" *Jesus Christ Superstar* (1973, from the rock opera by Andrew Lloyd Webber and Tim Rice), David Greene's *Godspell: A Musical Based on the Gospel according to St. Matthew* (1973) (composer Stephen Schwartz) offers a deliciously comic musical based on the parables and episodes of the gospel. From the Bethesda Fountain to the haunting presence of the World Trade Center, the backdrop of New York City opens up a fresh modern adaption of telling Bible stories.

Riffing derives from a musical exercise of jazz, a spontaneous improvisational turn in which musicians run wildly through unbridled notes. In film comedy, riffing (which rarely has an analogue in other fictional forms) can be seen as a sort of "goofing" or "miscellaneous bits."[2]

Riffing is that improvisational narrative that draws random bits together into a delightful show. While it may be difficult to see a film based on the Bible as riffing, *Godspell* achieves a comic version of the Bible that plays with parables under the grand scheme of Matthew's gospel of the life, death, and passion of Christ. It needed only a genuine resurrection to make it authentic good news.[3]

Godspell translates the parables of the Gospel of Matthew into vaudeville bits, with the story of the prodigal son acted out as a silent slapstick comedy ("I said 'kill the cow!'"). The gags flow serendipitously with the rhythms, pacing, and energy of the film, hopping from one bit to another. The parable of the goats and sheep divides the interchangeable group of disciples until the clownish Jesus invites all back into His flock. The comedy flows with various pericopae popping up until a somber eucharistic supper in which Jesus removes the paint from His disciples' faces (i.e. washes their feet) and prepares for His death. Yet the joie de vivre of the film infectiously summons viewers to sing "Day by Day," blending into the streets of New York City.[4]

Figure 6.1 With unbridled joy and divine playfulness, Jesus (Victor Garber) leads the motley disciples through Stephen Schwartz' rousing music. *Godspell*, Columbia Pictures Corporation, 1973. Author's screenshot.

The cinematic comedy of Jesus and His disciples occurs in other places. Cecil B. DeMille's silent version of *King of Kings* (1927) places Jesus with the little children. One cute-as-a-button young girl asks if Jesus heals broken legs. He nods. Then she asks Him to fix the broken leg of her wooden doll. He and the disciples smile at each other; then He twists twine into the joints and heals the toy. Comic moments occur in hagiographies, in the lives of saints as well. As we mentioned earlier, Rossellini's *Flowers of St. Francis* ends with a dizzy merry-go-round of the little brothers spinning in circles until they fall down. The direction they end up pointing to is interpreted as God's will. It is a joyous game of providence. To paraphrase an old saw, what seems like coincidence is actually God's way of remaining anonymous and still directing lives. And even as St. Francis was renowned as one of God's jesters, in St. Paul's language a "fool for Christ," he exuded the humor of the earth and the joy of the heavens. All nature and fools sing.

Music in the Bible is frequently joined by the glorious sounds of rejoicing. But frequently the expression of joy is occasioned by difficulty and suffering. While in exile by the rivers of Babylon, God's people weep and yearn for Jerusalem and are asked to "sing one of the songs of Zion." While their tormenting captors mock them with mirth, they will not sing and even hang their lyres upon the willows. Musical comedy is born in such trouble and looks forward to deliverance.

Following Moses' lead, Miriam the prophetess, Aaron's sister, takes a timbrel in her hand and sings (with all the women following her dancing with their own timbrels):

Sing to the LORD,
for he is highly exalted.
Both horse and rider
he has hurled into the sea.

Music's association with laughter dots many Hebrew Scriptures, with the Psalmist summoning "Oh come, let us sing to the LORD; let us make a joyful noise to the rock of our salvation!" (Psalm 95:1); "Make a joyful noise to the LORD, all the earth! Serve the LORD with gladness! Come into his presence with singing!" (Psalm 100:1); and "Then our mouth was filled with laughter, and our tongue with shouts of joy; then they said among the nations, 'The LORD has done great things for them' " (Psalm 126:2). Isaiah sees mirth connected to the lyre and tambourine (24:8). Each of them connects the goodness of God to expressions of musical praise and laughter. Rejoicing is musical laughter.

Even the work-oriented apostle James recommends the ancient virtue of *hilaritas*: "Is anyone cheerful? Let him sing praise" (5:13). Such a recommendation leads to the sub-genre of musical comedy films, where the music is infectious and the laughter contagious. Musical comedy transports the audience from the rivers of Babylon and lifts them to new heights of delight, even to the hills of Austria, which are alive with *The Sound of Music* (Robert Wise, 1965).

The musical comedy is best characterized as a sub-genre of joy and bliss, whether on *42nd Street* (Lloyd Bacon, 1933) or *Singin' in the Rain* (Stanley Donen, Gene Kelly, 1952). It carries its spectators toward heaven, or as Richard Dyer expresses it, toward a utopian vision. Utopia stands as any real or imaginary society, place, or state considered to be perfect or ideal. Spectators long for this utopian place as the Israelites longed for Zion, and it is music that connects us to that ideal location. Musicals offer an image of something better to escape into, or something we deeply want that our day-to-day lives do not provide. In one sense they offer "escape" and "wish fulfillment." In another, they create that world for which we feel we have been made. We are only pilgrims here, strangers in a strange land, looking for home. Thus musical comedies awaken the nostalgia for that sublime spot, over the rainbow or someplace in 19th-century St. Louis where we can find our paradise itself.

Dyer lists five needs that lie behind the longing for the utopian, five wants that beg to be fulfilled. Each is satisfied by a peculiarly matching characteristic supplied by musicals, gifts that splash the comedy films with ultimate pleasures and fulfillment.[5]

First is the category of *exhaustion* and *listlessness* in which life is experienced as unending and enervating work. Life is a grind or rut that one cannot escape. In answer, the musical comedy offers *energy*, an explosion of zest where dance and play and work become synonymous. Enthusiasm matches exhaustion and listlessness is overwhelmed and animated by vim, vigor, and vitality.

The second real need is *scarcity*, or poverty, both of physical needs and spiritual needs. The utopian response to sparse dearth of body and soul is naturally *abundance*, where wealth is shared and bread and wine spill over with gladness. The empty or half-filled glass is filled to overflowing.

Third, *dreariness* and *monotony* set a gloom over the community. The dull and tedious living of those condemned to routine or to boring tasks needs to be liberated. They are freed by the *intensity* and *passion* of the musical. What seems gray and bleak now breaks into rainbows and rejoicings. Even a lackluster monotony can be reframed in fresh and cheerful ways.

Fourth, the miserable experiences of *manipulation* and *exploitation* by others (or even by oneself to others) need radical transformation. What the musical offers in response is a genuine *transparency* and acts of *true love*. The masquerades of comedy are stripped and the confession of true selves ushers in honest and happy affection among the company of sinners turned into saints.

Finally, the musical comedy answers the modern problem of *fragmentation*, of individuals living life in isolation, waiting for Godot or finding no exit for their existence. Separated from each other, the audience is reconnected by song and laughter to *community*, to a fellowship of companions and friends, of people who will eat and drink and sing together.

Each need left to itself leads into its own dystopia, its own hell. One brief example may suffice, for now. The material prosperity of the late 1950s carried its own seeds of monotony for men in gray-flannel suits, making Madmen out of the routine-following, martini-drinking lonely crowd, who felt manipulated by a cultural climate that pushed for conformity.[6] In films, the opiate of the audience (snarked Luis Buñuel) "is conformity." The grand Arthur Freed musicals of the decade liberated spectators (even as filmmakers were desperately aiming to steal them back from the tiny screens in their living rooms) to live large with romancing, dancing, and singing in the rain.

New Yorker critic Pauline Kael worried that *The Sound of Music* (a.k.a. The Sound of Money) would singlehandedly unleash a wave of repression of artistic freedom. She eschewed its wholesomeness.[7] For Kael, the freshness of this film seemed mechanically engineered and manipulative in a Pavlovian way. But even with her cynical protests at this sugar-coated mush, she acknowledged, however begrudgingly, that its tug at the heart-strings worked, that she responded in a basic, universal way, even "humming those sickly, goody-goody songs." Utopia comes even to cynics and critics.

Emerging from the blessed cloister of a religious community, Maria (Julie Andrews) in *The Sound of Music* (1965) exudes the grace and exuberance of a young evangelist of joy. Released from her cell, she

Figure 6.2 About to leave the quiet sanctity of the convent, Maria (Julie Andrews) prepares to discover a few more of her favorite things. *The Sound of Music*, Robert Wise Productions, 1965. Author's screenshot.

spreads a gospel of effervescence as she dances into a dark and danger-ous world. Such a missionary of sprightly goodness is desperately needed as a governess for seven constrained children living in Austria in the late 1930s, where the Nazi hell is about to be unleashed. The story follows the von Trapp family as concert celebrities in Salzburg, Austria, just before fleeing across the Bavarian Alps into Switzerland.

Maria's new calling is to shepherd the über-disciplined children of Captain George von Trapp (Christopher Plummer), whose only musical training consists of the sounds of a military whistle calling them to atten-tion and obedience. Under his command they march well, but lack the delight of living well. Their regimented routine is militantly monotonous. The home is a model of rigorously enforced discipline and the mischiev-ous children secretly rebel against the restrictions that force them to obey rather than play. But they fear their father too much to be transparent before him.

When Maria arrives, the Captain blows his whistle. "Now, when I want you, this is what you will hear."

"Oh, no sir; I'm sorry, sir. I could never answer to a whistle. Whistles are for dogs and cats and other animals, but not for children and defin-itely not for me. It would be too ... humiliating." What she offers in return is the musical laughter of "My Favorite Things," "Do, Re, Mi," and "The Lonely Goatherd." She breaks down his stiff regimen and manipulation of his children (the first rule of his house *is* discipline!) and shows how they are little human beings who need his love.

Maria brings music back into the house and friskiness. When the Prioress wonders how does "one handle a girl like Maria?" she, and eventually the Captain, discover that it is like trying to bottle a sunbeam. She radiates wonder. In e. e. cummings' words, she teaches more than one bird how to sing rather than a thousand stars how not to dance. Nature, God's creation, comes alive as if it were a Hebrew festival. Even the hills clap their hands.

Into the dreary existence of the von Trapps, an existence where habits of good discipline petrify the children, comes this avalanche of laughter and music. For all those behind the walls of their constrained lives, she sees possibility: "When the Lord closes a door," she observes, "somewhere He opens a window."

Another more comic musical illustrates the same conditions that Dyer lists. *Sister Act* (Emile Ardolino, 1992) ushers one into the sounds of comic and joyous laughter through slapstick and music. Whoopi Goldberg is the wisecracking Deloris Van Cartier, a proverbial fish out of water, whose childhood harks back to Catholic school in 1968. When asked who can name all the apostles, she calls out, "John, Paul, George ... and Ringo!"

As the other children laugh, the nun calls her "the most unruly, disobedient girl in this school! Now, I want you to march right up to that blackboard and write the names of all the apostles alphabetically." She mischievously does so, but scribbles in big underlined letters, "John, Paul, Peter" and "Elvis," to another round of laughter.

"This is enough!" shouts the nun. "You are hopeless, and I wash my hands of you. Mark my words, Deloris. If you continue on this disruptive track, it will lead straight to the devil. Have you any idea what girls like you become?"

Little Deloris smiles. Now decades later, she sings at the Reno Moonlight Lounge. She is having an affair with casino owner Vince LaRocca (Harvey Keitel). This gangster/lover refuses to divorce his wife for her. He indicated that Father Antonelli told him in confession that if he got a divorce he would burn in hell for all eternity and so asks Deloris, "You want me to go against a priest and get ex-communicated?" Ironically, it will be the Roman Catholic Church which will protect and save her. When she witnesses Vince kill his chauffeur, she escapes and must be put in a witness protection program for her own safety.[8]

Her sanctuary is literally a sanctuary, a run-down San Francisco convent (actually St. Paul's Catholic Church in the Outer Mission District), located in a seedy, dilapidated block of homeless people, bikers, prostitutes, porno shops, and graffiti-marked slums. A sympathetic detective, Lt. Eddie Souther (Bill Nunn), hides her among white nuns, where no one would reasonably look for her. Masquerading as a nun, Deloris feels like Quasimodo in the belfry.

A strict and domineering Mother Superior (Maggie Smith) futilely tries to hold the failing convent together with a fortress mentality. When

Deloris meets her, she claims that there was "nothing wrong with my life. You know, before I came here, I had a career, I had friends, I had clothing that fit. Before I came here, I was okay."

"Oh, really," quips Reverend Mother, "From what I've heard, your singing career was almost non-existent, and your married lover wants you dead. If you're fooling anyone, it is only yourself. God has brought you here. Take the hint."

Out of the sleazy monotony of the Lounge and exploitation by her gangster boss, Deloris is taken in, however reluctantly, to become part of a community that will be transformed by music and laughter. She is told:

Reverend Mother: People wish to kill you. Anyone who's met you, I imagine. A disguise is necessary to protect us all. While you are here, you will conduct yourself as a nun. Only I will know who and what you truly are. You will draw no attention to yourself whatsoever.
Deloris: But look at me! I'm a nun! I'm a – I'm a penguin!

Told that from now on she would be known as Sister Mary Clarence, she is asked if she can handle the vows of poverty, obedience, and chastity. It's the third one that stumps her, "I'm outta here." While the poverty and austerity of the place are inherent tricks of the trade, the other nuns live a life of listlessness as well. As they try to sing "Hail Holy Queen Enthroned Above," the tune is horribly off-key and the choir ridiculously fragmented. One nun even sings three seconds behind everyone else.

Sister Mary Clarence brings more than a little rhythm to the choir. She brings an exuberant bounce, but also engages the former director, the elderly, acerbic, lanky, and deadpan Sister Mary Lazarus (Mary Wickes). They are instructed how to listen to each other. "That's a big key. Big key, you must listen to each other if you're going to be a group." None are left out. All are brought into the musical fold.

The church's services are sparsely attended. The priest repeatedly refers to the dwindling size of the congregation. However, at one Mass, the choir performs a "Hail Holy Queen" and then breaks out in a jazzy gospel rendition. Upset with the innovations, Reverend Mother accuses Deloris of trying to liven up church with popcorn and curtain calls, a sort of Willow Creek church. However, Monsignor O'Hara strategically calms the infuriated Superior, who even relents in letting the nuns go outside of the walls of the church to minister to the broken-down community. They clean litter and stand in front of porno shops. They tutor children and feed the hungry. As they serve the poor of the community, and as they sing contemporary songs with religious connotations, the parish begins to swell.

Belting out a sanctified version of 1960s rock hit "My Guy" by Smokey Robinson of the aptly named The Miracles, the choir sings "My God" after a lackluster rendition of "Crown Him with Many Crowns."[9] The reinvigorating Motown beat enlivens this flock of white misfits, who are

Figure 6.3 Sequestered in a church in a witness protection program, Deloris (Whoopi Goldberg) belts out converted hymns in *Sister Act*, injecting abundant life into staid church services. *Sister Act*, Touchstone Pictures, 1992. Author's screenshot.

funny in their own right. The shy Sister Mary Robert (Wendy Makkena) is revealed to be a diva and the eternally sunny and terminally cheerful Sister Mary Patrick (Kathy Najimy) brings a religious friskiness to the film. As she says, "I guess I've always been upbeat, optimistic, perky. My mother used to say that girl is pure sunshine. She'll either grow up to be a nun, or a stewardess. Coffee?"

Much of the humor centers on the practice of prayer. When Deloris asks what she is going to do in a place crazy with a lot of white women dressed as nuns, the detective Eddie says, "Pray." "Pray?" she asks incredulously. And pray the film does. The playful recognition of the forms of prayer invests the small transgressions with comedy. The incongruity of improper prayers contributes to the genial delight and intimacy of people talking to God in ordinary language.

At table with her new sisters for the first time, she is asked to give the blessing:

> Bless us, Oh Lord, for these Thy gifts which we are about to receive. And yea, though I walk through the valley of the shadow of no food, I will fear no hunger. We want you to give us this day, our daily bread. And to the republic for which it stands, and by the power invested in me, I pronounce us ready to eat. Amen.

Later, as the nuns seek to go to Reno to rescue Deloris, they approach a reluctant pilot, and begin a mess of prayers directed at altering his behavior. Threatening him with "May the Lord do to him what he is doing to us," he becomes a willing, albeit acquiescing, sky pilot helper.

Vince's two goons fear shooting a nun, but Vince tells them, "I know this woman, in the biblical sense, and she ain't no nun." As they are about to waste her, Deloris gets on her knees.

> *Willy*: What is she doin'?
> *Joey*: Oh, my God. She's prayin'!

Reciting the form of a prayer, Deloris makes her petitions known:

> Lord, I want you to forgive Willy and Joey, because they know not what they do. They're only doin' what Vince told 'em to do, because Vince is too chicken to do it himself! So he's called upon these two men to take care of his business! So I want you to forgive them, Lord. Espectum, espertum, cacoomb, toutu, eplubium. Amen!

When both Willy and Joey echo her "Amen," she socks them in the crotch and as they double over, she darts out of the room.

The other nuns arrive in Reno to rescue her, running amok through the casino. When Reverend Mother reveals the masquerade, that Deloris isn't a nun, they are surprised but amused. "Her real name is Deloris Van Cartier. She witnessed a vicious murder and has been hiding in our convent," she explains to the others.

The nuns query their Superior, "She ... she lied to us?" Another asks, "She wasn't a nun? But she made us sing so perfectly!" Then Sister Mary Patrick reflects and realizes, "Now that should have tipped us ..."

This revelation of her true identity leads not only to transparency, but to acceptance and a new community. Vince asserts that Deloris is "a broad. Y'got it? Just a broad!" to which Reverend Mother retorts, "I guarantee you she is no broad! She is Sister Mary Clarence of St. Katherine's Convent. She's a model of generosity, virtue, and love! You have my word for it, gentlemen, she is a nun!" The great comedy of spiritual transformation has begun.

The finale brings the house down as Deloris and the choir sing Peggy March's "I Will Follow Him." The words applied to God resonate with the multicultural congregation, infecting all with a contagious joy. Celebrating that "He" touched their heart, the choir belts out their commitment to follow Him "wherever He may go." They take comfort in the fact that nothing, neither a deep ocean nor high mountain, can keep them away from His love. They reach their climax vowing, "I love Him, I love Him, I love Him,/And where He goes, I'll follow, I'll follow, I'll follow." The entire congregation stands in a rousing ovation, including the Pope sitting, clapping, and enjoying the worship from the balcony. The overriding experience of this musical comedy is the laughter of joy. For C. S. Lewis, the purest laughter on earth dwells in the kingdom of joy, where volleys of laughter fall upon those who will receive them. As the old devil Screwtape observed, it occurs "among friends and lovers reunited on the eve of a holiday. Among adults some pretext in the way of jokes is usually provided, but the facility with which the smallest witticisms produce laughter at such a time shows that they are not the real cause." This laughter is a foretaste of heaven, or as Franz Joseph Haydn expressed the origins of his music, "When I think upon my God, my heart is so full of joy that the notes dance and leap from my pen."

Utopia sneaks in through musical comedy, feeding those longings and needs that keep us tethered to the petty problems of our lives. The making of a communal noise, whether song or laughter, breaks the bonds of gravity and gives a peculiar pleasure to human beings. Levity of body and spirit are unleashed, and the laughter is not only good for the lungs, but also for the sheer delight of comic fellowship.[10]

Notes

1 C. S. Lewis, *The Screwtape Letters* (HarperCollins, 2015). Screwtape did, however, adorn the cover of *Time* magazine in 1942 along with his creator C. S. Lewis.

2 Gerald Mast, *The Comic Mind: Comedy and the Movies* (Bobbs-Merrill Company, 1973), 7.

3 Of course, after Mel Gibson's controversial, but successful, *Passion of the Christ*, *The Onion* wrote that "Jesus Demands Creative Control over Next Movie" (March 3, 2004), 1. The Lord indicated that "I never should have given Mel Gibson so much license." He decided to take back the movie projects on his life, shepherding them from casting to marketing. In particular, He said, "Just look at *Godspell* – what the heck was going on there? It's time I reclaim My image." He complained that the movies did make His disciples "pop." "Some of those guys were real cut-ups, you know. Simon Peter could make you laugh tears of blood."

4 The song will be heard as a prayer spoken by Ben Stiller in *Meet the Parents* and form the content of the "grace" said before the meal, as Hollywood learns to pray from the movies.

5 Richard Dyer, "Entertainment and Utopia," in *Movies and Methods* (ed. Bill Nichols) (University of California Press, 1988), 220–232.

6 David Riesman, Nathan Glazer, and Reuel Denney, *The Lonely Crowd* (Yale University Press, 1961). But then the 1950s laughed at Jerry Lewis, who was his own lonely crowd.

7 Pauline Kael, *Kiss Kiss, Bang Bang* (Little, Brown, and Co., 1968), 176.

8 Brian Lowry, "Review: *Sister Act*," *Variety* (May 18, 1992).

9 A comic reorientation toward salvation occurs through gospel singing at baptisms and through a blind prophet in the Coen brothers' *O Brother, Where Art Thou?* See Michelle Cormier, "Black Song, White Song: Salvation through the Radio in *The Apostle* and *Oh Brother, Where Art Thou?*," *Journal of Religion and Film* 6 (2002), online at www.unomaha.edu/jrf/blacksong.htm (accessed October 10, 2015).

10 Scholar Rick Olsen cogently argues that both opportunities and dangers
   emerge when films like *Sister Act* seek to make the gospel relevant to contemporary culture. "Keeping the Fidelity in Stereo-Catechesis: Opportunities
   and Dangers Inherent in Transmediation of the Gospel," *Journal of Religion
   and Popular Culture* **14** (Fall 2006), online at http://artsandscience.usask.ca/
   religion/jrpc/articles14.html (accessed October 10, 2015).

7 Family Comedy

"Biblical stories," observes author Doug Adams, "are like grandparent stories."[1] Characters are rough, ambiguous, flawed, and thickheaded, but leavened with humor throughout. When parents moralize and try to set you on the straight and narrow paths, grandparents, Adams opines, remind you that you can mess up millions of times and it will still turn out alright. Grace and hope are introduced through their humor and unabridged tales. We may have rascals and scamps as uncles and cousins, even as parents, as grandparents are wont to tell, but even Jesus had Rahab, a prostitute, in His family tree.

Where the family is funny is at its conception, in the begets.[2] In one Christmas lectionary reading of the begets from the Matthew genealogy, one of the present authors stunned some sleepy saints and woke up the kids by explaining that the begets were all about sex. Rabbits beget other rabbits; asses beget other asses; everything begets, except lawyers and the elders of that church, because they were all men. The author has not to this day been asked to read Scripture in that church again.

The families of Scriptures do not always treat each other fairly. Jacob cheats his older hairy brother Esau out of his birthright for a bowl of porridge; his father-in-law Laban cheats him on his wedding night; Jacob returns the chicanery with his flocks and so on. Sometimes, families conspire against principalities and powers, as when Esther and her relative Mordecai conspire to overturn the wickedness of Haman, leading to the wild feast of Purim, where people cheer, hiss, and applaud when the principal characters' names are spoken in the reading of the comedy. Then they drink until they cannot tell the difference between the phrases "Blessed be Mordecai" and "Cursed be Haman." One is more than three sheets to the wind by the next dawn.

Fractured families and religion and comedy blend together quite snugly. In *Life with Father* (Michael Curtiz, 1947), autobiographical bits of Clarence Day, Jr. writing about his father, Clarence Day, Sr. (William Powell), appeared in the *New Yorker* magazine. These humorous and nostalgic recollections structure the comedy film. When little Jimmy Lydon's mother (Irene Dunne) wants to know why her son didn't kneel in their Episcopal church, he says directly, "I just couldn't." She asks, "Has it anything to do with Mary [their attractive house guest, Elizabeth Taylor]? I know she's a Methodist." "Oh no, Mother," he responds, "Methodists kneel. Mary told me. They don't get up and down so much, but they stay down longer."

The focus of the film is on Father Day's reluctance to be baptized and avoid going to hell. When the minister proclaims the doctrine of the baptismal office, he intones, "Except a man be born of water and of the spirit, he cannot enter into the kingdom of God. He that believeth and is baptized shall be saved – but he that believeth not shall be damned."

At this point, Father Day mutters, "Until you stirred Him up, I had no trouble with God. Oh, tarnation, Hallelujah! Amen." At the end of the film, Father Day steps out of his triumphal chariot carriage, and a policeman tips his cap and says: "Morning Mr. Day, going to the office?" To which Father replies, "No, I'm going to be baptized, damn it."

African-American family comedy spills over with religious significance, much of authentic African-American Christian faith being compromised and distorted.[3] The community of *Green Pastures* (Marc Connelly, William Keighley, 1936), while stereotypical and patronizing in many regards, moving from a perpetual fish fry to harp playing, communicates a curiously comic rendering of Bible stories such as Adam, Noah, and Moses. Noah gets the good line, "Forgive me for not recognizing you Lawd; I should have known the glory." God also tells Noah to make sure to label all the animals. This is bracketed around a Sunday school lesson, with bright, luminous children raptly listening to Mr. Deshee (George Reed) tell them about De Lawd (Rex Ingram), who has thousands of things to do in between the short breaths of humans, and asks all his charges, "Has you been redeemed? Has you been baptized?" The Pulitzer Prize-winning play was daringly adapted for the screen with its all-black cast. Not particularly religious himself, the white liberal Connelly sought to take religion seriously in an era of agnosticism, and while the play used "the ambiance, the milieu, of the Negro," it was about "more than race." It sought to infuse humor and humanity into what Connelly seemed to think was a bland and discredited set of beliefs.

Connelly, argues scholar G. S. Morris, created a safe "Negro folk religion" for the screen, but effected a significant change from the original book by making this gentle Uncle Tom God black, and not an old white Southern colonel. De Lawd may look terrible and powerful, but He forgives quickly the waywardness of His people. Discussing the Fall, Mr. Deshee asks the children what happened after Adam and Eve ate the forbidden fruit. One young girl answers, "Why, den dey felt yer' bad." The emphasis, observed Morris, is that the Fall is not a catastrophe for the unbelieving director, but a mushy liberal sense of faith as feeling.[4] While

Figure 7.1 Rex Ingram as "Da Lawd" actually adds joyous dignity to the pro-
ceedings in heaven in the Pulitzer Prize-winning adaptation. *Green Pastures*,
Warner Bros., 1936. Author's screenshot.

pushing the central act of the crucifixion off-stage, as if it were merely a
tacked-on ending for charming fairy tales, Connelly seemed more concerned about being an ethnographer capturing the charm of a passing
theology. Dead humans are now angels floating on clouds, smoking
ten-cent "seegars," and concerned with the fluffy beauty of their wings.
What makes the film infectious, however, is the joyous gospel music of
the Hall Johnson Choir.

Old Southern boy critic Joe Bob Briggs called *Green Pastures* the
"Gospel According to Sambo," recognizing it not only as strange, but joyous, black angels "wearing white choir gowns and paper wings, sitting on
papier-mâché clouds with fishing poles." Briggs concludes that the film's
gospel doctrine is more akin to popular theology than all the official film
versions of the Bible; its essential doctrine is "get out of that loose living
and come on down to the fish fry. We waitin'."[5]

Director Tyler Perry would revive a genuine faith and subvert old
stereotypes by inventing his grand and hilarious broken-family comedies.
His over-the-top exaggeration of the Madea character saw him playing
the elderly grandma in drag himself. Having experienced domestic abuse,
Perry found writing to be therapeutic. When his *Diary of a Mad Black
Woman* (Darren Grant, 2005) hit the screens, his honest, painfully funny
humor about dysfunctional families resonated with audiences, black and
white. While critic Edward Crouse argues that his films are filled with

"homilies aimed squarely and soppily at Christian sentiment," he concedes that what is exploited is the "human desire to love, and to be loved, with dignity ... and a kick in the ass."[6]

The tough, even thuggish, Madea harks back to slapstick, with destruction of property and physical humiliation inserted as normal activities. When a young girl threatens her with "I know Tae Kwan Do," she retorts, "And I know whoop your ass." What the film and its sequels do with their hilarious theatrical violence is embody the struggle between flesh and spirit, between being both a sinner and a saint, a battle too frequently chronicled by gospel songs.

Madea was a PG version of Perry's mother and aunt, women who would take no guff, but whose hearts of righteous faith and kindness would win out, however gruffly. While loving God, she isn't too biblically literate and can make a malapropism out of any verse. She promises she'll go to church when they have a smoking section. When talking about reading the Bible, she quips, "Every time I try to read the Bible ... and Jesus ... the one with all the words in red ... I open my Bible to that New Testimony and see all that red and I just give up. Jesus was talkin' way too much."

Madea strangles and pulverizes biblical texts with merry abandon. "Her" explanation in *I Can Do Bad All by Myself* (Tyler Perry, 2009) to a ward seeking to understand how to pray mixes biblical characters and cinematic trivia with chutzpah. When she borrows and pirates diverse bits of the biblical texts, Perry unleashes one of the funniest improvisations of textual riffing:

> Fadder God, God of Abraham, Isaac, and Jacob. God of Shadrech, Meshit, and de Billy Goat, who was in the fiery furnace that they barbecued on the day of Pentecost, when the Jewish people returned from the Sabbath day up on the mountain top in uhh, Ethiopia. Ah, God, Mary J. Blige.

Madea tells her young charge about Peter, one of "the twelve disciplines" who saw Jesus walking on water. As long as Peter kept his eyes on Jesus, he stayed afloat. But then he got distracted. In one of the most hilariously mangled compilations of Scripture and popular culture, Madea waxes eloquently on Peter's predicament:

> Jonah passed by in the belly of the whale. He looked down, Free Willy, with Jonah inside the belly and it made him distracted so he started to sink. He said, "Jesus, Jesus, help me." Jesus said, "I can't. I got to go to Calvary. I'm late." So Jesus went on to the cross. He said, "Don't worry though. I'm gonna send you a comforter. When the comforter come, you gonna be alright." So he's swimming. He try and swim. He was worried. And Jaws was coming. Spielberg did that Jaws thing. And he was surrounded. You know what happened?

Figure 7.2 Madea (Tyler Perry) attempts to pray to "the God of Shadrech, Meshit, and de Billy Goat, who was in the fiery furnace that they barbecued on the day of Pentecost." *I Can Do Bad All by Myself*, The Tyler Perry Company, 2009. Author's screenshot.

The young girl Jennifer fulfills the role of spectator, allowing the comic to set up her schtik, and asks, "What?" Madea merrily twists the story of Noah, as he rows up with the "St. Louis Arch" and saves Peter. Peter finds Eve on the ark and invites her to a show:

> They had tigers. You know, they had two tigers, two bears, two lions. You know how they had the male and the female. Well, Siegfried and Roy was there, and they had the two lions there. And them Lions jumped up and scratched Eve. That's how Eve get them two paws there. You ever see Eve with the paws? She got two paws right there. Read your Bible some time, honey. Read your Bible.

This last line punctuates the role of biblical reception in film comedy. "Read your Bible, honey. Read your Bible." It is the one way for a man or woman to get out of trouble, or maybe into it.

If comedy is a man in trouble, then Moshe and his wife Malli in *Ushpizin* (Gidi Dar, 2004) double their trouble as a married couple.[7] And what troubles! As Mel Brooks' old man in the 1963 Oscar-winning animated film *The Critic* lamented, "I was born lucky and that's it." So, it is the feast of Succoth (temporary dwellings). It is time for this Orthodox Jewish couple to remember the miracles that God bestowed upon the children of Israel as they left Egypt. Now they are commanded to make

Figure 7.3 Moshe (Shuli Rand) and Malli (Michal Rand) hope for a miracle on the Succoth holiday with their expensive citron. *Ushpizin*, Eddie King Films, 2004. Author's screenshot.

blessings on the Four Species: date palm branches, myrtle, willow, and citron. However, there is no money to buy an *etrog*, that special yellow citrus fruit used for the celebration.

Stumbling upon the most marvelous and beautiful citron, Moshe discovers it costs 1,000 shekels; he has no money and could only buy it "with God's help." His wife hides behind locked doors when the landlord knocks, praying "Father, make him go away."

When a friend asks how it is going with him, Moshe sighs and says, "Terrible, may His name be praised." Kvetching with God, he confesses to being sad and reads psalms for help. He can't make a decent living or give his wife a child, a need for which they say anguished prayers.

However, serendipitously and providentially, a generous lottery gift becomes available and the donor suggests they pick a number at random from a list. Number 35 turns out to be Moshe.

Clapping his hands in anguish, Moshe prays, "God Almighty we need a miracle. Please, hear our prayer, give a miracle!" His wife reads the 23rd Psalm, crying out to God, "He leads me beside still water. I shall fear no evil." Yet, she fears even opening the door when the inheritance of 1,000 shekels is delivered, finally slipped under the door.

They wildly celebrate the faithfulness of the Lord. A festival of exuberant praise and song breaks forth. Singing of the holiness of God, the saints praise His name for this "downright miracle. Father, thank you very much."

However, comedies require obstacles, and the miracles become trials. Eliyahu, a former thieving friend of Moshe, and Yoself, his cohort in crime, have escaped prison. They come to Moshe's house to hide from the

authorities and to take advantage of the Succoth holiday and its requirement to welcome guests and entertain strangers. These two *ushpizin*
(guests) want to steal rabbinic hats with fox tails to make a bundle. They
inappropriately play loud rock music during the holy festival. "Profanity!
Blasphemy!" shout the neighbors with outrage. These are not really the
holy *ushpizin*.

Sitting down with them for a meal, Moshe prays extensively while
Eliyahu tries to close the prayer with an early "Amen." Yosef drinks all
the wine, as the glass must be filled. The joy of the holy feast is strained
by the convicts' behavior, even as the couple try to bless these strangers.
They strain to practice genuine hospitality to these uninvited and dis-
agreeable guests.

Moshe reflects, "God wants us to realize that we are merely guests in
this world; we live in temporary dwellings." Little does Moshe realize that
God will ironically confirm this insight. The two convicts eat and drink
all the impoverished, barren couple have and then pester them about why
they have no children. Even when the two try to do good, making a salad
for their host, they use their food *and* the thousand-shekel lemon/citron
to prepare it. Malli cannot take it, and runs away.

The ending is a joyous fable, a promise fulfilled, as Malli returns home
beaming. She announces that she is pregnant and wants to name their
child Nachman. Absolved of his sins, Moshe exclaims, "I told you there'd
be miracles." The festive community dances, with even the criminal guests
returning with some semblance of respect for their hosts. Even the outside has been welcomed into the strict community, with music and dancing, laughter and joy.

The theme song in *Cold Turkey* (Norman Lear, 1971), Randy Newman's
gospel-flavored ballad "He Gives Us All His Love," opens up the comedy
of the economically challenged community of Eagle Rock (population
4,006) that takes a pledge to try and quit smoking – or go cold turkey –
for a month from June 1 to July 1, to win a bundle of money, 25 million dollars. Newman's lyrics, "He knows how hard we try; He hears the
babies cry; He's smiling down at us from up above; He gives us all His
love," speak of grace and hope for a distressed Iowan town.

The town is satirically packed with churches, from the First Baptist,
Eagle Rock Baptist, Immanuel Lutheran PLC, Our Savior's Lutheran MS,
Methodist, Congregational, the 1st Congregational UCC, the Church of
Christ Christian, and several cults of Christian Science and Reorganized
Latter Day Saints. It's a city in which "God's will is being done" but one
that also desperately looks for renewal, economically and spiritually.

In an advertising scheme to boost smoking, the Valiant Tobacco
Company doesn't expect any city to take the offer or complete it.
However, Reverend Clayton Brooks (Dick Van Dyke) is a determined
community leader for the beleaguered town. His generic Eagle Rock
Community Church sees the opportunity as a spiritual challenge. Yet,

as his congregation sings "I love the Lord down in my heart" repeatedly, Brooks preaches to sleepy, snoring men, old ladies, and flies in his service, asserting "I believe because I know in whom I believe," seeking to prepare his people for things to come. Unfortunately, his meek, mousy wife typed up his sermon inserting a section from *Holiday* magazine. He berates her with uncommon incivility.

When the bishop comes to town, he hears Brooks' plea to be sent to Dearborn, Michigan, out of this depressed area. He suggests a little prayer might help. Brooks decides to stay and help the city, urging them to quit their bad habit, reminding the people from Paul's First Letter to the Corinthians that "our bodies are the temples of the Holy Spirit." When they berate him for not having to give up smoking, the Reverend becomes weak with the others, taking up his old bad habit of smoking once again to show solidarity with his flock.

He and the mayor then persuade the rest of the town to join them, to complete the Lord's business. The tobacco company needs only one person to fail. One barters for a plot in the church cemetery. The town drunk, Edgar Stopworth (Tom Poston), decides he must leave town as he is incurable, humming his mantra, "The booze bone is connected to the smoke bone and the smoke bone is connected to the head bone and that's the word of the Lord!" Catholics cross themselves before giving up cigarettes. Many suffer frustration, eliciting quarrels, binge-eating (perturbed wife of the mayor Mrs. Wappler (Jean Stapleton) stuffs her face with tiny gherkin pickles), and even kicking the dog. When told that having sex is a viable substitute, Brooks and his addicted wife carry on a running joke of preparing the bed. When the challenge begins at midnight, the town is turned into a circus, with souvenir vendors, beer salesmen, and massage therapists to help citizens go "cold turkey."

The nadir of the moral experiment comes with the epiphany of Walter Chronic, lit with a halo like a saint (along with other immortals like David Chetley, all the newscasters are played by the comedy team of Bob and Ray), and the transformation of a church service into a television show. The congregation is directed to sing "Our God, Our Help in Ages Past" and smile for the television cameras. The city, behind the leadership of Reverend Brooks, takes an oath on a bible, "not a slab of bacon." (Comically, gangs of small boys wearing masks of the "hero," Reverend Brooks, run amok.) While the whole world prays for Eagle Rock to beat the big tobacco company, the gospel is compromised, exploited, and merchandized. The media tout that in the God business, there is nothing bigger than a symbol of practical and moral leadership, but it's two parts dung and one part inspiration.

It is his browbeaten wife who confronts the minister, whose image has been plastered on the cover of *Time* magazine, as the savior of the city. "How will it profit the whole world and yet lose its own soul?" Brooks counters, "Trap me with my words, eh?" She quietly answers, "I thought they were God's words."

The town succeeds and triumphs, but the gentle satire exposes the sinful nature of ordinary people, of political leaders, upstanding citizens, and religious families. After Reinhold Niebuhr wrote his book on *Moral Man and Immoral Society*, an apocryphal story relates that he wanted to change its title after looking more closely at his first subject. He thought the book should have been *Immoral Man and More Immoral Society*. Niebuhr sought to debunk the hypocrisy of those who became self-righteous, arguing for the doctrine of original sin. It isn't just the sin industries of tobacco and alcohol that ruin the world; at heart, it is as cartoonist Walt Kelly Pogo recognized, "We have met the ENEMY, and he is us," even if we are our own most ridiculous enemy.

The comedy of religion in British cinema stems from the English comic novel, from Henry Fielding and Jane Austen to Evelyn Waugh, with rich veins of social satire flowing through their pages. In the cleverly titled, frothy, and good-hearted *Keeping Mum* (Niall Johnson, 2005), Reverend Walter Goodfellow (Rowan Atkinson) is a failed Episcopal vicar and father. His family is falling apart; his preaching is dull; his lonely wife Gloria (Kristin Scott Thomas) is beginning an affair with her golf instructor (Patrick Swayze). His son Petey is bullied and his promiscuous daughter Holly seeks sexual thrills. Into their lives comes Grace (Maggie Smith), both literally and figuratively, who keeps mum about her own secrets. The coming of Grace not only brings death to sin, but kills the law that so burdens this family.

Atkinson had played the comic vicar before, from his sketches on *Not the Nine O'Clock News* to *Four Weddings and a Funeral* (Mike Newell, 1994), where, as the blundering cleric Father Gerald performing a wedding, he stands out with his misspeaking of the "holy goat" rather than "Holy Ghost" and "awful married wife." In an interview Atkinson complained that "many of the clerics that I've met, particularly the Church of England clerics, are people of such extraordinary smugness and arrogance and conceitedness who are extraordinarily presumptuous about the significance of their position in society." Atkinson concludes that they deserve the mud thrown at them.[8]

Providentially for the dysfunctional Goodfellows, housekeeper Grace arrives and starts solving problems. Critic Stephen Holden calls her "Mary Poppins' Dotty Doppelgänger"; she meddles and amends, metaphorically bringing God's free and unmerited blessing into this house of sinners. The incongruity of saving grace coming through murderous acts plays out like a vintage episode of "Alfred Hitchcock Presents."[9]

Practicing both goodness and judgment, Grace is a sweet, murdering granny who also reunites an estranged family. However, underneath the unusual concept of good things coming from serial murder, there lies a great source of religious discussion. We must be struck by the sword of satire, accosted by how strange Grace is and how she heals the Goodfellows, and only after this can we begin to see the salvation brought by Grace.

Grace Hawkins is an escaped convict who murdered her husband years ago; she is also Gloria's mum. As she has moved in with her heavy trunk of memories, the vicar gathers the whole family for prayer. She recognizes that he has a small sense of humor. "I like that. You're going to need one."

Walter starts, "Well, I don't think this occasion should go by without saying a few words." "Walter!" protests his wife. "Just a few words: 'Lord, thank you for this day. And thank you for bringing us Grace who has joined our family today and who we hope will be very happy here. And thank you also for Carl, Mark ..." (trying to ascertain his daughter's boyfriend's name).

"David!" she bellows.

"... whom we've also just met, but seems to be a very nice young man indeed."

"AMEN," says Gloria, "Who would like some tea?"

As the family awkwardly stand around, hands folded, Walter protests, "I meant every word." This bedeviled vicar tells Grace she is very welcome in their home. Reverend Goodfellow does not realize that Grace will become an agent of righteous judgment and ironic justice in their domestic crises. When Maggie Smith told director Niall Johnson that she wanted to wear all black and "be this black line running through the story," he agreed. "It sounded so good I didn't even ask her what it meant." [10]

Her first dark deed is the destruction of the neighbor Mr. Brown's incessantly barking dog, representative of the worldly noise that is distracting and distorting the focus of the Goodfellows. [11] When she seemingly steps over the line and murders the nosy neighbor himself, one is stumped by the quirky violence. Johnson comments in an interview that the plot is "like a black comedy, but the blackness of the humour is underpinned by the domestic view of it," once more highlighting the contrast between light and dark, religion and satire. She brings blessings by murdering what is not only evil, but just annoying. Here is a Grace that cleans out all of the leaven, no matter how small. The juxtaposition of bringing a sword to ensure goodness stymies one's understanding of just how Grace might work.

When she whacks the sleazy lover and voyeuristic golf instructor, Lance (Patrick Swayze), one almost cheers. Each act works to reintegrate the family by removing obstacles and temptations. When Gloria discovers that Grace is her long-lost mother and has been eliminating and disposing of problems, she exclaims, "You can't just go round killing people just because you don't approve of them." Grace responds, "You know, that's what my doctors used to say. It was the one point we could never agree on." Though her means are unorthodox, Grace cannot tolerate the sin working in the lives of her family, so she restores their domestic peace in the way she knows best.

Walter's preoccupation with his religious work renders him blind to serious spiritual matters in his own home. The troubling spiritual state of things points to how his religious teaching and his relationship with his family are lacking in passion, which we see related to humor as the minister starts to incorporate jokes into his sermon. Laughter and love co-mingle and augment each other.

Grace's first task is to help the dull preaching of her son-in-law by teaching him comedy. Walter Goodfellow tries some old jokes out that actually improve his ponderous sermons. Speaking in the voice of God, Walter confides, "I visit 2,000 years ago and meet this nice Jewish girl and they are still talking about it. Joking aside, it's true. Two thousand years later and we are still talking about it" [for the gospel] is "something worth talking about." The gospel of grace is leavened with parables and witticisms and as Walter recognizes, with "these jokes, things come alive. They really do!"

Grace tries to spur the oblivious vicar to renew his first love with his wandering wife, to rekindle the spark that made them lovers. Grace meets him in the chapel and asks: "Now, have you thought about sex?"

"Sex?" he gasps.

"The Bible is full of sex. Haven't you noticed?"

"The Bible?" he marvels.

"The Song of Solomon, for example."

"No," corrects the vicar, "now that is the passionate declaration of love from a devout man to God."

"No!" counters Grace in a matter of fact manner, "It's about sex."

"Right."

"Read it again, Reverend … and I'll make you a cup of tea."

He sits in front of the altar proclaiming "We beheld his *glory* full of *grace* and truth." Grace has revealed Gloria in all her intimate needs and desires. As Goodfellow turns pages, he catches on. "Let him kiss me with the kisses of his mouth, for Thy love is better than wine. His fruit was sweet to my taste."

The scene shifts from church to bedroom, where Gloria is undressing for bed and his voice-over continues: "His left hand is under my head and his right hand doth embrace me. Behold, thou art fair my love. Behold, thou art fair. Thy lips are like a thread of scarlet; thine eyes are like doves behind the veil. And comely is thy mouth." Goodfellow lies on his bed and takes off his reading glasses.

> Thy two breasts are like fawns feeding among the lilies. Thy navel is like a round goblet wherein no mingled wine is wanting. Thy belly is like a heap of wheat set about with lilies; let thy breasts be as clusters on the vine and thy mouth like the best wine. Open to me my dove for my head is filled with the draughts of the night. Come my beloved, let us see if the vine flourishes and the tender grapes and the pomegranates bud forth.

Figure 7.4 Only after Grace (Maggie Smith) enters his life will Reverend Goodfellow (Rowan Atkinson) be transformed from a dull Anglican vicar to a comic witness of God. *Keeping Mum*, Summit Entertainment, 2005. Author's screenshot.

The vicar rises from bed, meets his wife after she has finished brushing her teeth, and quietly embraces her and follows the lovemaking of the Scriptures. The Word of God is not only inspired, it is an aphrodisiac.

As the vicar from Little Wallop delivers the opening address of the Anglican Convention, he stumbles over his words as he speaks of "Cod's mysterious ways, I mean, God's mysterious ways. Cods will have to wait for their own convention." His deft adjustment with self-effacing and clever wit puts him at ease. Grace has breathed humor into his humility. "What is the difference between prayer in a church and prayer in a casino?" he poses. "In a casino you really mean it."

"All it takes is a little grace," he counsels. "A little of God's grace and our problems seem to fade away. Should we ask questions or enjoy the benefits? God tells us in Isaiah 55:8 'My ways are not your ways. I'm mysterious. Live with it!'"

Grace irons away and removes all obstacles to his marriage and his ministry, decisively and permanently. The black comedy in the film, with Grace doling out justice, serves to confront the viewer with questions about righteousness, grace destroying sin, temptation, the law, and judgment. Grace must kill to heal. Grace comes with violence, but brings spiritual and natural life more abundantly. It spreads throughout the relationships in the whole family. Grace's joyful influence leads Holly to stop sleeping with boys in vans and start baking pies instead, and Petey's bullies are taken out by Grace's enactment of judgment. The sexual sin of Grace's unfaithful husband, her first victim, and of Lance points to the destructive consequences of uncontrolled passion. Lance not only encourages Gloria's sin, but he also lecherously spies on Holly while she undresses. His comeuppance is with the iron of God.

Gloria recognizes the unexpected influence Grace has brought to her household. "Now, let me get this straight. My son is rid of his bullies; my husband has become a comedian; and my nymphomaniac daughter has discovered cookery." Noting that her family is unusually happy and not chaotic, she renders thanks to Grace. Person by person, Grace destroys the sinful and assists the Goodfellows, whose name, like Grace's, is also indicative of their ultimate role in the movie.

The *double entendre* of *Keeping Mum* juxtaposes keeping quiet about family concerns and taking care of one's own family. In making the family an ostensibly religious family, it foregrounds concerns such as the workings of sin, judgment, and grace. By means of benign humor, this divine comedy brings what is usually high and transcendent down to earth. Sinners are saved by Grace. In the end, Gloria writes to Grace that, "in all, I'd say our life here is complete. It just ambles along in its quiet and merry way," while the Goodfellow family holds on to spiritual Grace as they weather the sinful world.

Opening his *Anna Karenina*, Leo Tolstoi declared that "happy families are all alike; every unhappy family is unhappy in its own way." The truth is otherwise. All families are dysfunctional, some in greater ways that others. And all are doomed, unless rescued by the grace of God. One might just alter Tolstoi in one sense. All happy families know they mess up, but also know the comedy of their predicament and the mercies of God to restore them. Blessed be Mordecai.

Notes

1 Douglas Adams, *The Prostitute in the Family Tree: Discovering Humor and Irony in the Bible* (Westminster John Knox Press, 1997), 1.

2 See the Reduced Shakespeare Company's riff on begetting and the Good Book in *The Complete Word of God (abridged)* ("it's wacky; it's zany; a little profaney").

3 See Donald Bogle, *Toms, Coons, Mulattoes, Mammies, and Bucks: An Interpretative History of Blacks in American Films* (Continuum, 2001); Thomas Cripps, *Slow Fade to Black: The Negro in American Film, 1900–1942* (Oxford University Press, 1977), 25; Ed Guerrero, *Framing Blackness: The African American Image in Film* (Temple University Press, 1993).

4 G. S. Morris, "Thank God for Uncle Tom: Race and Religion Collide in *The Green Pastures*," *Bright Lights Film Journal* (January 31, 2008), online at www.brightlightsfilm.com/59/59greenpastures.php (accessed October 10, 2015).

5 Joe Bob Briggs, "The Gospel according to Joe Bob," *Film Comment* (April 1987), 54–55.

6 Edward Crouse, "We Are Family," *Film Comment* (March/April 2006), 42–45.

7 Moshe is played by Shuli Rand, who also wrote the screenplay, and Malli by his real-life wife Michal Batsheva Rand.

8 Will Taylor, "Rowan Atkinson: Church of England Clerics are 'Smug and Arrogant,'" *Telegraph* (September 25, 2011), cited in Sue Sorensen, *The Collar: Reading Christian Ministry in Fiction, Television, and Film* (Cascade Books, 2014), 87.

9 Stephen Holden, "Mary Poppins's Dotty Doppelgänger," *New York Times* (September 15, 2006); also see Anna Smith, "*Keeping Mum*," *Sight & Sound* **16**:1 (2006), 60–62.

10 Becky Day, "*Keeping Mum* Interview," Close-UpFilm.com (November 23, 2013), www.close-upfilm.com/features/Interviews/keepingmum.htm (accessed October 10, 2015). In this interview, Atkinson describes the particular challenges this clerical role presented: "I have to say I haven't played many serious roles [... and] I found it quite tricky to be honest. It's so easy to play Mr. Bean as he's such an extreme, whereas this character was closer to myself, you know, slightly dull."

11 We owe a debt to scholar Morgan Stroyeck for insights on this film.

8   *Picaro* Comedy

The *picaro* comedy follows an Everyman like a picaresque hero, a likeable character who is often a fish out of water on his or her curious, often providential, journey. According to Voytilla, two varieties of this comic pilgrim traipse across the landscapes of film comedies. The first is what he calls the catalyst fish, the trickster who makes things happen, as Ferris Bueller on his day off or Axel Foley as a Beverly Hills cop. Like Hermes, the character doesn't change much throughout the story, but alters those he meets. Even the wisdom of Apollo must bow to the wiles of such an impish *picaro*. Here, too, would be the anxiously hip, ironically smirking *picaro* of Woody Allen, who seeks to deconstruct virtues with a laugh. Allen pairs ultimate concerns with silly carnal desires.[1] Voltaire is reincarnated, but through a Freudian joke.[2]

The second kind of *picaro* is the wounded fish, the vulnerable underdog, or loser, who bumps into others and bounces from one place to another. Here the *picaro* is the Don Quixote fighting windmills, such as Chaplin or Buster Keaton. The young woman Amélie in *Amélie* (Jean-Pierre Jeunet, 2001) who finds a box of memories in her apartment, sees a wound in the world and tries to fix it. So too the characters of Tom Hanks in *Forrest Gump* (Robert Zemeckis, 1994) or Roberto Benigni in *Life is Beautiful* (1997) or Peter Sellers in *Being There* (Hal Ashby, 1979).

Picaros take the road less traveled. They follow their own drumbeats. They have a registered gait under the Ministry of Silly Walks, recognizable from way down the street. Chaplin's and Keaton's unique movements, as well as Lloyd's and Langdon's, are identifiable from any distance. Yet, they are not only peculiar and different, they usually walk alone. The *picaro* is by definition a singular creature. Keaton followed a curve like a boomerang in his features, in a seemingly hostile and resistant universe. He was a stranger in a strange land.

Hebrew prophets follow such solitary paths. The Wandering Jew stumbles across many troubles. The apocalyptic Ezekiel and the comically reluctant Jonah wander through strange visions and down detour paths, but end up doing what they were called to do and be, however begrudgingly. Curiously the Yiddish term "schlemiel" may be derived from the Hebrew character Shelumiel, whose name means "My well-being is God" (Numbers 7:36). Even so, such a *picaro* even blessed by God rarely sees things turn out perfectly. Yet as they open the Pandora's box, they find comic hope at the end.[3]

Usually the religious *picaro* will be a Protestant type, a pilgrim of the order of John Bunyan rather than one of Chaucer's entourage. But the comic religious *picaro* will have the humor of Chaucer, in all its hues. Protestant comic pilgrims like Jonathan Swift tend to be aggressive and satiric. Roman Catholic *picaros* are more akin to the rollicking G. K. Chesterton. The Roman Catholic imagination would highlight God as Loving Father rather than as Righteous Judge.[4] Two particular *picaros* command our attention in this chapter, one wounded and the other catalytic, and while the first is Anglican, he is more Roman Catholic, and the second, a Roman Catholic priest, acts much more Protestant.

We should first distinguish between these two tendencies of the Roman Catholic and Protestant imaginative characters. According to Andrew Greeley and Ingrid Shafer, the first is one who focuses upon the presence of God in the world, while the latter looks to His transcendence. The Roman Catholic tends to be sacramental and parabolic, while the Protestant is oriented toward preaching and doctrine. Those who adopt, adapt, and absorb and embrace culture are included among the Roman Catholics, while people who critique, reject, and reform culture tend to be Protestants. One might say that Roman Catholics emphasize the doctrine of creation while Protestants preach redemption.

For those who emphasize how we were created in the image of God, the dominant images of God are father, friend, or bridegroom, while those who see sin marring the divine image recognize God as judge, master, lord, king, or consuming fire. These latter clamor for holiness, justice, and moral righteousness, while the former sing of grace, abundance, and joy. The followers of the Protestant tradition, with its outspoken protesters and reformers, were generally stereotyped as severe and solemn pessimists regarding the world. The preoccupation of Puritans seemed to center on sin, on the need for personal and corporate repentance, and on striving to be kept unstained from this world.

In contrast, the Roman Catholic tradition informed much of the Italian Renaissance, with its zest, its exuberance, and its corruption due to religious optimism and freewheeling. The incarnational joy and earthiness easily became a spirit of carnival and carnality. Such a spirit was channeled into Chaucer, Rabelais, and into Baroque art and architecture. In particular, one can see it in one of the most compelling models of a hearty, robust, and joyous Roman Catholic artist. Art historian Charles Schribner described Peter Paul Rubens as a deeply devout Catholic humanist, scholar and linguist, skillful diplomat, enthusiastic lover of two wives (in succession), and tender father of seven children. His life was as filled with activities as his canvases, panels, and tapestries were teeming with richly (and quite scantily) dressed, bejeweled beautiful people, plump toddler angels, and powerful horses. Obviously for Rubens, the demands of devout faith, the pursuit of artistic excellence, and worldly fame were aspects of a seamless whole. Schribner makes the tongue-in-cheek comment that "Hollywood has yet to exploit Rubens' exemplary life on the screen."

Contrast the fun, frolicking, fluffy characters of Rubens with the harsh, monotonic sermons of Jonathan Edwards or the rational *Institutes* of John Calvin. Drama exists in Edwards' preaching as God dangles us like loathsome spiders over the pits of hell. The preoccupation with judgment and apocalyptic terror is strongly linked to the Protestant imagination. Perhaps one of the better Protestant films would be Clint Eastwood's *Unforgiven* (1992) or *Mystic River* (2003). *Babette's Feast* (Gabriel Axel, 1987) and *Big Fish* (Tim Burton, 2003), on the other hand, begin as Protestant and by the end are converted into charismatic Roman Catholic films. So too does *Places in the Heart* (Robert Benton, 1984) move from the sorrow of the Protestant life into the joy of the eucharist. Ingmar Bergman is Lutheran; Federico Fellini is near the Vatican. Paul Schrader is Calvinist in temperament even when he scripts for a Catholic like Scorsese. The Protestant Tom Shadyac (*Patch Adams*, 1998; *Bruce Almighty*, 2003; and *Liar, Liar*, 1997) fits the Roman Catholic mold, while Wes Craven is a back-sliding Evangelical from Wheaton College who is haunted by Christ and infused with irony.

Everyone combines a bit of each. Some days we wake up Protestant only to be transformed by a wife's kiss into a joyous Roman Catholic. Most of us teeter back and forth throughout our lives. However, it is the Roman Catholic in us that has all the fun, unless one is a Pentecostal.

In *Heavens Above!* (John and Ray Boulting, 1963), the incomparable (and inscrutable chameleon actor) Peter Sellers plays Reverend John Smallwood. An Anglican vicar, he demonstrates a blessedly oblivious call to charity and joy. Even as he is a wounded fish, he wanders into toils and dangers without realizing that he has been endangered.

When the apostle Paul examines the status of the Christian evangelist in his First Letter to the Church at Corinth, he asserts that God chose what is foolish in the world to confound the wise; what is weak to shame the strong; what is low and despised and things that are not to reduce the things that are, so that "no one might boast in the presence of the Lord." The lowly priest serves as court jester, outspoken, courageous, and somewhat ridiculous. Yet he will "turn the world upside-down" even while demeaned, slandered, and reviled. Yet, this court jester, like Lear's Fool, speaks truth.[5]

When the plum vicarage in Orbiston Parva becomes vacant due to the death of its drunken rector, the distinguished albeit conventional

Reverend John Smallwood's name is put forth as the most suitable candidate for this prosperous, elitist community. However, John Smallwood is also the name of a minor prison chaplain serving his ministry in obscurity. In one of those grand bureaucratic gaffes of filing mishaps, the church hierarchy blunders and sends the lesser-known, humbler saint to the vacancy. A man who truly believes the gospel is sent to a ritualistic, mostly lapsed, Anglican congregation. His calling is due to a "clerical error," a jest of which only he seems aware. He is truly a duck of God in the wrong pond. In one prison sermon he preaches idealism to a corrupt world, counseling "Judge not lest ye be judged" to a bunch of criminals. Smallwood is the kind of cleric who inadvertently follows the somewhat biblical admonition that if any man asks for your cloak, you should give him your pants as well. At the prison, Smallwood is left trussed in his underwear by a convict named Fred who steals his clerical clothes.

When he arrives at Orbiston Parva railway station, a cheerful and unpretentious Smallwood stands in the pouring rain after a station worker rudely tells him that there is no bus to take him to the church, until he meets a West African Christian, the garbage man, Matthew Robinson (Brock Peters), who offers him a ride under the notion that "we all gotta help one another." The two share a communing cup of tea while the hymn "Simple Gifts" plays cheerily in the background. This moment of charitable fellowship is followed by two men singing, "Praise the Lord! Ye Heavens Adore Him," while the next-door neighbors show nothing but irritation at the noise.

Smallwood replaces the grasping and manipulative churchwarden Major Fowler (William Hartnell) with Matthew, who experiences the racism of the community. While standing beneath a banner that proclaims "Love One Another," two women fight over a charitable handout and tell the new black churchwarden, "You don't belong here." The congregation may sing "All Things Bright and Beautiful" and "Lead Kindly Light," but its ethic is less benign.

In his *New York Times* review, critic Bosley Crowther grinned at how the film-making Boulting brothers were again making sport of British institutions "in a devilishly wry, satiric way." So, too, *Variety* found the Boulting brothers effectively employing their "rapier of ridicule."[6] Here the satirical target is the grand Church of England, outlining the foibles of men of the cloth. In particular, Crowther lauds the filmmakers' wit and audacity. Taking their cue from Malcolm Muggeridge, a former editor of the satirical magazine *Punch*, which has always poked fun at the British clergy with an astonishing air of impudence, they have whipped up a mischievous fable out of Muggeridge's idea about the way in which a truly Christian vicar upsets an entire community and makes for embarrassment in the upper echelons of the Church and government.[7]

Crowther's description of Smallwood points to his quintessential role as a *picaro*, in that this

> vicar is no common mortal, no pedestrian human – or perhaps he is. Perhaps it is because he is so mortal and human that he seems a freak. Anyhow, the candor and sincerity of the simple Christian doctrine that he brings ... are enough to puncture the complacence of virtually everybody in town and threaten the economic system when a unique spate of charity sets in.

The inhabitants of this town spend their hours of "daily devotions' in such rituals as playing bingo and watching Westerns on television ("Don't shoot me while I'm praying. Don't shoot! Aiiiee!"). The town is controlled by the Despards, whose factory produces Tranquilax medication as the only balm that modern society needs. The separation of wealthy and poor is laid out in an opening scene of a man washing his clothes in the commemorative fountain of this distinguished family, the single benefit the community gets from this class-conscious corporation (except for the sponsorship of a ladies' public loo).

Tranquilax, a dubious concoction that makes money for the town, benumbs the spiritual life of the world (along with television). Its commercial slogan, namely that "Life not worth living? Why suffer?" is wrapped in its ersatz trinitarian "three-in-one restorative" promise. In fact, the drug works triply as stimulant, sedative, and laxative. What more could one want or need? The escape of troubles through medication has supplanted the place of the Church of England in their tiny little lives.

The fussy and venal Archdeacon Aspinall (Cecil Parker) is mostly concerned with his donor base and so takes tea with the widowed Lady Despard (Isabel Jeans), the majority stockholder in Tranquilax. In their casual conversation, he exposes his own upper-crust hypocrisy. The discrepancy between traditional Church teachings on sex comes into comic view when Lady Despard banters about chastity, opining that the apostle Paul was a "very queer man." So, too, this queer little man, Smallwood, brings unintended consequences because of his devout altruism rooted in the Good News of the Christian message.

When told that he was not the archdeacon's first choice, Smallwood explains "I've never thought of myself as a clerical error before. ... If I've come to Orbiston Parva, it's because I was meant to come. I'm not packing it in now." Smallwood even rejects Lady Despard's contributions to the church building and organ fund on the basis that one should be helping one's fellow man. Lady Despard lists all of the renovations her family has funded, including the "dry rot in the pulpit," as evidence of the Despards' Christian faith. Smallwood reproves them both, saying, "To hear you talk, you'd think the Father, Son, and the Holy Ghost was a group of building merchants. Buildings aren't that important. We are

Figure 8.1 Mistakenly assigned to a snooty parish, Reverend Smallwood (Peter Sellers) seeks to live out the ways of the gospel with his one disciple, Matthew (Brock Peters). *Heavens Above*, British Lion Film Corporation, 1963. Author's screenshot.

the ones that want saving. It's people that converse with God, even before churches."

The bumbling Smallwood baffles everyone and is criticized because he "keeps bringing God into everything." However, Smallwood insists that complaints don't worry him, and quotes Luke 6:26 to Aspinall, "Woe unto you, when all men shall speak well of you! for so did their fathers to the false prophets." Few speak well of the underdog saint.

Smallwood does not bow to the uptight, upper-class twits who control the town; rather as a true believer he tries to revive the teachings of the Church. He is taken advantage of and misunderstood (a foretaste of Chauncey Gardiner in *Being There*), viewed as not only an eccentric but a trouble-making idiot. Smallwood remains a bit of a dolt, however, grabbing dog biscuits from a bowl as if they were snacks.

He honestly confesses to his congregation, saying, "I am not a good Christian, but I want to be, so I'm trying ... but it's not like joining the Co-op, you know, [and] your divvy depends not on how much you spend, it depends on how much you put in." The way to salvation is through Jesus, and being His disciple is essential to one's spiritual health. Smallwood stresses that "Jesus was quite clear about that. If we want to join his club, we've got to do as he told us, and live as he showed us. You can't dodge that fact, so there's no point in you trying." Smallwood reassures the flock that "I'm going to try to reopen negotiations with the Kingdom of God."

A series of quick shots exposes the spiritual lethargy of the congregation. One woman boasts that her family attends church during Easter, "but we are Christians, no doubt about that ... and I do think the church tries to do good, but you simply haven't got the time, have you?" A banker says the "need for Christianity has never been greater," relating it to banking, and a sophisticated woman tells Smallwood, "I think we're pretty religious around here, only you simply can't let it interfere with ordinary life."

Already Smallwood's joyful, loving presence is out of place in the materialistic, self-righteous environment of Orbiston Parva, yet not only must he deal with the overweening pride and prejudice of the Anglican establishment, but a local fundamentalist preacher (Kenneth Griffith) shouts fire-and-brimstone damnation, arguing that "It's only the fires of hell that keep the churches warm." His congregation will protest that Smallwood has employed unfair conversion tactics for converts.

At one point when Reverend Smallwood (Sellers) is preaching from the pulpit, a young boy is seen pumping the air for the little organ in the background while reading a copy of Nabokov's sensational novel *Lolita*. Sellers had played Quilty in Stanley Kubrick's 1962 film version of that book.[8]

His direct sermons challenge the hypocrisy of the congregation, being spiritually apathetic and comfortably lazy, holding to a form of godliness without the substance. Disturbed by his call to a Christian life, many call for his removal. However, he visits the matriarch of the village and stokes her fears about damnation. She "sees the light" and joins him in establishing an extravagant program of charity, which creates havoc for the local economy. Her generosity in distributing free produce from her own lands complicates business for the small shopkeepers. When she sells her shares in Tranquilax, the company's value crashes into worthless paper, factory workers are laid off, and unemployment runs rampant through the village. The trade union rails at the vicar.

Seeking to drum up faith and obedience, Smallwood critiques the spiritual apathy and emptiness of the congregation. He rues that "there aren't enough real Christians about to feed a decent lion." When he denounces their dependence upon Tranquilax, his words trigger damage to its stock. Shopkeepers complain about their lack of business due to the generous program of helping the poor. When one preaches and practices the gospel, there are consequences, to capitalist and Communist alike.

Smallwood also begins his renewal by inviting the Smiths, a tribe of gypsies forced off their land by Tranquilax construction plans, to live in his vicarage with the only stipulation being they must attend Bible classes. Mr. and Mrs. Smith (Irene Handl and Eric Sykes) are the comic foils as the poor, lazy, itinerant family masquerading piety so as to live and leech off of this gullible cleric. Their scruffy and grubby brood thieves and steals with licentious abandon. When Fred the former convict joins them, they scheme to steal lead from the church roof.

Yet even with Smallwood's labors on behalf of the poor, we are not given an idealized vision of these least of the kingdom. The scroungers and slatternly squatters who live off the welfare state are as greedy and selfish as those in power. The lack of money does not bring virtue. All have fallen short of the glory of God and are pretty mean. Human nature is filled with shrewdness, vice, and guile, and into such a world comes this gentle, genial, gracious vicar as a true antidote. Communism and socialism will not work, because people will not work if given the chance. Yet charity is demanded of those who would follow Jesus.

Having invited the colorfully immoral gypsies to be residential guests in the vicarage, the vicar seeks to persuade the Despard matriarch to open her house to vagabonds and vagrants and feed them all.[9] At this point, her class-conscious, seemingly senile butler, Simpson (Bernard Miles), shows himself to be a crafty old servant. Smallwood calls the people to denounce Satan and all of his works during a baptism; Simpson uses Scripture differently. He warns, "anytime you hear someone quoting from the Bible, better watch out, because it's probably the devil itself." He connives to dissuade Lady Despard from following Smallwood by contriving a "sign from God" to persuade his mistress that the time of charity is over. In fact, Simpson trades Scripture verses with the vicar. "Now I am going to quote you two bits of the Bible," he tells Smallwood: "Matthew 27:5, 'and he went out and hanged himself.' Luke 10:37, 'Go thou and do likewise.'"

The Boulting brothers take pot shots at psychiatry as well. When the archdeacon and Bishop Goodbody secure the professional services of Rockerby (Miles Malleson) to ascertain the psychological stability of Smallwood, he mistakenly interviews the wrong Smallwood (Ian Carmichael) and diagnoses him as having paranoid schizophrenia.

When Smallwood's effectiveness as a minister wanes, mainly because he is trying faithfully to follow Christ, Sir Geoffrey Despard opines that "nobody takes parsons seriously these days anyway." In their efforts to defuse the problem, the Church hierarchy sends him off to distant islands, but ultimately appoints Smallwood as "Bishop of Outer Space" when the little cleric seeks to counsel a nervous astronaut. When the anxious spaceman carps that the Church rarely practices what it preaches, Smallwood takes on the yoke of his brother, donning his space suit, exchanging it for clerical garb (once again). He is thus inadvertently sent into orbit around the earth, where he joyfully warbles hymns. It is his ascension after his life on earth.

As in the films of Luis Buñuel (*Nazarín*, 1959; *Viridiana*, 1961), those who seek to radically follow the teachings of Jesus are rendered hopelessly unfit for this world. The only place for such inept or naïve fellows, for such losers of this world, is in the heavens above. The *picaro* who seeks the Kingdom of God first and devoutly will soon discover that he was not made for this world, but for another.

The other kind of *picaro* underdog is more intentional in working his way through trouble. Fernandel as Don Camillo is the catalyst fish, the religious trickster, who gets tricked and punked as much as he gives. Like Smallwood, he converses with God and follows the gospel, but his humanity is much more bellicose and vulnerably comic.

From its early postwar publication in the satirical *Candido* magazine, Giovanni Guareschi (1908–1968) introduced his comic voice, the hot-headed priest Don Camillo (actually modeled on a partisan Italian Roman Catholic priest, Don Camillo Valota, who had endured the concentration camp of Dachau). The many adventures of Don Camillo mainly focused on his relationship to his friend and nemesis, Communist Mayor Peppone (Gino Cervi). Communists are curiously caricatured as having three nostrils. The two pull practical jokes on each other, as Peppone continually paints the hind end of Don Camillo's dog, Ful, a bright Communist red.

In Julien Duvivier's *Little World of Don Camillo* (1952), the story plays out in the village in the Po valley. The pugilistic priest converses with Christ who looks down from a crucifix above the altar. In one scene, after Peppone acknowledges in the confessional that he beat up Camillo in the dark and knocked some eggs out of his hand, the priestly confessor Camillo wants to pummel Peppone while the Marxist Catholic is kneeling at the altar rail. He asks Christ if he can beat Peppone up for Him. Christ says no because He had forgiven him and so must Camillo. The priest still wants to whack him with a candle. "No," replies Christ, "your hands were made for blessing." To which Camillo mutters, "My hands, but not my feet," so Christ allows him to land a thunderbolt kick to Peppone's underside. At this, a penitent Peppone remarks casually, "I've been expecting that for the last ten minutes. I feel better now." "So do I," exclaims Don Camillo, and it seems that even Christ was pleased too.[10] The gentle and very endearing humane satire shows two flawed men of good will from radically different political positions engaged in trying to do what is right.

Don Camillo is wonderfully human: he regularly loses his temper, engages in fisticuffs and brawls, earning reprimands for impatience and self-control from the crucified Christ, who continually chides his servant, emphasizing the role of conscience as the messenger through which God's Holy Spirit speaks. He rebukes him, and not his adversary, when he is sarcastic toward his enemies. The novels illustrate the spiritual dimension of ordinary people, incorporating "satire as a branch of morality."[11] When the *crocefisso* looks down at Don Camillo, He asks, "Where did you get that cigar, Camillo?" Don Camillo answers, "Peppone had two. I think I took it without asking him. You know he believes in equal distribution of wealth."

When Don Camillo complains that after Peppone had won an improbable election he came to light a candle, he tells Jesus that Peppone

Figure 8.2 In his ongoing debates with the crucified but living Christ, Don Camillo (Fernandel) is roundly reprimanded for not loving his neighbor as himself. *Little World of Don Camillo*, Produzione Film Giuseppe Amato, 1952. Author's screenshot.

blasphemed by coming to thank God for having helped the cause of the Marxists, "of those that deny You!" Jesus answers:

> Don Camillo, he came to thank God, he didn't thank the head of his party. He didn't ask the head of his party to let him win: he prayed to God. He doesn't deny God; on the contrary, he recognized God's power. One day he will understand everything that today he doesn't because he doesn't know the truth. The way that leads to the truth is not at all easy for everyone.[12]

In fact, Jesus tells Don Camillo that Peppone actually voted for the Christian Democrats and not for his own party (and, he reminds his puffed-up priest of his own inconsistency in that he voted for his friend Peppone and, by extension, the Marxists). The tales revolve mostly about the proper love of one's neighbor as a reflection of the love of God, a telling Horatian satire for a divided country of *paisans*.

As one who fought in the war and endured the loneliness and hardships of a German POW, Guareschi saw satire as humor's weapon, a powerful and beneficial weapon, like the cannon to the science of artillery. "When the alarm sounds, humor dons a uniform and arms itself. It becomes satire. It becomes mean and implacable."[13] As such, the effect of satirical propaganda is prompt and instantaneous. The humorous vignette endures, poking fun and demolishing an adversary. It is not a simple, trite comic story (the "preferred drink of slower minds"), but a perspective in which the humorist looks calmly at the serious condition of the world that many see as cataclysmic and sees "the funny side of the issue."[14] The priest learned a freedom of spirit even behind the barbed wire, telling his Nazi captors that "it's pretty easy to regulate what's on the outside but only God the Father can command what's inside. And you can't do a damn thing about it, Lady Germany."[15] (Like Viktor Frankl in Auschwitz and Aleksandr I. Solzhenitsyn imprisoned in the Gulag Archipelago, Guareschi found a deepening of faith and humor in the camps.)[16]

After the war, Guareschi attacked the Communists and capitalists as much as the fascists. Dictatorships were the institutional negation of humor and thus social enemies. He viewed humor as an antidote to the power of politics, leveling the playing field and combating the pompous rhetoric of oppressors:

> Humor is the declared enemy of rhetoric because, while rhetoric puffs and flares everything up, humor takes rhetoric down and strips it to the bone with vicious criticism. Against rhetoric's power to enflame egos with its depiction of war as glorious flag-waving, sustained by the allegory of ghostly heroes mounted on white horses, humor describes war in such a way as to calm hearts and awaken reason.[17]

According to Guareschi, the humorist knows how to discover the latent comedy in human events; it "unveils the comedy and the illogical in any situation." It can diagnose the disease and recommend a potential cure, but it must be honest with itself before it exposes the enemy. Thus Don Camillo and Peppone share the same strong, stubborn traits and both are exposed and healed with humor. "Humor does not destroy. Humor reveals what needs to be destroyed because it's bad. Humor heals anew. Humor destroys only the equivocal. It strengthens what is substantially good."[18]

In a column against the liberal changes wrought by Vatican II in the Roman Catholic Church, the reactionary Guareschi expressed his sarcasm in palpable ways: "A very wise decision was to abolish the famous 'Index.' Doing that kept some liberal conciliar Fathers from proposing to put the Gospels on the Index." With tongue firmly planted in his cheek, he spoke of

> replacing the traditional altar with the cordial "buffet-table" designed by Lercaro; substituting Gregorian chants with catchy modern tunes; and introducing microphones in church along with loudspeakers and other electronic mechanism – useful only if the power doesn't go out – to remove from what was once the Mass that austerity and magical air of mystery that gave it the cold feeling of a religious rite.[19]

Guareschi sketched one whimsical illustration for the magazine *Il Borghese* in which he denounced the liberalization of the Church, with a priest being asked why a group of Marxists were entering a church. "Are they attacking the church?" "No," says the priest: "they're going to have the flag of the International Association for the Spread of Atheism blessed."

In a trailer for a 1963 film directed half by Guareschi and half by Pasolini, withdrawn shortly after release, the humorist attacks his atheist comrade, declaring that "dictatorships do not tolerate the humor of those who are afraid. At the doorstep of the vast, gloomy Communist empire, with the blood of millions who have been assassinated, history has written: 'It is forbidden to laugh here!' "[20]

Trying to get Italians to take themselves less solemnly and to be humorous, Guareschi admonished: "The person who doesn't know how to laugh doesn't know how to rule. We Italians, we're serious. We're so serious we provoke laughter. ... Let's become more serious. Let's learn to laugh." The key is to love and forgive one's enemies, even as one laughs with them.[21] In fact, laughing can be a sign of such forgiveness.

Unlike Jonah, the biblical *picaro* who gripes and complains when God forgives the Ninevites, Don Camillo rejoices in God's grace. He may try to take the devil by the tail and whip it, but the comic priest with the funny face embraces the image of God imprinted upon every other face and loves them, *imago Dei risibilis*.

In his remarkable theological reflections on laughter, Kuschel posits a problem of the Greek origins of laughter.[22] Homer, he notes, shows that the laughter of the gods has "no compassion for the weak, no mercy for the afflicted, no sparing of the innocent, no solidarity with the victims. [It] rings out over the battlefield with its piles of corpses." Even in Aristotle's positive perspectives on laughter, laughter concerns the lower, second-class category of men and women, the slaves, fools, and shameless rascals, not the heroic (*arête*). The Scriptures, on the other hand, point to the foolishness of all individual men and women. The Christian view is much more egalitarian, leveling, and funny. Jesus, the apotheosis of the *picaro*, brings a messianic jubilation, both a forgiveness of fools and a pleasure in their company. He was after all a "glutton and a winebibber," a friend of tax collectors, drunkards, and sinners.

W. H. Auden opined that a Christian society could produce comedy of "much greater breadth and depth than classical comedy." In the Christian *picaro*, the laughter of heaven took on a body, and brought laughter to earth, bringing hope and joy to those who have been excluded and marginalized. "For Christians whose laughter stems from the spirit of joy and happiness, and who feel particularly committed to the despised and outcast," an ethic of laughter will arise.[23] In identification with those who are despised and exploited comes salvation soaked in laughter. There is divine *gelos* in the divine pathos.

Notes

1 Gary Commins, "Woody Allen's Theological Imagination," *Theology Today* 44:2 (July 1987), 235–249.

2 The trickster remains a staple in the global history of comedy, as one who audaciously breaks boundaries and challenges the status quo. William Hynes listed six characteristics of the trickster: ambiguity, deception, disguise, upending of status, uncertain origins, and a "sacred and lewd *bricoleur*" (one who playfully transforms any object into an aid to mischief). *Mythical Trickster Figures: Contours, Contexts and Criticism* (University of Alabama Press, 1997). See also Eric Weitz, "Trickster," in *Encyclopedia of Humor Studies* (ed. Salvatore Attardo) (Sage Publications, 2014), 776–778. The trickster can be depended upon to disrupt and subvert our usual expectations of behavior and morality.

3 Some film comics (e.g. Charlie Chaplin, the Ritz brothers, Sid Caesar, etc.) frequently begin as schlemiel children, "miniature comedians operating in a non-receptive context," dedicated to spreading chaos and affirming the absurdity of life, ignoring rules and devising games that "seem formulated by a Mad Hatter." Seymour Fisher and Rhoda Lee, "Schlemiel Children," *Psychology Today* (September 1980), 66, 73.

4 Ingrid Shafer, "Introduction: The Catholic Imagination in Popular Film and Television," *Journal of Popular Film and Television* 19:2 (1991), 50–57.

5 Yet one must recognize the ineffectual and incompetent comic clergy who merely serve as the butt of the jokes. Examples include the mediocre but proud Dr. Primrose in Oliver Goldsmith's *The Vicar of Wakefield*, the pompous Mr. Collins in Jane Austen's *Pride and Prejudice*, the stupid islanders in *Father Ted*, and the quintessential bumbling Father Mulcahy in *M*A*S*H*; these are ridiculous without being "fools *for Christ's sake*." See Sue Sorensen, *The Collar: Reading Christian Ministry in Fiction, Television, and Film* (Cascade Books, 2014), 70–71.

6 Staff, "Review: *Heavens Above!*" *Variety* (December 31, 1962).

7 Bosley Crowther, "Review: *Heavens Above!*" *New York Times* (May 21, 1963). One of the typical *Punch*-style jocular asides occurs when a train master announces the next station and addresses a compartment full of clerics, saying, "Last supper, gentlemen." Special thanks of acknowledgment go to my former student Morgan Stroyeck for her insightful and delightful analysis of this film.

8 Pauline Kael, "Britain: Commitment and the Strait-Jacket," *Film Quarterly* 15:1 (1961), 4–13.

9 Francesca Orestano, "The Rev'd William Gilpin and the Picturesque; Or, Who's Afraid of Doctor Syntax?" *Garden History* 31:2 (Winter 2003), 163–179.

10 Giovanni Guareschi, *The Little World of Don Camillo* (trans. Una Vincenzo Troubridge) (Pellegrini & Cudahy, 1950), 19–20.

11 Alan R. Perry, *The Don Camillo Stories of Giovannino Guareschi: A Humorist Portrays the Sacred* (University of Toronto, 2007), 186.

12 Ibid., 61.

13 Ibid., 30.

14 Ibid., 31, 32.

15 Ibid., 34.

16 Steve Lipman, *Laughter in Hell: The Use of Humor during the Holocaust* (Jason Aronson, 1993), 14–15. In Solzhenitsyn's *Gulag Archipelago*, a man is arrested for merely smiling at something in *Pravda*: "the fact of smiling at the central organ of the party was in itself sacrilege." Aleksandr I. Solzhenitsyn, *The Gulag Archipelago* (trans. Thomas P. Whitney) (Harper & Row, 1973), 283.

17 Perry, *Don Camillo Stories*, 38, 39.
18 Ibid., 43, 44.
19 Ibid., 167.
20 Ibid., 151.
21 Ibid., 189. My friend and colleague Fred Wiseman pointed out that loving one's enemies takes on a wholly different connotation in Guareschi's *Comrade Don Camillo* (Farrar, Straus, and Giroux, 1964). The funny priest and his Marxist adversary take their ideologically charged students to Berlin, sharing the trip for economic reasons; while they debate theology and ideology in the front of the bus, the good Communist and Christian kids are busy screwing each other in the back.
22 Karl-Josef Kuschel, *Laughter: A Theological Reflection* (trans. John Bowden) (Continuum, 1994), 6–7.
23 Ibid., 122.

9   *Film Blanc* Comedy

When an angel of the Lord stood in the path of the stubborn prophet Balaam, he did not recognize him. His donkey did. When Peter had been placed in prison, with four squads of soldiers guarding him, the church fervently prayed for him. An angel of the Lord suddenly appeared and roused Peter and led him out of prison to the house of Mary, the mother of John Mark. When he knocked at the door, a servant girl named Rhoda answered and in her joy, went to announce to those gathered in prayer that Peter was at the gate. They said to her: "You're crazy!" and maybe "it's his angel." As the saints kept praying for his release, Peter kept knocking. They had a hard time believing that God's angel had really helped Peter. Even angels get involved in biblical comedies.

In his *Institutes of the Christian Religion* of 1536, Reformer John Calvin defined angels as "dispensers and administrators of the divine beneficence toward us. They regard our safety and undertake our defense, direct our ways and exercise a constant solicitude that no evil befall us." Although very little comedy inhabited the systematic mind of the Geneva theologian, he set up the baseline for cinematic depictions of these messengers of God.

Angelic comedies do provide the help that human characters need, often by holding up mirrors to their predicaments. They insert the divine help that succors and saves them. In *Grand Canyon* (Lawrence Kasdan, 1991), Los Angeles businessman Kevin Kline is almost hit by a passing vehicle, narrowly avoiding becoming a "wet bug stain on the front of a bus," but is grabbed by a stranger and yanked back to the curb just in time. Turning to thank the young woman whose quick thinking saved him, he notices that she wears a Pittsburgh Pirates baseball cap, the equivalent of a halo from his favorite baseball team. "Was that a real person or was that something else," he wonders, "you know, sent from *somewhere* else?" His trip to Miracle Mile on Wilshire Boulevard is arrested by an uncertain sign from above, but one that saved him with divine beneficence. "Some," the Book of Hebrews tells us, "have entertained angels without knowing it" (13:2).

Biblically, angels are fearsome creatures, even if made a little lower than humans.[1] In sacred literature and art, seraphim are wondrously terrible and mysterious. They frequently begin their pronouncements with the words "fear not." Few cinematic angels need to allay the fears of their charges; rather they are quite chummy. At least they are not like Raphael's chubby little cherubs. Accurate portrayals are not to be expected, but rarely do we get angels with wings (although little wings are often pinned onto breast pockets); most are plainclothes messengers. One (Clarence) even wears his nightshirt.

Calvin Theological Seminary professor emeritus Andrew Bandstra discerned five ways in which the Bible describes the work of angels. First, they are God's messengers, which is what the word "angel" originally meant. As God's messengers, they terrified people so that they often had to preface their message with "don't be afraid." Second, angels praise God (Revelation 5:11). Third, they exercise God's providential care, protecting and guarding His children. (While Peter is rescued from prison and Elijah finds help escaping from Jezebel, the Scriptures provide no support for the romantic notion that each person has his or her own personal guardian angel.) Fourth, the key duty of the angels is to encourage God's people to obey Him. Obedience here (*upo-akouw*) means to be put under the hearing of, namely to listen to, Him. Finally, angels carry out God's justice, not just offering supernatural sentiment.[2]

Catholic journalist G. K. Chesterton ruminated that "Angels can fly because they take themselves lightly," and no less an authority than the Angelic Doctor himself, St. Thomas Aquinas, "leaves the Christian with a wide field for his fun. He does so on the authority of the Philosopher" – revelation and reason in perfect harmony – "who, we are reminded, 'posits the virtue of *eutrapelia*, which in Latin we call *jucunditas*, enjoyment.' His conclusion rejoices smiling Christians."[3] One hilarious and miraculous comic fantasy flies forth in Vittorio De Sica's surreal neo-realist film, *Miracle in Milan* (1951). In this fable for grown-ups, a magic dove is given to a poor boy, Toto, found as a baby in a cabbage patch. An old woman, who becomes an angel, helps him and in a shanty town beggars get brooms to ride off into the heavens, where "good day really means good day." The rich and greedy may inherit the earth and its oil, but the meek get a roller-coaster ride to a better place.[4]

Film critic Peter Valenti identified the supernatural comedies of the 1940s as examples of *film blanc*, films that featured such benevolent supernatural beings who intervene in human affairs.[5] (No doubt, more cinematic curiosity is raised by such *fallen* angels as Lucifer and his minions, but we will ignore them in this section.) In contrast to the gritty, dark *film noir* of the postwar period, such films as *Here Comes Mr. Jordan* (Alexander Hall, 1941), *It's a Wonderful Life* (Frank Capra, 1946), *Angel on My Shoulder* (Archie Mayo, 1947), and *The Bishop's Wife* (Henry Koster, 1947) presented divine agents that are sent to set things right.

During the time of war and impending death for many men, the stories about heaven and an afterlife, however fanciful, comforted a nation worried about its loved ones. After death a mortal meets with a kindly representative of the world beyond (mostly heaven), has a Hollywood love affair, and finally transcends mortality by escaping the spiritual world for the material universe. Even though many reflect the *film noir* dark shadows of the 1940s, as comedies they still affirm life and light and love.[6] While mortals in these B-feature films make mistakes, they are saved by their basic human goodness. Even God and the omnipotent powers of the universe allow a semi-Pelagian heresy to win out.

These divine white comedies included several elements. First, their protagonists would confront some crisis in life, either failure or death. If the latter, the hero might die or be on the verge of death, but would surely be emptied of hope. Second, they become acquainted with a kindly representative of the world beyond, sent from heaven to earth to encourage or protect their protégés.[7] Third, they experience a budding love affair, and finally, an angelic being would help them transcend their crisis, whether by escaping the spiritual world and returning to earthly existence or overcoming their despair. Their epiphanies have changed little over the years, as angels from Charlie Chaplin's *The Kid* (1921) to those in Jim Robinson's *The Music Box* (1979) look like merely human characters with fluffy wings and haloes, but creatures overflowing with joy.[8]

One classic *film blanc* emerging out of World War II, where one hoped that supernatural forces were at work in the mortal world, was *The Horn Blows at Midnight* (Raoul Walsh, 1945). Listening to the Paradise Coffee program ("it's heavenly" and "the coffee that makes you sleep"), an inept and mediocre band trumpeter (Jack Benny) falls asleep, only to dream he's the angel Athanael who has been appointed to sound the last trumpet for the end of the world. Battling fallen angels, he does manage to save a young woman from suicide.

More typical is the wartime drama *A Guy Named Joe* (Victor Fleming, 1943), in which a bomber pilot Major Pete Sandidge (Spencer Tracy) becomes a guardian angel to a younger pilot Ted Randall (Van Johnson) after he dies in a World War II battle. He must decide whether to sacrifice his own romantic interest, fiancée Dorinda Durston (Irene Dunne), to this new man. In this sentimental and somewhat sappy story, the ghost with the good heart gives up his earthly "possessions" in a noble and patriotic gesture. Individual tragedy could be turned to social good and sentimental comedies. Although Pete dies, as Christ also died, he has made a contribution that will be remembered and embodied in others.[9]

Theologian Neil Hurley found expansive religious symbolism in Frank Capra's films, even as promoting a three-tiered universe of hell, purgatory, and heaven that marks the *Divine Comedy* of Dante. He traced a common pattern of a naïve man-child hero who finds himself entangled in a web of compromise, suffers the pangs of hell (bad conscience, disgrace) and with the aid of a woman, purges himself through a public confession of complicity and atonement, leading to a happy ending. The victim/hero is himself the battlefield of good and evil forces.

Capra, however, achieved an inner radiance of comic warmth and life-affirming uplift. "For Frank Capra, universal drama is a redemptive one in which sacrifice and atonement are central factors, not only for individual integrity, but also for success, romance and the common good of democratic communities."[10] Capra offered a sort of "un-crucified Christ" for American civil religion, with his focus upon the resourceful and resilient little guy, who overcomes political obstacles and personal humiliation with heart and humor.[11]

The archetypal *film blanc* is Roman Catholic director Capra's somewhat dark parable, *It's a Wonderful Life* (1946). Clarence Oddbody (Henry Travers), a clumsy and frumpy Angel Second Class, needs to earn his wings. An opportunity arrives when George Bailey (Jimmy Stewart) has come to the end of his rope. Financial problems have afflicted his life and he desperately needs help. The film opens with a chorus of prayers interceding for him as he contemplates a suicidal jump into a river on Christmas Eve. Pretending to drown himself, Clarence tricks his charge into doing what comes naturally to him: helping others.[12] In essence Clarence saves George's life by getting George to save his.

In a trick of "what if" Clarence transports George from his present life in Bedford Falls to a bleak world in which he didn't exist. The film is able to juxtapose the tragic consequences of a missed life, intimating that all life is sacred and that every life is important. Capra's populist concern for the ordinary man was, as he put it,

> A film to tell the wary, the disheartened, and the disillusioned, that no man is a failure! To show those born slow of foot or slow of mind, that each man's life touches so many other lives. And that if he isn't around it would leave an awful hole. I wanted to shout, "You are the salt of the earth!" and *It's a Wonderful Life* is my memorial to you.[13]

Persuading George that one man can positively affect the lives of so many others, George realizes how grateful he is for what he has. Capra had experienced his own "visitation" after the success of his 1934 romantic comedy *It Happened One Night* in which he had been feeling sorry for himself after so much success. A little man entered his room, confronting Capra as a coward, just as Adolf Hitler bellowed from a radio broadcast. The anonymous little man issued a challenge to the self-pitying director to preach the good news of America to America. Capra had his religious calling to preach.[14]

In *It's a Wonderful Life*, Clarence shows George what the repercussions would have been if George had not been born, how tragic and

Figure 9.1 As comedies begin with some obstacle or frustration, George Bailey (Jimmy Stewart) had lost all hope in a dark Christmas season; but through the guidance of an angel, Bailey comes to learn the significance of his life. *It's a Wonderful Life*, Liberty Films (II), 1946. Author's screenshot.

sad life would have been for others. Coming to realize how rich he is in friends, George sees afresh that he is surrounded with family and loved ones. A bell rings, indicating that the balding junior angel has graduated and got his wings. Laughter around the Christmas tree resounds with the deepest sign of film comedy, joy.

Critic Stephen Brown noted how the camera work often approximates God the Father's point of view, depicting a world "ultimately under the reign of a good God."[15] The divine presence appears when George has his first romantic meeting with Mary (Donna Reed) and his last supper with his father. Central, however, is the instant that George stops calling on Clarence to get him back to his precious life and calls out to "God" on the bridge: it immediately starts snowing, showing that he is back in the real world.

In comparing inspiration in British and Hollywood films, *New York Times* critic Bosley Crowther points to Capra's homely hero in a small American town, Bedford Falls, whose circumstances compel him to stay at home, ending up running a two-bit "Building & Loan" shop. When his dithery uncle misplaces a large sum of the company's money, the greedy shark of a town banker tries to grasp their company. Utterly depressed, George goes to jump off a bridge, wishing he'd never been born. Clarence Oddbody persuades George that he "really had a wonderful life. Don't you see what a mistake it would be to throw it away?" Through a divine flashback, George is given the opportunity to see what might have happened: the cozy tavern becomes a gin mill, and – heaven forbid in a movie – the quaint movie theater is a lurid burlesque stage.[16] Praying to be kept alive for the sake of others, George looks smug and sentimental to Crowther, a "figment of simple Pollyanna platitudes."

However, since its first release, *It's a Wonderful Life* has garnered a devoted following, as it echoes both the loneliness and joy of the holiday season. Its celebration of family, friends, and divine intervention rings a little bell every Christmas, moistening up not a few eyes.

In contrast, *Stairway to Heaven* (Michael Powell and Emeric Pressburger, 1946) offers a more sophisticated flight of fancy, where RAF pilot Peter Carter is caught between earth (in color) and heaven (in monochrome); at least in Carter's hallucinations he thinks he is being summoned to the afterlife just when he falls in love with an American WAC. Carter asks for a stay of sentence and the heavenly court hears the case, just as he is undergoing a brain operation.

However, time changes opinions; some four decades later, film critic Roger Ebert found *It's a Wonderful Life*, this "ultimate small-town homily," disarmingly simple, with humor and bite.[17] The comedy depends upon the ritual humiliation in which a character descends to his or her low point, followed by the ritual victory, an optimism shown by Capra in the "Christmas Catholic" and his "ecumenical church of humanism" where he used comedy to "warm people to my subject … first I entertain then I get them in a spirit of laughter and then, perhaps, they might be softened up to accept some kind of moral precept. But entertainment comes first."[18] The redemptive quality of Capra's populist comedies is charged with a sense of innocence and justice.[19]

The genre of *film blanc* wafted out of the heavens of Hollywood after the war, bringing fantasy, comedy, and whimsy into sentimental films. Angels descended with ease into the lives of ordinary citizens on earth. Benign, even goofy angels try to fix bureaucratic mistakes in the afterlife, as in *Here Comes Mr. Jordan* (1941). Boxer and saxophonist Joe Pendleton (Robert Montgomery) is prematurely separated from his body by an overzealous bureaucratic angel, Messenger 7013 (Edward Everett Horton); thus the efficient Mr. Jordan (Claude Rains) must intervene and correct the mistake of the celestial collection agency. Jordan watches over the upward traffic of souls who must "cross the *Jordan*" to enter the Promised Land. Company policy demands that they find a "new body" for Joe to inhabit until his time is ripe. Hierarchy rules, so much so that after heavenly clerical errors, Jordan can extinguish memory. Actually, this ability to evoke amnesia in human consciousness runs counter to biblical narratives, where people too vividly remember their encounters.

When the film was remade in 1981 as *Heaven Can Wait* (Warren Beatty, Buck Henry), the suave and dapper James Mason plays the high-ranking functionary Jordan who must correct the inept error regarding the prize fighter Joe Pendleton (Warren Beatty), who will (aptly) become the dumb quarterback of the City of the Angels Rams and will conveniently get in shape in time to win the Super Bowl for the team. A middle-class bureaucratic angel disobeys the law of "Probability and Outcome" and takes Joe before his time, with his original body cremated. Nevertheless, Jordan unflappably asserts that "There is a reason for everything. There is a plan." Not only do angels make mistakes, but bodies are interchangeable, almost suggesting Church father Origen's heretical opinions on interchangeable birth.

The masquerade of divine messengers stems in part from Hebrews 13:2, where the author reminds his readers to not forget to "entertain strangers; for thereby some have entertained angels unawares." St. Paul describes angels as thrones, dominations, powers, virtues, and principalities, with Pharisees embracing them and Sadducees rejecting them. Cinematic angels must camouflage themselves in human form or remain invisible to all except those to whom they reveal themselves. The comic potential of characters talking to invisible persons plays off the possibility of lunacy, a sort of craziness that borders on a loss of reason and sanity itself.

An angel (with the voice of James Whitmore) representing the Archangel Gabriel thunders from the heavens at foul-mouthed manager Aloysius X, "Guffy" McGovern (Paul Douglas) of the Pittsburg Pirates (in last place) in *Angels in the Outfield* (Clarence Brown, 1951). A bit perturbed, he would not have intervened except it "seems someone down there is sending up a lot of prayers."

"Someone praying for me? Gee," says the big-mouthed Guffy, and by the way, are there "ball players in heaven?" "Plenty of ball players," responds the angel, "but very few managers."

However, continues the angel, before "I answer those prayers, I have to clean you up." He sets down certain rules for Guffy to follow. First, cut out the blasphemy. Second, start treating your fellow man with more respect and understanding. Third, "love and stop slugging thy neighbor, hear me?" When Guffy asks for a sign, the angel says, "Look for a miracle in the third inning."

Fresh, naïve reporter Jennifer Paige (Janet Leigh) is assigned to follow the Pirates and discovers a moppet from St. Gabriel's Home for Orphan Girls. Bridget White sees an angel behind each player. When questioned, she allows that she prays every night, every morning, and sometimes during arithmetic.

Both Guffy and Paige informally adopt Bridget and take her to ball games and to Guffy's home to celebrate his birthday. Paige unfortunately cooks veal with leather rather than olive oil, but the problem of the dinner is otherwise. "What's the matter, Bridget?" Paige asks.

"Grace," answers the orphan. "Grace who? Oh yeah, grace, I almost forgot," mutters Guffy. Bridget prays: "O Lord, make us truly thankful for these thy gifts which we are about to receive. Amen."

Guffy comes under scrutiny for acknowledging that he does in fact hear from angels and that they have helped his Pirates toward winning

Figure 9.2 Manager Guffy (Paul Douglas) seeks divine guidance from the Heavenly Coach. *Angels in the Outfield*, Metro-Goldwyn-Mayer (MGM), 1951. Author's screenshot.

the pennant. But he has a more difficult challenge not getting into fights. When a nun is asked "Is it always right to turn the other cheek, Sister?" as Guffy got walloped when he tried, she responds, "Well, the meek shall inherit the earth."

Kneeling at second base talking to the angels, he learns that one of his old friends whose pitching skills have declined is about to be signed up "in the Spring for the Heavenly Choir team." Guffy has learned that human relations are more important than winning and puts him in as his starting pitcher for the game which will decide if they win the pennant.

At a hearing with the baseball commissioner on Guffy's sanity, a psychiatrist is brought in who dismisses all religion as an invention and attempt to explain mysteries.[20] However, the defense admits three clergymen: a minister from Trinity Church, a rabbi, and an Irish priest. When asked about the existence of angels, they quote Exodus: "Behold I send an angel before them," and the testimony that the Angel of the Lord encamps about His people.

But Guffy's nemesis, Fred Bayles (Keenan Wynn), challenges them: Why would an angel ever watch over such a profane and foul guy as Guffy?

The priest answers with the parable from Matthew 18:12: "If a man have 100 sheep and one of them goes astray …" Both poignancy and humor mark the rescue of Guffy and eventually of his Pirates. In the remake of *Angels in the Outfield* (William Dear, 1994), the orphaned kid

Roger (Joseph Gordon-Levitt) prays a politically correct, gender-neutral prayer, "God, if there is a God, if you're a man or a woman ... I would really like a family; my dad says that will only happen if the Angels win the pennant, so maybe you could help them out a little, amen, or a-woman." The tagline for this Los Angeles Angels team to win the pennant is "Ya gotta believe!"

Defending Roger, Maggie Nelson (Brenda Fricker) argues:

> My name is Maggie Nelson. I take care of foster kids. One of these boys is the child who can see angels. He could stand up right now and tell you what's going on and I'd know you'd just laugh at him. But, when a professional football player drops to one knee to thank God for making a touchdown, nobody laughs at that. Or when a pitcher crosses himself before going to the mound, no one laughs at that either. It's like you're saying it's okay to believe in God, but it's not okay to believe in angels. Now, I thought that they were on the same team.

The apotheosis of the *film blanc* occurs with God Himself setting up an interview with a somewhat befuddled supermarket assistant manager, Jerry Landers (John Denver), in Carl Reiner's direction of *Oh, God!* (1976). God (George Burns), appearing in various guises such as a taxi-cab driver and hotel room-service attendant, wants Landers to be His messenger to a skeptical world.[21] Theologians try to discredit him and the media mock him as a nut case. God acknowledges that the last miracle He did was the "1969 Mets; before that, you have to go back to the Red Sea." Reiner takes some shots at the audience for *The Exorcist*, mocking those who now believe in the devil just because a little girl wet the rug and threw up some pea soup.

With an early environmental message, God lambasts His earthly creatures for killing His creation. He accuses them of "turning the sky into mud. I look down; I can't believe the filth. Using the rivers for toilets, poisoning my fishes. You want a miracle. *You* make a fish from scratch. You can't. You think only God can make a tree? Try coming up with a mackerel."

In particular, God calls Landers to confront a fund-raising fundamentalist preacher (an easy target in the 1970s), one Reverend Willie Williams (Paul Sorvino), who drags Lander into court. Trying to prove God's existence, Landers argues that God could appear as a witness if he so chooses. The judge, losing patience, is about to charge Landers with contempt when the leisurely God saunters in, takes the stand, and swears over the Bible, "So help me Me; if it pleases the court, and even if it doesn't please the court, I'm God, your honor." He performs a few card tricks and then disappears. His voice, like the Cheshire Cat, continues, as He tells the packed courtroom: "It can work. If you find it hard to believe in Me, maybe it will help to know that I believe in you." Of course, while God always hears, He confesses that sometimes He doesn't listen.

Landers, who loses his job and feels like a failure, is revisited by God, who puts him in company with Johnny Appleseed, reminding him that the seeds he has planted will eventually take root. After God tells Landers He won't be coming back, Landers asks what if he needs to talk with Him. "I'll tell you what: you talk, I'll listen." This easy, humanistic God, one that many people like to believe in, is a tame, malleable divinity. When Landers confesses that he doesn't go to church, God responds, "Neither do I." Who wouldn't want a cigar-smoking George Burns to oversee his or her life? It may be a delicious idea, but it is only whipped cream, the kind of spiritual nutrition one gets from *film blanc*.

Peter Valenti's category of *film blanc* with angelically oriented films, featuring angels' benevolent supernatural intervention in human affairs, exists in the realms of comedy, with laughter among the heavenly hosts. Much of the humor is generated by characters interacting with unseen presences. However, these cinematic angels are more than ombudsmen, but very fallible creatures themselves, awkwardly helping to usher in fanciful comic *deus ex machina* endings. Some of the men and women they assist on earth, but some they guide to the heavenly realms. The author of the Book of Hebrews asks, "Are not all angels ministering spirits sent to serve those who will inherit salvation?" (1:14). If they are, then it is through these divine films these messengers bring the good news of hope nestled in humor.

Notes

1 See Christopher Deacy's admirable work on eschatology, especially "Angels in Scripture and Film," in *Screening the Afterlife: Theology, Eschatology and Film* (Routledge, 2012), 156–158.
2 Andrew J. Bandstra, "A Job Description of Angels," *Christianity Today* (April 5, 1993), 21.
3 M. A. Screech, *Laughter at the Foot of the Cross* (Westview Press, 1997).
4 This fantasy satire suggests a "childlike view of Dostoevski's *The Idiot*." Pauline Kael, "Miracle in Milan," in *The National Society of Film Critics on Movie Comedy* (ed. Stuart Byron and Elisabeth Weis) (Viking, 1977), 261.
5 Peter L. Valenti, "The *Film Blanc*: Suggestions for a Variety of Fantasy, 1940–45," *Journal of Popular Film and Television* 6:4 (1978), 294. See also Martin Norden, "America and Its Fantasy Films: 1945–1951," *Film and History* 12:1 (1982), 1; and Andrew Sarris, "The Afterlife, Hollywood-Style," *American Film* (April 1979), 25–27, 77.
6 Sarris, "The Afterlife," 25–27, 77. Sarris argues, convincingly, that the films tell us "more about the times in which they were produced" than the times with which they were concerned. Some, like *Stairway to Heaven*, are based on the premise that a "mistake has been made in heaven and that the individual is granted the right of appeal and the possibility of restitution for the unauthorized snuffing out of his life" (77).

7 Frequently the portrayals of a charitable providence overlooking this mortal world were comic themselves. A liberal theology suggested that individuals could improve their situations. For some, this offered a Pollyanna view of the world clashing with the violence and realism of turbulent war and post-war times. Some critics see fantasy films as a way to enhance the human image of the self, seeing in them an opportunity to renew the soul without God. Constance Markey, "Birth and Rebirth in Current Fantasy Films," *Film Criticism* **14**:7 (Fall 1982), 14–25.

8 James Gullo, "Hollywood's Heavenly Host," *Premiere* (January 1991), 22.

9 Peter L. Valenti, "The Cultural Hero in World War II Fantasy Film," *Journal of Popular Film and Television* 7:3 (1979), 310–321.

10 Neil P. Hurley, "The Divine Comedies of Frank Capra," *America* (April 20, 1985), 322–324.

11 Jeanine Basinger, "America's Love Affair with Frank Capra," *American Film* (March 1982), 46–51, 81.

12 Jeanine Basinger, *The "It's a Wonderful Life" Book* (Knopf, 1986); Frank Capra, *The Name above the Title* (Vintage Books, 1971); and Peter L. Valenti, "The Theological Rhetoric of *It's a Wonderful Life*," *Film Criticism* 5:2 (Winter 1981), 23–33.

13 Capra, *Name above the Title*, 383.

14 Ibid.

15 Stephen Brown, "Optimism, Hope, and Feelgood Movies: The Capra Connection," in *Explorations in Theology and Film: Movies and Meaning* (ed. Clive Marsh and Gaye Ortiz) (Blackwell, 1997), 232. Brown adds that when we view life from an eschatological perspective, from the salvific work of Christ, we find that our existence can be seen as something meaningful and providential, not merely random or accidental.

16 Bosley Crowther, "The Spirits Move: A Comparison of Inspirations in British and Hollywood Films," *New York Times* (January 12, 1947), 1.

17 Roger Ebert, "Don't Miss Jimmy Stewart Talking to the Shrubbery or Donna Reed Losing Her Bathrobe," *TV Guide* (December 24, 1986), 4, 6; Richard Corliss, "Our Town: George Bailey meets 'True,' 'Blue,' and 'Peggy Sue,'" *Film Comment* 22 (November 1986), 9–17.

18 Capra, *Name above the Title*, 93.

19 Brian Rose, "*It's a Wonderful Life*: The Last Stand of the Capra Hero," *Journal of Popular Film* 6:2 (1977), 156–166; Morris Dickstein, "It's a Wonderful Life, But …" *American Film* (May 1980), 43–47.

20 Looking for celebrities to acknowledge the presence of angels, Bing Crosby in a cameo as himself playing golf sinks a putt and says "thanks" to the heavens.

21 "Review: *Oh, God!*" *Variety* (December 31, 1976), online at http://variety.com/1976/film/reviews/oh-god-1200423958/ (accessed October 21, 2015). At one point, Reiner conceived of Mel Brooks playing God and Woody Allen as Landers.

10 Clergy Comedy

The biblical descriptions of men called to be priests and Levites (and they were all men) and the men and women called to be apostles and pastors are remarkably human, fallible, and flawed. They are thus candidates for comic characterization.

St. Peter, the man given the keys to the Kingdom, however, plays comedy better than anyone. With Peter having denied Christ three times, Jesus asks him if he loves him (Do you *agapeo* me?) and Peter merely responds that he likes (*philia*) Jesus. When the Holy Spirit calls Peter to bring the gospel to the Gentiles, Peter is sleeping on a roof, dreaming about eating non-kosher food. (In fact, the Gospel of Mark, which is mainly about Peter, is all about food!)

Wannabe clergy who usually turn out to be frauds and shams inhabit the Scriptures, from the false prophets that Amos rails against to the hilarious sons of Sceva in the Book of Acts (19:13–20). Itinerant Jewish exorcists set up business by seeking to chase out evil spirits. When the seven sons of Sceva commanded an evil spirit to come out in the name of "Jesus whom Paul preaches," the demon answered and said, "Jesus I know, and Paul I know, but who are you?" The evil spirit leaped on the brothers and overpowered all seven, so that "they fled out of that house naked and wounded." While engendering fear among all those who heard of it, the story also advertised the wild and comic consequences of bogus preachers.

God's clerical saints are funny, from St. Lawrence who jested during his martyrdom about being turned over on the grill ("I'm done on this side") when he is being tortured for his faith, to St. Francis who rejoiced with all creation and is known as the jester of God. The Irish St. Dunstan, originator of the lucky horseshoe, was even celebrated in poetry:

> St Dunstan, as the story goes,
> Once pull'd the devil by the nose
> With red-hot tongs, which made him roar,
> That he was heard three miles or more.

For Voltaire, the first priest was "the first rogue who met the first fool," an indication of the skepticism that many moderns have toward clergy. As Erasmus was prone to praise fools, rogues, and clergy, so numerous silly films pop up to bolster that image. Cynical faith healer Jonas Nightengale is a barnstorming fraud in *Leap of Faith* (Richard Pearce, 1992). *Saving Grace* (Robert M. Young, 1985) situates a new pope, Leo XIV, in an Italian village to learn of life among the peasants. And Ivan, the rose-colored, Edenic minister of *Adam's Apples*, keeps showing kindness to his seemingly irredeemable neo-Nazi parolee (Anders Thomas Jensen, 2005). The intrusive and irritating Reverend Frank in *License to Wed* (Den Kwapis, 2007) overextends his welcome in helping a young couple towards marriage; he mirrors Mark Twain's description of the preacher who "never charged nothing for his preaching, and it was worth it, too."

Even a slapstick comedy like *Big Momma's House* (Raja Gosnell, 2000) places Cedric the Entertainer as "the Reverend" who champions forgiveness in his congregation. In contrast, Reverend Deke O'Malley exploits poor blacks with promised trips back to Africa in Ossie Davis' *Cotton Comes to Harlem* (1970), followed by Richard Pryor playing the immoral cuckolded Reverend Lenox Thomas trying to get revenge in Michael Schultz's *Which Way is Up?* (1977). The era of civil rights in which preachers often stood in the vanguard of social justice also portrayed black clergy as comics, with Flip Wilson as the Preacher in *Uptown Saturday Night* (Sidney Poitier, 1974), Richard Pryor as wonder preacher "Daddy Rich" in *Car Wash* (Michael Schultz, 1976), and Harry Belafonte as the titular con-man preacher in *Buck and the Preacher* (Sidney Poitier, 1972). The apotheosis of black clergy, Reverend Cleophus James, pastor of the Triple Rock Church, rocks in *The Blues Brothers* (John Landis, 1980), with James Brown as the inimitable Reverend James (and Kathleen Freeman as Sister Mary Stigmata, also known as the Penguin).

As we have seen, clergy reside in *film blanc* as well as other films. As a choir sings "Hark! The Herald Angels Sing" over the image of a nativity scene at a department store, a tall, handsome angel named Dudley (Gary Grant) responds to the prayer of a harried bishop (David Niven) in Robert Sherwood's screenplay for *The Bishop's Wife* (Henry Koster, 1947): "God, can't you help me?" Explaining the situation to his charge, the debonair scamp of an angel confides that "you're known to be a good man, Henry, and you were heard. We're everywhere helping people who deserve to be helped." The Pelagian heresy of human goodness underlies the selection of the bishop for special help. However, Henry's obsession with financial and other worldly matters has created a crisis deeper than the mere construction of a new building.

Dudley's actual mission is to transform the bishop from his obsession over money and building programs to recognize the supreme importance of his neglected wife. With a casual and whimsical élan, Dudley rushes in where fools might fear to tread. Dudley does his work in indirect ways,

Figure 10.1 The much too debonair angel Dudley (Cary Grant) connects with the bishop's neglected daughter and wife (Loretta Young) much more than the preoccupied clergyman (David Niven). *The Bishop's Wife*, The Samuel Goldwyn Company, 1947. Author's screenshot.

waking the bishop to the reality that Dudley has charmed, even seduced, his wife, child, servants, and dog. He discovers that his vocation is not to build cathedrals, a pastime that leads him to ignore the very things most valued by God. In a curious twist, Dudley finds himself falling for the innocent and alluring Julia (Loretta Young), the bishop's wife. He skates into her affections. When she protests that she never knows when Dudley is joking, he quips, with one of the most telling theological lines about comedy, "Ah, I am at my most serious when I'm joking."

Hokum comedy sneaks in with biblical citations. When Dudley and the bishop's wife Julia visit the atheist Professor Wutheridge (Monty Woolley), they share wine. However, in reference to the stories of both Elisha and the widow's oil and the wedding at Cana, Dudley keeps filling up the glasses without the bottle, leaving the doubter with the miracle of a wine bottle that never runs out. The crusty unbeliever does buy a scrawny Christmas tree. However, by the end, the professor is writing again and back in the church at the Christmas Eve service, where the choir sings "Grant us, Lord, salvation."

Dudley's mission is to get the workaholic cleric to notice and appreciate his beautiful wife. In slapstick fashion, Dudley uses his "super powers" to glue Henry to a chair and thus delay him. Dudley tells Henry that he is "sacrificing [his] principles for the cathedral. These are lean years. There are so many needy." Discovering that an old melody resonates with a particularly wealthy woman, Dudley uses it strategically to sway her from funding the new cathedral-building program to helping the less fortunate.

However, his own wings of desire infect Dudley as he spends more and more time with the enchanting Julia. Confiding in the married woman, he whispers "few people know the secret of making a heaven here on earth. You are one of those people." He is almost an angel who would fall (or, like Wim Wenders' heavenly visitor in *Wings of Desire*, exchange the immortal for the mortal). Such flaws make angels human and, thus, more humorous. But his vulnerability awakens Julia to the danger of this divine being who complains of being tired of an existence where "one is neither hot nor cold, hungry nor full."

When the bishop tells Dudley he was praying for a cathedral, the angel responds "No, Henry, you were praying for guidance." What he receives is a Christmas revelation that they should never forget the birthday of the child born in a manger and find what *He* would want in his stocking, which turns out to be "loving kindness, warm hearts and the stretched out hand of tolerance, all the shining gifts that make peace on earth." *New York Times* critic Bosley Crowther dismissed the film: "Most of us have some dark misgivings about the tact of the makers of films when they barge into the private area of a man's communication with his God."[1]

Dudley sees his difficulty: it was "in me. When an immortal finds himself envying a mortal entrusted to his care, it's a danger sign." Such was the crisis of Genesis 6:4, where the sons of God went to the daughters of men and had children with them. Surely, this must be a taboo. The same predicament occurs with Denzel Washington as the angel Dudley in a remake, *The Preacher's Wife* (Penny Marshall, 1996). At St. Matthew's Baptist Church, set in a contemporary New York venue, Reverend Henry Biggs (Courtney B. Vance) has problems. From mounting debts necessitating the closing of the church's youth center and a sputtering boiler to a declining congregation, he wrestles with his own spiritual crisis. Talking to himself he is overheard by God. "Lord, I'm a little tired. I sure could use some help."

The minister and his choir-director wife Julia (the very charismatic Whitney Houston) find their romance flagging as he attends to the needy and to a mercenary encroaching developer, Joe Hamilton. (As one congregation member characterizes Hamilton's commercials on television: "That man is so oily, you could fry chicken on his smile.") *Variety* found director Penny Marshall's modern musical fairy tale a sentimental throwback to another era of bank mortgages, Christmas pageants, and a cardboard villain, but one that still works pleasantly, especially, as they put it, with the "sizeable African-American audience."[2] Unlike the Cary Grant vehicle, this one sings with energy.

What is important to this Dudley is the attractive Julia; so the film takes on more sexual tension than is shown in Cary Grant's flirtation with Loretta Young. Julia is a strong, determined woman and her husband is left feeling inadequate in many ways.

This Dudley (Denzel Washington) acknowledges how much competition there was to be sent to earth. He corrects the notion that angels have wings as a bad literary cliché. Angels seem to want the taste of earth, to smell the roses and touch the flesh. But he is called to be an aid to a clergyman who has lost his sense of what is important to God. Dudley arrives to help Henry renew both his personal faith and his hope that he can make a difference in the lives of his parishioners.[3]

Peculiarly, the *film blanc* moves from the mysterious workings of divine intervention as the answer to prayers into secular sermons on just how good humans have it on this planet during their short span of time. Angels envy us. They want to breathe air, kiss, and eat. One has only to watch Wim Wenders' *Wings of Desire* (1987) to see how miserable existence is for these supernal creatures who must eavesdrop on human conversations. Becoming human, an angel is able to drink coffee and bleed and meet the trapeze artist he fell in love with, but as this is a German film, there is not much *Freude*.

Clergy are mostly mere pawns on the stage of comedy. They are what fiction writer Robertson Davies has called the *Fifth Business*:

> [Y]ou don't know what that is? Well, in opera ... you must have a prima donna – always a soprano, always the heroine, often a fool; and a tenor who always plays the lover to her; and then you must have a contralto, who is a rival to the soprano, or a sorceress or something; and a basso, who is the villain or the rival or whatever threatens the tenor.
>
> So far, so good. But you cannot make a plot work without another man, and he is usually a baritone, and he is called in the profession Fifth Business, because he is the odd man out, the person who has no opposite of the other sex. And you must have Fifth Business because he is the one who knows the secret of the hero's birth or comes to the assistance of the heroine when she thinks all is lost. ... The prima donna and the tenor, the contralto and the basso, get all the best music and do all the spectacular things, but you cannot manage the plot without Fifth Business! It is not spectacular, but it is a good line of work.[4]

The question of who the cleric is in film comedy is that he or she is usually Fifth Business, neither hero nor heroine, villain nor confidant, but an essential character that propels the play into its comic denouement. It is a very good and humble part to play.

Notes

1 Bosley Crowther, " Review: *The Bishop's Wife*," *New York Times* (December, 10, 1947).
2 Leonard Klady, "*Preacher's Wife*," *Variety* (December 14, 1996).
3 Kevin Thomas, "A Heavenly Persuasion," *Los Angeles Times* (December 13, 1996).
4 Robertson Davies, *Fifth Business* (Penguin Books, 1970), x.

11 *Reductio ad Absurdum*

One of the more outrageous sub-genres of comedy must be the *reductio ad absurdum*, which is often realized as black comedy and farce. In this odd category one follows or applies an idea, theme, or trait to its logically absurd conclusion. A simple task or mistake is taken and magnified into chaos or craziness. Unrestrained logic leads to the ridiculous. If Dionysus did not loosen up Apollo and the other gods, everything would be destroyed (even then, Dionysus might muck it all up a bit anyway). In Euripides' *Bacchae*, when Pentheus with his iron-clad authority will not recognize the importance of the vine and ecstasy in the life of his polis, the women go mad and tear him apart.

Take, for example, Laurel and Hardy's *Music Box* (James Parrott, 1932), in which they take a piano up a staircase, or Tom Shadyac's *Liar, Liar* (1997), in which a lawyer must tell the complete truth for a whole day. Each logical premise results in illogical behaviors. By stubbornly following the logic of the absurd, one falls into laughter. The insanity of war addressed in both *Duck Soup* (Leo McCarey, 1933) and *Dr. Strangelove: Or How We Learned to Stop Worrying and Love the Bomb* (Stanley Kubrick, 1964) takes the serious business of total destruction and points to its inanity. So, too, *Being There* (Hal Ashby, 1979) suggests that television prepares one for success in this world and a facade for being wise.

The 2005 City of the Angels Film Festival, showcasing a series on "Divine Comedy: Spirited Laughter," raised questions for Professor Craig Detweiler of whether such savage, anarchic comedies as Mel Brooks' *Blazing Saddles* (1974) or the Coen brothers' *The Big Lebowski* (1988) had rendered notions of God irrelevant.[1] Detweiler slyly points to the Book of Ecclesiastes, where one like Woody Allen despairs of life, but tells readers to enjoy their food and wine and embrace their spouses.[2]

A biblical paradigm of *reductio ad absurdum* appears in narratives like Nebuchadnezzar being turned into an ass or the slavish adherence to the Preacher Koheleth's summation of all life as vanity in the Book of Ecclesiastes. In his view even laughter becomes madness, like the crackling of burning thorns.

One hopes for what Cheryl Brumbaugh-Cayford sees as "God's Presence in the Absurd" in which a revival of comic imagination of festivity and fantasy may help restore God's people into what is right. She juxtaposes the power of the oppressed to speak out against oppressors in the passage of Daniel 5, where God's handwriting on the wall comically undoes Belshazzar, who is then ridiculed by his queen mother.[3] J. R. C. Cousland distinguishes between the comic (which provides a happy resolution) and the comical (which provokes laughter) in the apocryphal Book of Tobit. Tobit (whose name means "good") is a righteous and pious Jew living in Nineveh; his own tribe of people ran off with Jeroboam's idolatrous cult of the bull. Tobit faithfully gives alms to the poor and tries to bury his countrymen in proper fashion. He sends his son Tobias to collect a debt in a far off country.

In this country another faithful servant of God, Sarah, lives in misery. Sarah's problem, like the Wife of Bath, was that she couldn't keep a husband. Every man she married (and there were seven so far) was kidnapped and killed by the demon of lust, Asmodeus, on their wedding night, just before the union could be consummated. Female sexuality could not be more frustrated, or fatal.

Into such a "miserable" world, literally a world needing mercy, the angel Raphael appears as a kinsman to lead Tobias, rescue Sarah, and heal Tobit. Comical, even farcical, elements abound in the book (blindness caused by bird feces, a father digging a grave for his future son-in-law on the wedding day, an attack by a giant fish who tries to swallow Tobias' foot – in a world where humans are supposed to have dominion over the natural world – and stock characters of inept physicians). The wild absurdity of Tobit and Sarah's world where one suffers shame for righteousness and even prays for death seems to counter a good and happy ending. Yet the comical and comic will wed, even as righteousness and bliss may one day kiss one another.

However, in his disguise Raphael introduces Tobias to Sarah and they fall in love. To protect Tobias from Asmodeus, Raphael writes a prescription of burnt fish heart and liver extract (from the fish that tried to bite Tobias) that will drive the demon into Egypt. The gall from the fish will be used later to heal Tobit's blindness from the bird droppings.

In the upside-down world of comedy, the obstacles come first, with an echo of the prophet Amos recognized by Tobit, "Your feasts shall be turned into mourning, and all your mirth into lamentation." But in the topsy-turvy world of God's intervention into these depressed lives, the comic triumphs as the world of the faithful Israelites is put right and the divine comedy ends with a wedding. Sarah's father had been digging a grave for Tobias, expecting the same to happen to him that happened to the other husbands, but when the fumes drove old lust away, he hosted a double feast.[4] As Sarah's father sang and prayed to God on the morning after the honeymoon, finding the couple asleep but alive in the bridal chamber, "Thou art to be praised, for thou hast made me joyful; and that is not come to me which I suspected; but thou hast dealt with us according to thy great mercy." (As the last endnote of the book, Tobit happily gets to hear of the destruction of Nineveh before he dies at a ripe old age.)

Breaking the curse of Asmodeus is the ancient equivalent of escaping the time warp in director Harold Ramis' *Groundhog Day* (1993). Comedian Bill Murray plays Phil Connors, an acidic and obnoxious television weatherman who is condemned to relive the one day the mammal comes out of his hole to see how long winter is going to be extended. If Phil the groundhog emerges on a sunny day and sees his shadow, winter will last six more weeks. For Phil the smug human, the one day of February 2 in Punxsutawney, Pennsylvania will seemingly last forever. The film chronicles the transformation of a callow wiseass to a caring human being as it follows him through a Punxsutawney purgatory. Yet, as Phil must learn, he cannot save himself.

The film, described by Janet Maslin of the *New York Times* as half Capra/half Kafka, has been claimed by various religious traditions, working like a spiritual Rorschach test for projecting one's beliefs onto its narrative.[5] It suggests the Buddhist belief of *samsara*, the endless cycle of rebirth one seeks to escape, or the Jewish practice of *mitvahs* (good deeds). As University of Notre Dame professor Michael P. Foley points out, even the Wiccans could celebrate the film because February 2 is one of their four "great sabbats."[6]

Ramis, co-writer (with Danny Rubin) as well as director, had inspired *Animal House* (1976) and *Ghostbusters* (1984). Raised Jewish and married to a Buddhist, he claims to be an agnostic. Ramis infuses the story with a bit of light-hearted romanticism while he asks existential questions. Phil comes to do his job, quite perfunctorily and begrudgingly, and then tries to leave this hick town as soon as possible. But a snow storm that the weatherman did not foresee restricts them from leaving Punxsutawney. When he wakes up at 6:00 the next morning, the radio cheerfully blares out the Sonny and Cher song "I Got You Babe," a sweet promise from a hidden god. The repetition of the lyrics will become increasingly annoying.

Phil finds that he is stuck reliving this one day, February 2. Grounded by a blizzard (which he failed to predict), he finds himself in a liminal state, a sort of purgatory where he needs to learn what loving others actually is. With his selfish, centripetal mode of living, the question is will Phil see the depth of his own sinfulness and repent of it? Contemptuous of others, Phil declares all people "morons."

The burning question of "What if there were no tomorrow?" condemns Phil to a Sartre-like room with no exit. Phil rushes through Kübler-Ross' five stages of loss: denial, anger, bargaining, depression, and acceptance. He tries to cope, to bargain, to manipulate, even to commit suicide, all to no avail. He refuses to live by "their rules." As Foley

Figure 11.1 Acerbic weatherman Phil Connors (Bill Murray) must undergo his own purgatory to discover the value of *kairos* time over *chronos*. *Groundhog Day*, Columbia Pictures Corporation, 1993. Author's screenshot.

shows, Phil is stuck in the Nietzschean quagmire of discovering there are no consequences to his actions, and becomes Machiavelli's Prince. He steals, assaults, mocks, and exploits. He memorizes a sexy homeroom teacher's name the better to seduce her later. Even when he tries to do good deeds, his life revolves around his own needs. As Kenneth Turan, critic of the *Los Angeles Times*, noticed, "He pigs out on pastries, drives with abandon, seduces women and flouts the law. Does any of this make him happy? No, it does not."[7]

Hints of his need are presented throughout. A beggar is constantly ignored each morning as Phil goes his merry way. An old high school acquaintance vainly seeks to sell him life insurance every morning. He steps in a mud puddle. He does exploit the limits of human knowledge, becoming quite all-knowing for this one day. He recognizes repeated events: a dog barks or a truck appears. *Heidi II* plays at the theatre; a man chokes. He exploits this knowledge by getting to know what women want and even tries his manipulative schemes on Rita (Andie MacDowell) by memorizing her favorite Baudelaire poem, learning French, and playing Ray Charles' "But You Don't Know Me" on the piano. Rita, however, has been to Catholic school and is better prepared to resist his Machiavellian maneuvers to seduce her.

Several points illumine the religious aspects of the film. First is the relationship of talent to producer. Rita is the producer, a gracious and easy-going woman in charge, but Phil argues that the "task of a good producer is to keep the talent happy." So the producer God is relegated to a job to make the world a pleasant place for each of us to serve ourselves. One cannot manipulate the love of God. Phil sees himself as "a god, not the God, but a god." Challenged by Rita, who affirms there is a god and you are not it, he asks, "how do you know I'm not a god? Maybe he's been around for a long time." Yet, his growing omniscience is futile; as a jaded weatherman, he tells the Groundhog Day spectators, "I'll give you a winter prediction; it's going to be cold; it's going to be gray; and it's going to last the rest of your life." Ennui becomes despair no matter how many questions on *Jeopardy!* you can answer.

The film plays with the idea of time, of two kinds of time, *chronos* and *kairos*.[8] *Chronos* conveys the typical calendar perspective, the basic sequential chronology of our lives. Its best tropes are a metronome or a treadmill of life, a repetition of ordinary events that give stability and normalcy to life, but if drawn out into an eternity, become a living hell of sameness. One becomes stuck in such a rut of mundane time. On the other hand, *kairos* gives a distinctive, unique experience in which time stands still, in which one tastes life beyond time in a surprising and memorable moment.

The Scriptures address both kinds of time. Ecclesiastes declares that "for everything there is a time." *Chronos* fits here. But in his Letter to the Galatians (6:9–10), the apostle Paul admonished his readers, "And let us not grow weary in doing good, for in its own time [due season, *kairos*] we shall reap a harvest *if we do not give up*. So, then, as we have time [opportunity, *kairos*], let us do good to all persons." In the same passage, Paul warned the caustic listener, "Do not be deceived; God is not mocked" (6:7). The verb mock, meaning to turn up the nose at, characterizes the smug behaviors of Phil, who sows to his flesh.[9] The consequences of such sowing lead to corruption and the delusion that there are no consequences for carnal and selfish actions. However, such self-deception leads to death, a sort of suicide of the soul. So Paul recommends perseverance in doing good.

Chronos counts the minutes and hours and days; it is quantitative. *Kairos*, the most opportune and supreme time, is experienced in qualitative ways. For Aristotle, *kairos* is important rhetorically as it is a right word in its proper season. Most curiously, the Greek word *kairos* also means weather. Thus, this oblivious weatherman who should be able to prognosticate the *kairos* does not recognize his ignorance of *kairos*.

In this small town much like Bedford Falls in Frank Capra's *It's a Wonderful Life* or Seahaven in Peter Weir's *The Truman Show* (1998), Phil must find his way out of his predicament. Yet he is unable to help himself, in spite of the grand American civil religious principle of Benjamin Franklin's "God helps those who help themselves." The growing awareness of one's helplessness and need for help spurs Phil to surrender, to give up and let himself be bought by the Pearl of Great Worth,

Rita. Scholar Audrey Farolino points out how the film thus moves from a Kafkaesque tale to a Capraesque ending.[10]

Stuck in what seems to be Nietzsche's repetition of the eternal, the metaphysical quandary allows one peculiar characteristic of comedy films: running gags. As animator Paul Terry waxed ridiculously that if one mouse is funny, a hundred is a stitch, so the gags of the film escalate like comic snowballs. Each day brings a little deviation from the standard fare of meeting Ned Ryerson, the whistling belly-button insurance "bing" salesman, stepping in a puddle ("watch out for that first step, it's a doozy"), and Phil's unending stream of insouciant patter. (One very apt gag tribute was a cable television company's continuous offering of the film for 24 hours on February 2.)

In the Gospel of Mark, the author writes about the appointed time in the purpose of God (1:15). One is told to redeem the time (*kairos*), which is what Rita will do.

Dancing in the gazebo, Phil seeks to romance Rita, but one can't manipulate the love of God. Slapped on one cheek, he says, "If you need help on the other cheek, let me know." Her reproof is part of his spiritual instruction that slowly transforms him. He gives money to the beggar and brings coffee to his friends. However, when he tries to resuscitate an old man, he fails. The man dies. In an adaptation of Charles Dickens' *A Christmas Carol*, Bill Murray had played the selfish and cynical Media Scrooge. In *Scrooged* (Richard Donner, 1988), he also had to learn the limits of his world, and only a glimpse of eternity will shock him into humility. Having made himself into a local god, Phil is stuck until he realizes he has limited power.

But he starts to see more. When Rita stands in the snow, he observes, "You look like an angel." But knowledge and good deeds are not enough. Then he must confess: "I am a jerk."

He is asked, "Is this what you do with eternity?" His slow transformation begins with his own realization that even in this frozen world of time, "Only God can make a tree."

Rita is the key. When we first see her doing the weather against a green screen, we see only her head and hands. She is part spirit, and prophesies to Phil in ordinary language: "It's cold out there." Yet, the seer of seers, the prognosticator of prognosticators, cannot see his own future or present predicament. When he begins to realize that he is going to experience the same repetitive things his whole life, he asks what would it be like if every day was the same damn thing and nothing you did ever mattered? A guy downing his beer at the bar mutters, "That about sums it up for me."

Confessing that "I'm not that smart," Rita is wiser than he, but her wisdom is disguised in vulnerability. Only when Phil puts himself up for sale, does his redemption draw nigh. At a fund-raiser for eligible bachelors, Phil puts himself on the auction block. One carnivorous bidder wants him, but Rita outbids them all by emptying the contents of her check-book, paying the odd sum of $339.88 for him. Rita, whose name stems from the Greek for "pearl," buys Phil from his life of shadows. The kind and patient presence of Rita, the pearl of great price, redeems Phil from his selfishness. It is, as Foley explains, "a happy peripety; rather than Phil buying the pearl with everything he has, the pearl buys him with every-thing she has." "God" has redeemed this fool with everything she has, sacrificing her all for his bliss.

Her 12 years in a good Catholic school hint at her core. She saves him: "You are mine! I own you." The producer has claimed her talent and rescued him from his egotism. The man who has hogged the ground has been released from his purgatory into the arms of comedy. No longer does he have to wake up with merely the strains of "I've Got You Babe," for he has been got. The distinctive miracle of *kairos* has triumphed over the repetitive moments of *chronos*. So the apostle Paul speaks again: "Let us not be weary in doing good, for in its own time we shall reap a harvest if we do not give up."

The Sisyphean task of challenging the universe also occurs in Mark Joffe's wacky Australian comedy, *The Man Who Sued God* (2001), as it attacks the absurdity of insurance companies' claim that an accident for which they have no liability is "an act of God."

A divorced Steve Myers (the great Celtic actor Billy Connolly) is a big Irish lawyer turned fisherman who explains he was a "better lawyer but a happier fisherman." However, when lightning hits and destroys his boat, his only source of livelihood, he discovers that he can't sue the insurance company. When he reads a St. Mark's Church sign that quotes the Book of Job, asking "Who will listen to your complaint against God?" he real-izes his complaint is thus with God.

Chagrined and at a loss, he decides to take God's prominent repre-sentatives to court and so files claims against the Roman Catholics, the Anglicans, the Presbyterians, and the Jews. Like the beginning of an old joke, a cardinal, a bishop, a Presbyterian, and a Jew are summoned into the bar of the court.

Myers hates the way that the insurance companies use God as a lying mechanism, so he goes to the Good Book to find precedent for his seem-ingly irreverent actions. He finds in Ecclesiastes 1:9 that there is "noth-ing new under the sun." He argues that if God exists, He would not be offended and probably shares the same sense of justice.

The comic satiric farce runs amok with fundamentalists who accuse him of blasphemy and being the Antichrist and a sardonic journalist, Anna Redmond (Judy Davis), who joins him in his quixotic quest, even as she has her own secret axes against the insurance companies to grind.

When he acknowledges that he doesn't have a chance in suing one of the world's biggest insurance companies, he decides to sue God. "So if God does exist, the churches must be liable." To which the journalist

Anna laughingly replies, "And the churches can only win the case if they prove God does not exist." This conundrum that God might not exist separates Church defendants from insurance companies. One wag suggests that "If God exists, I don't think He sits around sinking little boats."

The defendant then becomes God, as an entity with local, i.e. earthly, representatives, the churches and synagogues. If they wish to deny liability by denying the existence of God, then they are guilty of misleading or deceptive trade. When a judge decides that the case has merit, the religious leaders join together, determined not to "make a martyr of this man." Each seeks direction. The Roman Catholic priest prays before a crucifix. The Anglican prays, "In these troubling and perplexing times, may You bring help to us Your humble servants." The Presbyterian reads the *Financial Review*. These four representatives are seen as persons accountable to and responsible for their employer.

A formidable Council of Churches and Jewish Synagogues conspires to beat down this ridiculous claim. The Presbyterian declares that "an Act of God should be taken seriously." Asked what it means, the rabbi says, "it means what it says." When one cleric suggests they pause a minute for wisdom, the rabbi mutters, "Mystery, chystery, we need clout." When asked what the three other Christian clergy are doing about the case, he again quips, "They're all praying; they should be praying for better lawyers."

In the courtroom, stained-glass windows are adorned with the virtues prudence, justice, temperance, and charity. Each of these cardinal virtues lets light into the somber courtroom. Judge Bonaface sits before the dignitaries of a Roman Catholic cardinal, Anglican primate, Presbyterian moderator, and rabbi. When someone sneezes, each adds to a running gag: "Bless you." "Bless you." Bless you." "Mazel tov!"

In his Irish/Scottish accent, Myers reminds the clergy that "He who does not love his brother does not love God (John 4)." They are seen in collusion with capitalist corporations, making lots of money. Myers challenges the clerics: "Last year, your company gained profits of 6.2 billion. Did you remember to thank God for it?"

Myers, accused of being a fornicating crank, looks in the Scriptures to find some help in his time of trouble, even if they provide only a moral victory. He rejects certain proverbs: "He that digs a pit" (which suggests that he himself will fall into it) and one about how there will be carcasses where the eagles shall be gathered together. He finds material on cockatrices, but doesn't know how to incorporate it …

Myers confronts a minister, pointing out that if he "can't explain an act of God to me (and the other religious leaders), how can the shady characters in accounting tell me?"

Myers devises several clever strategies to confound the lawyers. He starts, "Isn't it one of God's commandments that we mustn't take his

Figure 11.2 Prosecuting his own case against an "act of God," Steve Myers (Billy Connolly) takes religious leaders as representatives of the Almighty to court to pay for damages by their CEO. *The Man Who Sued God*, Australian Film Finance Corporation (AFFC), 2001. Author's screenshot.

name in vain? Isn't that exactly what they [insurance companies] have been doing?"

Responding to how this constitutes a legal fiction, namely a lie, the clergy equivocate. On the stand, the cardinal allows, "It comes close to it, I would concede."

When asked if what Myers was proposing was blasphemy and how he could tolerate it, the cardinal answers candidly and quietly, "To be truthful we haven't given it a lot of thought." It is then that Myers brings out his moral artillery. "Is it because the churches' wealth combined could easily pay off the third world's debt? As massive shareholders in financial institutions, including Global Insurance? What are you doing in bed with these people?"

The ensuing confession of the cardinal on the stand turns the question around: "It is true Mr. Myers, that we are not perfect. We've been on the wrong side of things very often. We are sinners. We are blind to much injustice. We have blood on our hands. Guilty, no question."

Myers protests, "I didn't ask for your confession." The cardinal continues:

> Sure, it would take eternity to hear it. I wonder if you recognize any of the same flaws in yourself, a little intolerance perhaps, a little too much self-love. I don't know about your God, Mr. Myers, but my God is an eternal well-spring of love, hope and inspiration for millions. He moves mountains. Yes, how does your faith compare with that God? It's a poor world without faith you know.

Humbly, Myers says, "I know."

> Do you? I mean Love of God. I mean feeling God work on your
> heart. Have you felt that? Compared to that, the loss of your boat
> is nothing. A speck of dust. Not even a speck. Who knows God may
> have been trying to teach you that.

Myers inquires seriously, "It was a sign?" "I wouldn't rule it out,"
concludes the cardinal. To which Myers says, "You are excused, Your
Eminence."

Realizing that the lawyers will work to extend the court case indefin-
itely and finding everything unraveling, in addition to the compromised
firing of Anna, his beloved journalist (and an accusation that she has a
specious agenda for exploiting this ludicrous story for profit), Myers goes
and sits in a pew in church. He gazes up at the crucifix. Viewing Jesus
on the cross, he confesses that he hasn't "got a prayer," just like Jesus.
He goes to a synagogue, where the clean-up maintenance man finds his
briefcase papers on the floor and tells him, "You've dropped your case."
Suddenly, the man's offhand remark is a sign and a revelation. The word
of the Lord comes to him clearly: drop your case.

He returns to Anna and asks, "How does a moral victory sound to
you? A lot to be said [for such an ending]."

With all its whirling energy, the film ends up as a jocular sermon on
God's providence, on the signs He sends to spiritually blind and deaf
people. At an earlier point, Myers explicitly asks for a sign from God,
staring at the heavens, but turns away with his dog, just as a falling star
shines across the heavens. A sign appears on a church marquee that
points him to John 4:20. In the background one espies the Southern
Cross building.

As they return to the courtroom one last time, we view the last window,
with the theological virtue of hope. The confession of the cardinal on the
stand and his own musings have led him to consider how "All things move
toward destruction, only love hath no decay." To such a dilemma, he pon-
ders aloud, "How can I sue God for an act that led me to this woman?"
This whole adventure has been a sovereign act of love. "Pax vobiscum."

Myers has made his point indelibly; however untenable the insurance
company's stance, it is highly unlikely that the churches would challenge.
As soon as he withdraws his case, a white dove crashes through and shat-
ters the stained-glass window of the courtroom, the one underscoring
charity. It flies in and perches on the judge's bench. The primate declares,
"It's a sign!" The cardinal exclaims, "A miracle!" The Presbyterian moderator announces, "A winged messenger." The prosecuting attorney Gerry
Ryan ejaculates, "It's a f***ing cockatoo!"

Myers realized that the insurance god is a false one, but that he
had missed the point of the lightning strike on his yacht until the end.

He finally realizes that he can't sue a God that led him to Anna, the red-headed woman he loves, by sinking the boat that had led to this case. So he resigns and leaves the courtroom rejoicing. Love has indeed conquered all.

Leaving the courtroom, someone suggests that they will "soon be able to prove that God doesn't exist." He is asked whether that claim was made in a science magazine. No, comes the reply, "the *Presbyterian Monthly*." The irony of liberal denominations sawing off the branch on which they sit is carried to its absurd conclusion.

The reduction of human narratives to absurd status, of being unable to win against the world, the devil, injustice, and death, and yet being saved in weakness, stands as a witness to the Christian gospel. The fools that emerge are not those of the Book of Proverbs, but of the apostle Paul's First Letter to the Corinthians, where he proclaims that one becomes a fool for Christ's sake, believing in a promise that the foolishness of God is wiser than men and the weakness of God is stronger than men. God chooses the foolish things of the world to put to shame the wise and to bring to nothing the things that are.

Let no one deceive himself. If anyone among you seems to be wise in his age, let him become a fool that he may become wise. The absurdity of Paul's wisdom is borne out in Phil and Myers; the fools become wise.

Want to make God laugh, goes the old Jewish joke: "Tell Him your plans." The quintessential *reductio ad absurdum* film comedy plays on the notion that a human can play God. Tom Shadyac's *Bruce Almighty* (2003) explores the outlandish speculation of what would happen if God bestowed His "powers" on a mere mortal. Shadyac's film strips and rips apart the nobility of the creature aiming to be creator.

Given God's powers for a day what would one do? What if those powers found themselves in the hands of a Buffalo news reporter who possesses the same mannerisms as Ace Ventura and Lloyd Christmas of *Dumb and Dumber*? Utter chaos is precisely what ensues when God (Morgan Freeman) bestows divine powers upon Bruce Nolan, while bestowing the audience with the power of laughter. And perhaps the reason we laugh so fruitfully lies with the film's ability to highlight the divide between God and His human creatures.

The film's inciting incident finds Bruce (played by the wackily charismatic and rubber-faced Jim Carrey) at his worst. After he is fired from his job, gets beaten up by a gang, bickers with his girlfriend (Jennifer Aniston, appropriately named Grace), and has his rug soaked by his dog's urine, he cries out to the heavens. Nolan questions God's seeming proclivity for picking on him and him alone, exclaiming, "He should be the one fired."

Well, the narrator of *The Shawshank Redemption* has something to say about that. Enter Morgan Freeman as God, tranquilly offering sage advice and possessing a sort of unspoken wisdom one would imagine the

Holiest of Holies having. Additionally, he wears a dynamite ice-cream suit. Morgan Freeman–God–Holy Ghost greets Bruce in a warehouse, disguised as a whimsical janitor with an all-knowing smile. He offers the troubled Bruce a chance to assume his role for a while, giving him an opportunity to walk a mile in his sandals (which he will undoubtedly wash afterwards with fine perfumes). Maybe, Freeman's God speculates, Bruce can do a better job (yeah right). One caveat is that Bruce can't alter free will. Kevin Thomas of the *Los Angeles Times* opines, "It's a Presbyterian universe out there," mixing up the emphases on Arminian versus Calvinist theology.[11]

This, of course, is where the magic, a.k.a. miracles, happens. Bruce immediately demonstrates the fatal flaws of man, using God's powers exclusively for his own selfish gain. Uncommitted in relationship and petty in his aspirations, the immature Bruce uses his special gifts to blow up a woman's skirt, enlarge his girlfriend's breasts, vanquish thugs, and create another confusion of Babel in the tongues of his smarmy competitor Evan Baxter (Steve Carell).[12] He rarely stops to consider utilizing the powers to benefit others (other than completing satisfying Jennifer Aniston). This comedy of superiority reigns as this godlike Loki runs amok. Stephen Holden of the *New York Times* calls Carrey's Almighty "selfish, capricious, and shortsighted," pointing out, a bit too literally, that although it may be "a sweet idea to lasso the moon and bring it a little closer to your window, the meteorological implications of such tampering could be catastrophic."[13] When Carrey takes a page out of *It's a Wonderful Life* by pulling this stunt, thousands in China suffer from the monumental sea risings. (One of Bruce's first miracles is to part a bowl of tomato soup like the Red Sea.) The rift between God and man is in place for a reason. Our minds often only comprehend the immediate, demanding fleeting gratification rather than mapping out the ramifications of a certain action. It must be nice to be all-knowing.

Critic Roger Ebert summed up this sentiment with bravado:

> The problem with playing God, the movie demonstrates, is that when such powers are entrusted to a human, short-term notions tend to be valued higher than long-term improvement plans. Bruce's short-sighted methods work fine for himself, but not so well for everyone else; when you're God, you can't think only of yourself.[14]

Bruce Almighty conveys that only one is worthy, omnipotent, and graceful enough to embrace all the problems of the world we live in.

When Bruce finally does discover that he has the ability to help people, he neglects it. Upon hearing the hundreds of thousands of prayers in his head, he distills them into an email inbox appropriately named "Yahweh. com." Once he sees the immense amount of prayers, he answers "Yes" to all of them, dismissing the notion of taking time with the population's

Figure 11.3 Endowed with divine powers, Bruce Almighty (Jim Carrey) plays God with unbridled mischief until he discovers his own selfishness. *Bruce Almighty*, Spyglass Entertainment, 2003. Author's screenshot.

struggles, problems, hopes, and faith. The result, as one could imagine, is tumultuous.

Instead of directly embracing God's greatest role as a consoling Father who listens to us, he plays the role of the wealthy stepdad, giving in to whatever his children want. Often the children find that what they desire does not actually make them truly happy. Alternatively, it is the wisdom that trickles down from the Father that will guide them to the path of righteousness. This path that Bruce provides is one littered with thorns, rocks, and barren emptiness.

But the film wouldn't be funny if Bruce had led the people of Buffalo down a righteous path. The massive rift between God and man supplies the much-needed humor in a divine sense. Holden's review for the *New York Times* praised the film because it manages not to sound "dogmatic while playing cannily into a cultural climate in which the will of God is invoked with increasing frequency and fervor." Perhaps this is why the rift between God and man has become so immense. Instead of valuing Him as a figure to engage in conversation with, we have grown so distant that He is either an object of contempt when the bad happens or a source of wonderful praise when the good occurs.

The film is far from theologically airtight (one sentimental homily tends to emphasize that miracles reside within each person), but the position it places its protagonist in is priceless. Tom Shadyac finds a way to close the rift between God and man in some places, but leaves it open in others. Obviously, Bruce Nolan is far from perfection, but he maintains a willingness to change. Ultimately, by crossing the bridge at some points, other enlightenments become available, perhaps even leading to a yearning to cross the bridge completely.

While Morgan Freeman (as triune electrician, janitor, and boss, Shadyac quipped) permits Bruce Nolan to experience his side of the coin on the miracle/power/divine intervention walk of life, he does not experience the selflessness, wisdom, and, most importantly, grace (which is why his relationship with his girlfriend, GRACE, suffers tremendously towards the end of the second act) necessary to the Father's perfection. And therein lies the comedy. Bruce is not truly Almighty, mighty, yes, but he lacks the "All." While it may be fun to part your soup like Moses and make Steve Carell blabber incoherently on live television, it is not fulfilling, nor is it eternally fulfilling.

Bruce's humanity shines through at every turn within *Almighty*. Not surprisingly, he might remind one of a demi-god from Greek antiquity. Heck, in the modern age, Zeus probably would have revved up Jennifer Aniston's libido and made the Buffalo Sabres win as well. But that is not the essence of the Christian God. God helps His creation, providing guidance, wisdom, and comfort, even dying for them. And that is where Bruce plummets into the rift as if he were Thelma or Louise. He falls short of the Almighty. But from these shortcomings comedy inadvertently arises. Would it have been as funny if Bruce had kissed the Hispanic gangsters on both cheeks instead of making a monkey come out of their rears? Well, maybe not. But God's power in the hands of Bruce and his inability to see past his human, tragic flaws inspire the comedy. And when you've "got the power," a tragic flaw is about the most hilariously bad thing you can have.

Only when he is prompted to eavesdrop on the prayers of his girlfriend does pathos enter his life. Conviction of his selfishness compels him to kneel down and confess his sins, in the middle of a highway. The light streaming onto him is not divine, only an oncoming Mac truck. It is this apocalypse, this revelation, that leads him to stand humbly before the Almighty, learn to pray from the heart (not like a Miss America contestant), and receive his redemption.

Two final wild parodic films reduce the apocalypse to carnivalesque comedy in dealing with the spirit world. In *Ghostbusters* (Ivan Reitman, 1984), Dr. Peter Venkman (Bill Murray) drolly announces to the mayor that "This city is headed for a disaster of biblical proportions."

The mayor asks skeptically, "What do you mean, *biblical*?"

Venkman's colleague, Dr. Ray Stantz (Dan Aykroyd), explains: "What he means is Old Testament, Mr. Mayor, real wrath of God type stuff. ... Fire and brimstone coming down from the skies! Rivers and seas boiling!"

Other ghostbusters add: "Forty years of darkness! Earthquakes, volcanoes ..." "The dead rising from the grave!" After which Venkman sums it all up in a wildly exaggerated form of logical absurdity: "Human sacrifice, dogs and cats living together ... mass hysteria!"

"All right, all right!" concedes the mayor, "I get the point!" So, too, in comedy, the logical point is stretched to its silly extremes that we might not reduce our lives to mere rationality.

Our last *reductio ad absurdum* comedy comes from the raunchy and dilatory comic stream of Seth Rogen and James Franco, their apocalyptic *This Is the End* (2013).[15] Once upon a time, deep in the heart of the Hollywood hills, James Franco had a party. A slew of celebrities hammed it up, sang about taking their panties off, and avoided a coked-up Michael Cera at all costs. What if, amidst this bacchanal of revelry, the dispensational idea of a Rapture spontaneously occurred? It's not too farfetched according to Matthew 24:36: "of the day and hour knows no man." So why couldn't the Book of Revelation come to pass during a James Franco house party? Seth Rogen and Evan Goldberg, writers of *Superbad* and *Pineapple Express*, transform this rumination into reality, penning and directing a film that most likely closely reflects the actions the Judd Apatow bunch (Seth Rogen, James Franco, Danny McBride, Craig Robinson, Jonah Hill, and Jay Baruchel) would take in the event that they were actually "Left Behind."

As the Rapture begins, righteous believers are beamed up into heaven, while the celebrities inside Franco's house don't even realize anything has happened. When Rogen and Baruchel inform them that something is awry, do these Hollywood celebrities begin repenting of their lavish lifestyles filled with immoralities and depravity? They do not. Instead James Franco informs everyone to party on, revealing that the In 'n' Out Hamburger truck is on its way (though that is about as close to heaven on earth as one can get). However, upon venturing outside, the majority of the partygoers are devoured by Satan's sinkholes, as only the film's main characters remain.

Thus, the actors' quest for redemption begins (whether they know it or not). However, that path to redemption is chock-full of Rogen's signature phallic gags and jabs at their fellow actors' careers. But surprisingly, *This Is the End* introduces a novel type of humor within this revelatory world, almost biblical. A certain sequence spoofs films such as *The Exorcist* and *Rosemary's Baby*, as Lucifer decides to possess Jonah Hill who has prayed a phony – and decidedly mean-spirited – prayer.

Quite rapidly, however, we see how Rogen and Goldberg can work phallic humor into a topic as morbid as possession, as the sequence that follows is hysterical. Once the demon dwells inside of Jonah Hill (ask not how he got there in the first place), it is portrayed as a gossipy middle school girl, provoking the would-be exorcists with shallow taunts. When Baruchel tosses water onto Hill exclaiming, "The Power of Christ compels you!" the demon responds, with classic Jonah Hill sarcasm, "Does it, Jay? Does it compel me?" Rogen and Goldberg place a modern spin on such tropes, rendering hilarious the subjects that often terrify us.

Figure 11.4 After one act of self-sacrifice, James Franco reveals his true smug arrogance and is duly rejected by the blue Rapture light. *This Is the End*, Columbia Pictures, 2013. Author's screenshot.

The path towards their redemption is peppered with such gags. Besides performing an exorcism on Hill, Rogen and Goldberg chronicle just how this group of man-children would operate in the event of the biblical end of days. The answer, we find, is not well. They run out of water, are attacked by a murderous Hermione Granger, and pursued by Satan's arsenal of ravaging beasts. All the while their friendships come apart at the seams, as each one is often too selfish to care about anyone but himself.

Ultimately, letting go of their selfishness holds the key to redemption in God's eyes. Craig Robinson discovers this notion first, as he sacrifices himself for his self-proclaimed best friends in the world. His last words on earth are a battle cry of "take your panties off" as he charges at a fiery hell-beast in their path. However, instead of being devoured, a majestic stream of blue luminescence surrounds him and he is whisked off into heaven. Robinson wears an ear-to-ear grin across his face, finding himself unable to resist the supreme happiness of salvation.

Upon witnessing such a miracle, the remaining guys try and take Craig's example, deducing that being good must get you saved. They immediately compliment each other superficially, flattering each other with praise for how smart or funny the other is, a stark contrast to the preceding scenes. However, once they realize these remarks aren't cutting it, they understand they must take the path Craig did, perhaps the hardest path of all in their eyes: placing others before themselves.

For a moment, it seems as though James Franco will be saved, as a blue beam embraces him when he saves his pals from Danny McBride's post-apocalyptic Donner Party. However, Franco takes too much pride in his act of salvation, flipping off McBride with the brazen bravado of a double bird, and uttering some not so nice things along the way. We assume Mr. Franco was not familiar with what often comes after pride. Franco plummets to earth due to his exhibition of smug arrogance, devoured by the group of Kenny Powers-driven cannibals. Franco neglects the grace that was given to him, remaining ensnared in the petty arguments of earth.

Ultimately, Baruchel performs one last good and noble – sacrificial – deed and finds himself drawn up into heaven. However, as he grasps the hand of Rogen to lift him along, Rogan is denied entry. This is when Rogen shows the first bit of recognition of the weight of sin as he lets go of his friend's hand and falls back into the gaping maw of the demon. It is this sacrifice – a recognition that each person is responsible for his own sin and must come to an understanding of such in order to (in this narrative world, at least) be cleansed. This allows Rogen to join Baruchel as they both zip up into heaven, laughing in each other's arms. Such is the divine happiness of salvation, as the *eschaton* promises the grand laughter of paradise. It is a culmination of laughter, the sort of laughter found at a wedding feast: constant, jubilant, and joyous. When Rogen and Baruchel arrive at the pearly gates, Robinson is there to greet them, the same smile plastered across his visage. The three skip into paradise where the redeemed ride Segways and listen to the Backstreet Boys (did I say paradise or sixth circle of Dante's inferno?). Their laughter is real and constant, much like audiences' throughout this film.

What's interesting about *This Is the End* is that Rogen and Goldberg have endowed such seemingly despicable characters with the opportunity to find redemption. It's almost as if they're mirroring the concept of grace from some higher outside source. The late Roger Ebert took note of this, finding that "even at the lowest moments of terror and hilarity, there's an undercurrent of hope and redemption for those who seek it."[16]

Who would've thought that the man who once bickered with Paul Rudd about how they knew the other was gay would be penning a film chronicling a scenario in which the Book of Revelation came to fruition in modern day Los Angeles? In fact, Betsy Sharkey of the *LA Times* observes, "the destruction so closely mirrors predictions in the Book of Revelation, if not for the scandalous behavior the film would probably appeal to a very unlikely subset of the population."[17] It is a prophecy of things to come, though not accurate in the slightest, highlighting once again that the Bible is easily interpreted in various ways. And while we may not have asked for it, we received it (much like Jonah Hill's character does from a well-endowed demon), and can only hope when that Day of Judgment arrives, we're not the ones stuck in James Franco's house.

The absurdity of these films is rooted in a reality hyper-extended. In the wacky world of comedy, one can imagine such hyperbole. The fantasies of ordinary mortals can play in the cosmos of God, and remembering whence they came, laugh at the grand incongruity of such vanity.

Notes

1 Craig Detweiler, "Divine Comedy at the Cineplex," *Christianity Today* (February 27, 2006).
2 See Ronald D. LeBlanc, "Love and Death and Food: Woody Allen's Comic Use of Gastronomy," *Literature/Film Quarterly* 17:1 (1989), 18–26.
3 Cheryl Brumbaugh-Cayford, "God's Presence in the Absurd: Thoughts on Christian Social Action," *Brethren Life and Thought* 42 (1997), 74–77.
4 J. R. C. Cousland, "Tobit: A Comedy in Error?" *Catholic Biblical Quarterly* 65:4, 535–553.
5 Janet Maslin, "*Groundhog Day*: Murray Battles Pittsburgh Time Warp," *New York Times* (February 12, 1993).
6 Michael P. Foley, "Phil's Shadow: Lessons of *Groundhog Day*," *Touchstone* (April 2004), online at www.touchstonemag.com/archives/article.php?id=17-03-012-v (accessed October 10, 2015). We have drawn upon Foley's insights with unbridled delight and appreciation.
7 Kenneth Turan, "Bill Murray's *Groundhog Day*: It's Déjà Vu All Over Again," *Los Angeles Times* (February 12, 1993).
8 Robert Jewett, "Stuck in Time: *Kairos, Chronos*, and the Flesh in *Groundhog Day*," in *Explorations in Theology and Film: Movies and Meaning* (ed. Clive Marsh and Gaye Ortiz) (Blackwell, 1997), 155–166.
9 See Horace, *Satires* I, 6, 5; II, 8, 64; *Epistles* I, 19, 45, "naso suspendis adunco."
10 Audrey Farolino, quoted in Robert Jewett, "The Deadly Deception of the Flesh in *Groundhog Day*," in *Saint Paul Returns to the Movies: Triumph over Shame* (Eerdmans, 1999), 101.
11 Kevin Thomas, "Not Quite Divine," *Los Angeles Times* (May 23, 2003).
12 Also, in a scene included in the DVD's "deleted scenes," Bruce is seen setting the back of Evan's head on fire – making him appear to be a Hindu deity as viewed from the front. This explains the smoldering that is seen coming from Evan's shoulders in the scene that was included. This scene if included would have made Bruce seem more vindictive and dangerous as a god, rather than just befuddled and misguided.
13 Stephen Holden, "Film Review, *Bruce Almighty* (2003): God's Power as an Ego Trip for an Id," *New York Times* (May 23, 2003), online at www.nytimes.com/movie/review?res=9D02EFD81F3EF930A15756C0A9659C8B63 (accessed October 10, 2015).
14 Roger Ebert, "Review: *Bruce Almighty*," May 5, 2003, online at www.rogerebert.com/reviews/bruce-almighty-2003 (accessed October 10, 2015).
15 In *The Name of the Rose*, Brother Jorge warns that comedy would enable men to laugh at everything. "Can we laugh at God? The world will relapse into chaos." This film is about that end of the world for these slackers. R. Lamm, "Can We Laugh at God? Apocalyptic Comedy in Film," *Journal of Popular Film and Television* 19:2 (1991), 81–90.
16 Roger Ebert, "Review: *This is the End*," June 12, 2013, online at www.rogerebert.com/reviews/this-is-the-end-2013 (accessed October 10, 2015).
17 Betsy Sharkey, "Review: *This is the End*: A Towering Inferno of Fun," *Los Angles Times* (June 11, 2013), online at www.latimes.com/entertainment/movies/moviesnow/la-et-mn-this-is-the-end-review-20130612-story.html (accessed October 10, 2015).

12   Multi-Leveled Comedy

The multi-leveled plot, also known as ensemble comedy, mixes several groups of characters, interacting and brought together over one unifying event. It compares and contrasts various responses of social groups to the same stimulus or setting. The sub-genre has a bit of upstairs/downstairs comedy to it as in Shakespeare's *Midsummer Night's Dream* or the mix of numerous elements in *The Gods Must Be Crazy* (Jamie Uys, 1980), where an African bushman, bumbling game warden, lovely school teacher, African revolutionaries, children, and animals play their parts. So, too, Woody Allen's ensemble piece *Hannah and Her Sisters* (1986) follows the prodigal paths of different characters throughout a year between Thanksgiving meals.

The biblical paradigm for the multi-leveled plot fits the story of Jacob, Esau, and Laban, or even the Bible itself. However, one of the more curious episodes in the Gospels also conveys diverse comic responses to a miracle, namely the story of the man born blind in John 9.

The episode starts with a typical Jewish question from Jesus' disciples: "Rabbi, who sinned, this man or his parents that he should be born blind?" The opening gambit parallels the nature of comedy with an obstacle or tragedy in the beginning. Human suffering exists. Bad things happen to people, and so for the curious disciples, there must be some badness in this man's genes or his own behavior.

Jesus throws a curve, reversing their expectations with a jolt. Neither sinned, He responds. This is all a set-up for a grand comedy, to display the works of God in the light of day. Watch this, He tells them, and then as if it were a crude vaudeville stage, Jesus spits onto the ground and makes mud. "Here's mud in your eye," He says to the blind man. "Now get out of here and go wash it out in the pool named Sent." This happened on a Sabbath day when the music halls were supposed to be closed.

The simple act then becomes a communal comedy, of numerous players coming on stage to complicate the matter of one miracle. When the neighbors see him, they are confused, arguing whether this was the man they used to see sitting and begging. Some think it is he, while others say, no way. He *keeps* saying, like a running joke, "I am the one!"

But his former handicapped state is now juxtaposed with sight. How did this happen, they ask? He tells them simply that Jesus made clay, anointed his eyes, and said to go and wash and he went and washed and *presto!* Where is this guy, they ask. Don't know, he shrugs.

The plot thickens and complicates with the arrival of the Pharisees, who pronounce that Jesus cannot be from God as He does not keep the Sabbath. But the incongruity is too much for others who said, "How can a man who is a sinner perform such *signs?*"

The man formerly blind is called on stage and declares Jesus must be a prophet. The Jews then doubt whether he was ever blind, so they call up the parents. Asked about their son's condition and the healing, they respond like Woody Allen's parents, "We know he is our son, and that he was blind; but how he now sees, we do not know; or who opened his eyes, we do not know. Ask him. He is of age; he can speak for himself!"

When they return to interrogate the man, they pounce on him and demand that he give glory to God as this man is a sinner. His retort carries the logic of common sense to the bureaucratic pressures of the religious leaders: "Whether He is a sinner, I do not know; one thing I do know, that whereas I was blind, now I see."

As they persist in questioning and pestering him, he answers that he has told them repeatedly all that happened. "Why do you want to hear it again? You do not want to become His disciples too, do you?" He exposes their ignorance and prejudice with delightful clarity. Having no other recourse, they dwindle into *ad hominem* arguments and say, "How can you teach us as you were born entirely in sins" putting him out of the synagogue.

The story comes full circle after the merry-go-round of characters, with Jesus returning and restoring balance. To the man born blind, He reveals the Son of Man. To the Pharisees, He tweaks their obtuseness with a final quip. He explains that He came into this world that those who do not see may see; and that those who see may become blind. The Pharisees retort, "We are not blind, too, are we?" And Jesus says to them: "If you were blind, then you would have no sin; but since you say, 'We see,' your sin remains."

There are, in biblical scholar Mark Biddle's terms, moments of "gotcha!" in Jesus' public debates with those who opposed His ministry.[1] The triumph of His wit occurs as well with a mélange of characters, with overlapping, jockeying, conflicting, opposing, and balancing people of all sorts, a zoo of human animals that writer Frederick Buechner labels *Peculiar Treasures.*

Two French films supply peculiar treasures and religious dimensions to the multi-level plots: Marcel Pagnol's adaptation of the Jean Giono novel *La femme du boulanger* (*The Baker's Wife*, 1938) and *L'auberge rouge*, produced twice (*The Red Inn*, Claude Autant Lara, 1951; Gérard Krawczyk, 2007).

Figure 12.1 The community cannot partake of the baker's bread until his prodigal wife is returned, a sweet parable of God and his wayward chosen Bride. *La femme du boulanger (The Baker's Wife)*, Les Films Marcel Pagnol, 1938. Author's screenshot.

In *The Baker's Wife*, the eponymous comely young Aurélie (Ginette LeClerc) has run off with one of her husband's customers, the marquis' shepherd (Charles Moulin), leaving her forlorn husband (Raimu), the baker of living bread, behind. Like Gomer with Hosea, the bride wanders into adultery and idolatry. She is young, foolish, and faithless and a scandal ensues from her selfish behaviors. She has run off with him on the marquis' horse.

The baker goes to church for comfort, but the austere young priest obliviously preaches an ironic sermon about every wife's need for a Good Shepherd. So, he goes to the tavern, gets uproariously drunk and weeps into his wine, lamenting that "I invited this fellow into my house for a cookie," he says, "and he took all I had."

But while the cuckolded baker still loves her, he neglects his calling and will not bake any more bread until she returns. The community, at first dismissing the transgression as merely a private affair, begins to realize the social implications of sin, namely that the supply of the baker's sumptuous bread has stopped. At first mocking him, the Provençal villagers become hungry for his bread and are thus forced to work together, to be a community and restore the wayward younger wife to her husband. The teaming of the Communist and the Roman Catholic cleric, enemies at first, shows the grace lurking behind the need to work together for common bread and the Bread of Life.

It takes a village to make such a multi-level comedy, and director Pagnol offers sweet and revelatory vignettes to provide a pungent metaphor of the people of God, amidst the "the scandalous – and terribly inconvenient – defection of the baker's wife." As film critic Frank Nugent observed, "After all, even a righteous curate must have bread, and even a profligate marquis and a heretical school teacher: in the face of a common emergency they must set aside their normal enmity and combine against the foe," all theists who seek the Bread of Life.[2]

What strikes the viewer of this poignant comedy is the pathos of the great clown Raimu as the baker. Nugent described him as having

> something Chaplinesque about his inability to recognize the harshness of the world. His deception is comic, but it is tragic too; just as there is tragedy in his refusal to resent the mocking villagers who drunkenly bring him antlers. He tries to commit suicide, but that act was not of their doing: it was a bewildered recognition of the bitterness in his own soul, a gesture of despair wrung from his heart rather than by their deeds. It is this undercurrent of tragedy, this steadfast air of dignity that is at once the secret of his funniest scenes, the quality that prevents his film from toppling into farce.[3]

What Nugent has implicitly described is that same story of Hosea and Gomer, of God and Israel, of God and His motley Church. God is ready to die for His wayward bride. And at the truly hilarious end, the wife is brought back and forgiven (and the marquis even gets his horse back) and the baker rejoices. He begins his baking again, and even makes five extra loaves for the poor. A eucharistic comedy celebrates the *koinonia* of a broken village who depend upon a baker.

In the second French comedy, *L'auberge rouge*, multi-level shenanigans take place around a roly-poly priest. The macabre multi-level comedy is more akin to the ruse and treachery of Jacob's sons over Shechem's betrothal to Dinah in Anita Diamant's novel *The Red Tent* or of David having to get 100 Philistine foreskins for his marriage to King Saul's daughter. Themes of killing, cannibalism, and pig-feedings may obscure the delightful heart of the film: that both justice and grace abide.

Gérard Krawczyk's 2007 version follows the 1951 version starring the comic genius Fernandel. In the mountainous setting of the Pyrenees in the 19th century, two innkeepers, Pierre and Rose Martin (Christian Clavier and Josiane Balasko), vainly tried to make ends meet until they discovered the nefarious but profitable practice of murdering their guests. Their adopted deaf son Violet (Fred Epaud) conveniently disposes of the bodies with his hungry pigs.

When a traveling coach carrying *commedia dell'arte* stock characters, a wandering cleric Père Carnus (Gérard Jugnot) and his young seminary charge, and a man with a bear converge upon the bloody inn, another

Figure 12.2 In her effort to keep the priest (Gérard Jugnot) alive, murderous inn-keeper Rose Martin (Josiane Balasko) confesses her ongoing crimes to him in the sanctity of the confessional. *L'auberge rouge* (*The Red Inn*), Les Films Christian Fechner, 2007. Author's screenshot.

series of special sacrifices is in the offing. However, the wife, Rose, cannot and will not kill the priest. She questions him about the sacred nature of the sacrament of confession and discovers that in a private confessional, no information can be shared or exposed by the priest, no matter how heinous a crime is confessed. So, speaking through an iron grid, she tells all to the shocked cleric. Meanwhile their comely daughter and the theological neophyte fall in love.

In the rustic *Kammerspiel* setting, the other sinners go blithely on their way, unaware that death stalks their every choice. Even going to sleep, committing adultery, or trying to escape eventuate in being fed to the pigs and used to stuff a scarecrow. Based on a true story of two 19th-century hostel murderers who eventually went to the guillotine, in this vaudeville farce, the priest tries to save the lives of his fellow travelers without violating the confessional. Each minor story layers upon the others, with stock jokes and ingenious set-ups cleverly designed for the providential denouement.

The multi-leveled plot highlights the truths that everyone is important and everyone is comic. The eye of God is upon the ducks and turkeys of the world as much as the sparrows. The actions of each character touch upon the lives of others. No man, as John Donne wrote, is an island. It is as if characters in the Chaucerian pilgrim stories suddenly met altogether in the cathedral at Canterbury, all under the judgment of their vices and all under the grace of God. The ripple effects of each man's comedy and each woman's humor, of their peccadilloes and trespasses, of their acts of charity and kindness, shape the destiny of their fellow citizens and travelers. As Augustine pointed out, the resurrection was God's joke played upon Satan, and its consequences continue to this day.

Notes

1 Mark E. Biddle, *A Time to Laugh: Humor in the Bible* (Smyth and Helwys, 2013), 102.
2 Frank S. Nugent, "The Screen: The French Are Telling the Scandalously Funny Story of 'The Baker's Wife' at the World Theatre," *New York Times* (February 27, 1940).
3 Ibid.

13   Parody

Parody thrives on making fun of other forms and genres, of imitating them by lampooning their generic qualities. Its etymology reaches back to the prefix *para* (alongside, opposite) and the noun *ode* (song, lyric poem) suggesting an imitation of a familiar and established artistic form. Religious parodies proliferated among the mystery and morality plays of the medieval era, retelling the story of Noah and his nagging wife in a distinct comic frame.[1]

Director Mel Brooks remains the cinematic master of parodying film Westerns, horror films, and Hitchcock (e.g. *Blazing Saddles*, *Young Frankenstein*, *High Anxiety*) by lampooning the conventions and codes of horror films, Westerns and biblical epics in recognizable ways. Impishly, he distorts the old forms for laughs and punctures our expectations with, well, the unexpected.

The parody is frequently an original narrative based on a familiar work or text. It usually incorporates a multiplicity of targets (such as Mel Brooks' subtexts on Germans and prayers in his films) and includes gags, stunts, and what is known as anomalous surprise, namely an unpredicted violation of audience expectation (e.g. Brooks' use of the Glenn Miller hit song "Pardon Me Boy" or Igor's hump that changes sides on his back).

No other biblical text approaches this sub-genre as much as the story of Jonah. The form and expectation for a biblical text on a minor prophet is set up with the narrative's inclusion in the Holy Scriptures. However, the content and treatment delightfully violated all expectations of prophetic behavior and divine judgment. The original work seems to parody the typical story of one of God's chosen seers in every way possible.

Scholar John Miles, Jr. argued that Jonah was a biblical parody in several distinct ways.[2] First, one takes a familiar literary text or familiar style and exploits it for humor. In the Book of Jonah, Miles sees the proximate target not simply as Jewish life, but as the style of Jewish letters in biblical prophecies. What we laugh at is a style so standardized in biblical literature that it is easily recognizable with its clear stereotypes of the summoning Deity, the unworthy prophet, and the wicked sinners deserving judgment. It is replete with stock scenes of a calling, a judgment, and the loud decisive action of God.

Not only does Jonah rush the opposite way (to Tarshish rather than Nineveh), but as a prophet he is both stubbornly disobedient and petulant. A prophet is usually called by God and sent out. Jonah runs the other way. He gets on board a ship, finds a comfortable stall, and falls asleep snoring, even while God sends a horrific storm that terrorizes the crew. When he confesses that he is responsible for the upheaval on the seas, the sailors are so frightened that they will not toss him overboard, but he encourages them for their own safety to hurl him into the sea. A great fish swallows him and after three days hurls, or spews or vomits, him back onto land. Other prophets righteously suffer the vicissitudes of their vocation, but Jonah invites his troubles.

Jonah begins with the formulaic calling of the prophet and what usually happens with the humble reluctance of prophet to accept the call. Biblical stalwarts from Moses to Gideon to Isaiah all demur when God calls them. Jonah exaggerates their trepidation with his own chutzpah. He just refuses to go and decides to "run away," as in a Monty Python sketch. The book spoofs the iconic character of the Hebrew prophet.

Second, when the Lord produces a sign of His omnipotence (a storm at sea), the prophet does not take off his sandals or fall prostrate; he falls asleep. Miles identifies this as Chaplinesque sangfroid: "Okay, I'm the one you want," he tells the sailors, "just throw me in the sea."

Third, the story parodies the psalm of deliverance and thanksgiving from the belly of the fish, a parody of Psalm 130 where one cries to God from the depths. Jonah descends into the pit with water, where a "veritable flood of water imagery" inundates the prophet, all for comic effect. He even has seaweed wrapped about his head. The big fish is told to vomit him out, a vulgar response like Baal gods relieving themselves or King Eglon supposedly going to the toilet after Ehud has stabbed him.

When he finally gets to Nineveh, Jonah reluctantly preaches his pitiful, succinct sermon, doing the bare minimum to get by in obeying God. His sermon in Hebrew to the Ninevites consists of only five ambiguous words: "In forty days, Nineveh turns!" But there are several anomalous surprises for him, and for the reader. He expects, maybe even hopes, that the Assyrian pagans will reject his message and he will go home, or maybe take another cruise to Tarshish. But, unexpectedly, the king turns; he repents and calls the whole kit-and-caboodle to lament and cry out to the Hebrew God. They fast and put on sackcloth and ashes.

Then comes another anomaly. Jonah had decreed that not only the people, but all the livestock had to do the same. Sheep and goats and cows had to forgo grazing and drinking, had to pray mightily to the Lord, and to change their behavior. To think of a heifer in sackcloth and ashes is to imagine a Gary Larson *Far Side* cartoon, a comic incongruity which no other prophet could evoke.

Fourth, the rejection of the prophet by a king does not occur; rather after a jejune and banal sermon (only five words), the king, all the people of Nineveh, and all the resident cows respond with repentance. They are all convulsed with sackcloth and ashes, leading to a burlesque of prophetic success. Where else does a prophet have such enormous success?

Then Jonah sits and stews under a gourd tree in the hot, sweltering sun of the desert winds. He is the only one who remains unrepentant after his merciful God has showered His grace upon everyone and everything. Jonah even complains that God shows mercy and loving-kindness and that He has a "long nose," which in Hebrew means He is patient and doesn't flare up with anger. Jonah would prefer a short-fused, short-nosed God. He didn't want the Assyrians forgiven.

Finally, after the worm eats the bush that shades Jonah from the heat, God points out Jonah's hypocrisy and how the erstwhile prophet cares more about the plant and his own comfort than the potential destruction of many men, women, and children. And then, God reminds him in one last anomalous gag, "and besides that, many cows" (4:11). One suspects that all the other prophets laugh at this sorry parody imitation of a man of God.

Finally, the book concludes with the whinnying complaint of the prophet to God (4:2): "Didn't I tell you this would happen?" His own frustrated sense of *Schadenfreude* (why didn't bad things happen to bad people?) places Jonah in the sardonic character of Sholem Aleichem's Tevye. But it is God who treats Jonah as a kid; He kids him and shows grace to all.

Scholar Wes Gehring outlined seven characteristics of parody. First, parody requires the basic imitation of a familiar genre or auteur. The audience must recognize the object of spoofing. Second, it must be funny. This is the fundamental commandment. Third, in its imitation of a recognizable form, it may shed light on it and offer some educational insights, but its core reason for existing is to evoke laughter.

Fourth, it should not be confused with satire, which has a totally different motive of reform. While the two may overlap, the parody plays while satire works. A parody may have satirical elements, such as when Brooks' *A History of the World Part I* (1981) mocks the anti-Semitism of the Middle Ages with a Busby Berkeley musical number. But social commentary and critiques are generally the *modus operandi* of satire, not parody. Parodies are broader and more fun, puncturing the work of a genre or author. However, Gehring sees a more subtle and nuanced imitation that can bring the original form more into focus in what he labels a "reaffirmation parody."

Fifth, parody merrily mixes time and space; as "indeterminate genre," it is not limited to a geography or time period. A parody of a biblical story could be written in a different context or genre altogether. Sixth, film parody involves a compounding phenomenon as it is often peppered with eclectic references to other structures or texts. In the Book of Jonah, the stupidity of other religions is parodied as sailors pray each to their own private gods to no avail. Compound parody plays homage to other bits, texts, and sources.

Seventh, the parody self-consciously draws attention to the fact that it is self-reflective. It shows itself to be a parody. It is a joke and it doesn't disguise the fact; yet it doesn't flaunt it. Jonah moans over his fate and wants to die because a worm ate his shade plant. The gourd was destroyed not by a lion or an earthquake, but a worm.

Mel Brooks explains that in parody, one should "never try to be funny. The actors must be serious. Only the situation must be absurd. Funny is in the writing, not in the performances. And another thing, the more serious the situation, the funnier the comedy can be."[3] Jonah did not try to be funny in this dire situation of the death of all Nineveh, but he was.

Both Brooks and Woody Allen capture the absurdity of the Jewish predicament. In *Annie Hall* (1997), Allen parodies the American family dinner when he imagines himself sitting at table with Diane Keaton's Midwestern Protestant family. The suspicious grandmother spies this invading Jew at the Thanksgiving table as an Orthodox Rabbi. Like old Hebrew prophets who kvetch with God, both directors spoof God and His ways. "If God had wanted us to fly," quips Brooks, "He'd have given us tickets." Or look at Jewish history, Brooks advises: "Unrelieved lamenting would be intolerable. So for every ten Jews beating their breasts, God designated one to be crazy and amuse the breast-beaters. By the time I was five, I knew I was that one." At Chautauqua Rabbi Robert Klein told of the Yeshiva University rowing team that was always beaten by Harvard. They sent a spy over who came back and reported: "We've been doing it all wrong. Only one shouts and the others row."

Brooks also took on the Christian God in parodying the Last Supper. Playing a stand-up philosopher serving as a waiter called Comicus, he stumbles into the upper room where Jesus and His disciples have gathered. As the Lord confides that one of them will betray Him that night, the disciples ask "Who?" At that moment, Comicus shouts "Judas," which startles the betrayer, but Comicus continues, "Do you want a beverage?" Brooks inserts the typical blasphemy of saying the name "Jesus" in the Lord's presence, but when da Vinci tries to paint a portrait of the group, he persuades them to all sit on one side of the table. Comicus lingers behind Jesus with a silver plate shining like an aureola, the radiant luminous cloud in many medieval paintings. Brooks had earlier, in his classic *2000 Year Old Man* with Carl Reiner (1975), caricatured the Man from Nazareth as thin, nervous, wore sandals, came into the store a lot, but never bought anything. So, too, Episcopalian Robin Williams extended Brooks' caricature by arguing that Jesus was Jewish: "Some people say Jesus wasn't Jewish. Yes, of course he was Jewish: 30 years old, single,

Figure 13.1 As the Jewish waiter at the Last Supper, Mel Brooks parodies the sacred art of Leonardo da Vinci. *A History of the World Part 1*, Brooksfilms, 1981. Author's screenshot.

lives with his parents, come on! He takes his father's business; his mom thought he was God's gift. He's Jewish; give it up!"

In *Zelig* (1983), Woody Allen parodies the comic metamorphosis of an American Jew, who assimilates too easily into American culture.[4] His parodies of prayers and piety infuse many of his writings and stand-up routines. "If it turns out that there is a God, I don't think he's evil. But the worst that you can say about him is that basically he's an underachiever." Allen's evidence against God is the creature man himself. Allen is able to take the believers' notion of hope and turn it into selfishness. "If only God would give me some clear sign! Like making a large deposit in my name in a Swiss bank." But he reminds his critics, "To you, I'm an atheist. To God, I'm the loyal opposition."[5]

In *Hannah and Her Sisters*, Max von Sydow's curmudgeon of a character, reflecting on television evangelists, gripes "If Jesus came back and saw what was being done in his name, he'd never stop throwing up." Ironically, Sydow played the character of Jesus in one of the most boring epics, George Stevens' *The Greatest Story Ever Told*, described by the *Time* critic as the longest story ever told. (And for film audiences, when Jesus says He's coming back, it's not a promise: it's a threat.)

Both directors enact parodies of religious behavior, mostly the forms of prayers. From *Blazing Saddles* to *The Producers*, Brooks inserts petitions to God. In *The Producers* (1967), his greedy corporate businessmen stand to pray to the Almighty: the American Dollar. In explaining his ability to spoof the mores and beliefs of humanity, Brooks confessed "Shakespeare said hold the mirror up to life; I held it a little behind and below."[6]

In his parody of the Western, *Blazing Saddles* (1974), Brooks situates the town meeting in a church, but one without hymns. They do sing "The Ballad of Rock Ridge" that affirms total depravity in its last line: "our town is turning into shit." Prayers are parodied as well, with the ersatz preacher in black asking God if their prayers really work or "are we just jacking off?" When the nasty Hedley Lamarr (Harvey Korman) wants his assistant Taggart to round up every vicious criminal varmint in the West, he lists them in ascending despicability:

> I want rustlers, cut-throats, murderers, bounty hunters, desperados, mugs, pugs, thugs, nitwits, dimwits, vipers, snipers, con-men, Indian agents, Mexican bandits, muggers, buggerers, bushwhackers, horns-wogglers, horse-thieves, bull dykes, train robbers, bank robbers, ass-kickers, shit-kickers, *and Methodists*.

Perhaps what is most different from satiric comedy is parody's requirement of affection, of a lighter and more playful tone toward the text. It helps to be a fan of the target parodied.

Jesus almost seems to use a comic formula, "the Law says to you, but I say ..." He does not abolish the Law, but He employs its form to show more profound truths. Man was not made for the law, but the law for the good of man. When He said that Sabbath was made for man and not man for the Sabbath, one looks to see a sly smile: rest was made for human beings, not that we should work hard at resting. The joke is there for those who have ears to hear.

One of the most provocative parodies, with generous dollops of satire and taboo comedy, was *Monty Python's Life of Brian* (Terry Jones, 1979), in which the British blokes sought to spoof the biblical epic. After Terry Gilliam's large animated graphics (and titles designating "Judea AD 33, Saturday afternoon. About tea time") mock the giant Hollywood Bible films, the story follows the holy star in the sky guiding three wise men. Immediately the echo of previous narratives of the nativity protrudes. As they enter a mangy manger, we realize with them that this is *not* the Holy Family; the film chronicles the misadventures of an ordinary bloke named Brian Cohen, who is mistaken for the Savior. Brian is not Jesus, but the parallels of his life spoof many biblical episodes and the ways that religious followers twist the truths of their leader.

The Python group confessed that their own upbringing had little more than hymn singing and beatings in the Anglican tradition. As some of their own vicars didn't take the Gospels that seriously, they became functional atheists. Commenting on the film, John Cleese and Michael Palin acknowledged the pitfalls and dangers of doing a story around biblical times. Wrestling with ancient texts, they tried to insert comedy into them. Their most basic premise, and one that infused the project with their humor, was that human nature has not changed much since those days. People still exhibit the same arguments, the same foibles, and the same human imperfections. Cleese thought, "What would I have been thinking then in this dirty, smelly, seamy way of living?" The troupe sought to demystify the great moment with making the world common and vulgar, not with straight white teeth and pressed bath robes. False and confusing prophets are covered in mud, ranting away spreading discontent, with one so completely boring and uncharismatic, that no one listens to him.

Second, the film shoots its quills at the gullibility of followers, of people who do not think for themselves, and who follow a crowd mentality. The Jewish historical situation was infected with messianic fever, seeking out someone who would deliver them from oppression and institute the Olam HaBa (the world to come), including followers of Judas of Galilee and Theudas in the first century. Monty Python found such credulous true believers funny. Brian shouts out, "Look, you've got it all wrong! You don't NEED to follow ME. You don't NEED to follow ANYBODY! You've got to think for yourselves! You're ALL individuals!"

"Yes!" shouts the crowd, "We're all individuals!"

"You're all different!" asserts Brian.

"Yes," the crowd obsequiously echoes, "we ARE all different!"

To which one man in the crowd stammers, "I'm not ..."

What bothered Terry Gilliam was that too many people held to a God who couldn't take a joke. Reading the Gospels he found Christ saying very profound and wonderful things; so that wasn't where the silliness was found. However, His followers were the joke. Their interpretation of His good news of peace, love, and charity was misused so that over the next 2,000 years, all kinds of killing and torturing were done in His name.

This tendency of men to misinterpret the Scriptures is showcased in a scene dealing with the Sermon on the Mount, where the real Jesus stands at a great distance from a group of listeners. Blessed are the peacemakers is misinterpreted as "Blessed are the cheesemakers," to which one woman asks "What's so special about the cheesemakers?" She receives an "enlightened" explanation, "Well, obviously, it's not meant to be taken literally; it refers to any manufacturers of dairy products."

When Mr. Big Nose thinks that Jesus has just said, "Blessed are the Greeks," he is about to protest, when he discovers, "Oh, it is blessed are the MEEK! Oh, I'm glad they're getting something; they have a hell of a time."

When Brian comes upon a group of lepers begging, one calls out "Alms for an ex-leper." The satire on the healing of the leper is directed not at the Messiah's ministry, but at the laziness of human nature that leads people to declare themselves victims and to depend upon a dole. He complains, that while being healed by a do-gooder, he has lost his livelihood and would appreciate it if the Lord would make him a "bit lame in one leg in the middle of the week." Someone who should be grateful is shown to be a complainer. He asks if Brian would give him half a dinar for his life story, a shot across the bow for those who transform their testimonies into money-making enterprises.

The comic momentum of the parody rolls out like the Red Sea with a multiplicity of targets: Jewish salesmen sell stones and beards (for women, not allowed to attend such executions, must disguise themselves as men)

*Figure 13.*2 Monty Python's satire of religious fanaticism includes the schismatic rise of denominations' emphases upon such seemingly minor details as sandals: are they to be raised on high or cast down? *The Life of Brian*, HandMade Films, 1979. Author's screenshot.

for a ritual stoning, custodians pick up body parts at the Coliseum after the children's matinee, and the Monty Python jab at the political far left of the 1970s (and indirectly religious sectarian and denominational politics), where groups so similar spend their time bickering over details. The revolutionary Judean People's Front can't agree with the People's Front of Judea, spending more time on labels and rhetoric than acting and fighting with each other about who is more doctrinally pure.

While offensive to many (and for good reason), the film also works as a reaffirmation parody, subverting prejudices in order to bring one back to original doctrines. One scene, for example, shows the proliferation of denominations as a group of religious/political Jews debate. When lunatics think that Brian is their savior (when he tries to deny it they argue that of course a real Messiah would deny it), they start arguing and split up into different sects. When Brian leaves a shoe behind, the group divides into the Shoeites and Sandalites, sounding a lot like an Islamic schism. Pieces of a dropped and broken gourd are gathered by the faithful, with one deleted line noting that a man found a "piece of gourd that passes all understanding." Kenneth Turan noted the sheer audacity of the film's biblical buffoonery.[7]

References to biblical passages sneak in. When the conflated story of a master giving talents to his two sons begins, a cynic challenges, "What were their names? You don't know. He's making it up." One blind man stands before a ditch and declares "I can see." He throws away his cane and immediately falls into the hole, putting an image to Jesus' words about the blind following the blind. The film, the troupe argue repeatedly, is not about faith but about following authority blindly. Their clear message is "Think for yourself."

The most controversial aspect of the parody is the crucifixion scene.[8] The Python group dismissed most of the protesters as pigheaded fruitcakes, rejecting them too facilely as dumb and posturing as absurd idiots. They saw them as people pretending that they were Christians when they are not really following Christ. They disparaged the renowned former editor of *Punch* magazine, Malcolm Muggeridge, whose behavior in a televised debate they found quite nasty, as he had missed the early sections of the film and so didn't quite catch on to the premise of the film. Nevertheless, the cheap laughs regarding death by crucifixion troubled many.

Crucifixions were common, they argued. And people did jeer and mock at the death of Jesus. Ironically, they insert another sales booth, where an entrepreneur is hawking little souvenir crosses, a precursor of the religious jewelry conglomerate turning a form of torture into necklaces. What they do in the scene where Brian and many others are lifted onto the cross is not as blasphemous as it might seem. That is how the Romans executed many rebels of that time. Brian's fellow revolutionaries do show up and read a commending resolution on his behalf, sing "For he's a jolly good fellow," and depart quietly (while another fanatic group shows up and commits mass suicide just to show the Romans how serious they are). Someone suggests, looking at the silly sots, that it's only a joke, folks, but it is not. When Brian is about to be released, the film parodies the final sentimental scene of *Spartacus*, where everyone claims to be "Brian." "I'm Brian and so's my wife."

What this parody achieves is to point out the words of Paul, that the cross is foolishness to the Greeks and a scandal to the Jews. It is both funny and offensive to tradition. Eric Idle's cheery and cheeky song, "Always Look on the Bright Side of Life," lifts the film into the disturbing theme of grace. Brian is Everyman, not the Man Who is God, and Everyman is condemned to die. While all have been found guilty, the song sounds like a Disney musical conceit whistled in the dark, even suggesting an unintentional hint of resurrection. As the Pythons noted, we do come into the world to die. While meant as a nihilistic notion that we come from nothing and go to nothing, the song still hints that there might be something else for which humanity was intended. There may be a bright side. And only a parody could whisper it amidst the dark laughter.

Notes

1 Martha Bayless, *Parody in the Middle Ages: The Latin Tradition* (University of Michigan Press, 1996).
2 John Miles, Jr., "Laughing at the Bible: Jonah as Parody," *Jewish Quarterly Review* 65:3 (January 1975), 168–181.

3 Maurice Yacowar, *Method in Madness: The Comic Art of Mel Brooks* (St. Martin's Press, 1981), viii.

4 Ruth Perlmutter, "Woody Allen's *Zelig*: An American Jewish Parody," in Andrew Horton (ed.), *Comedy/Cinema/Theory* (University of California Press, 1991), 206.

5 Allen quips that his parents' values are "God and carpeting." His mother-in-law carps on with God about "salvation and interior decorating." See Gary Commins, "Woody Allen's Theological Imagination," *Theology Today* 44:2 (July 1987) and Doris Donnelly, "Divine Folly: Being Religious and the Exercise of Humor," *Theology Today* 48:4 (January 1992), 6.

6 Philip Fleishman, "Interview with Mel Brooks," *Macleans* (April 17, 1978), 8.

7 Kenneth Turan, *Los Angeles Times* (August 17, 1979), n.p.

8 See Richard Webster, *A Brief History of Blasphemy* (Orwell Press, 1990), 27ff. The front page of *Variety* highlighted columns by Jewish, Protestant, and Roman Catholic leaders: *Variety* (August 22, 1979), 3. However, its Swedish marketers exploited the film with an advertisement announcing "This film is so funny that they banned it in Norway."

14   Satire

Classic satire presupposes a standard against which vice, folly, and hypocrisy can be compared. It combines both moral purpose and wit, using ridicule and mocking in an effort to improve the world. The satiric work of Isaiah against those who make gods and stools out of wood sets a paradigm for the dark and funny satires of Luis Buñuel and the Monty Python troupe.

Satire employs various forms of caricature and ridicule to taunt, scoff, mock, gibe, spoof, tease, blame, shame, scour, and puncture, all to *improve* society. Its use of wit and humor has a purpose: to reform some vice or folly or stupidity. And within the history of the Christian Church, vice, folly, and stupidity reign with popes and bishops, pilgrims and Baptists.

It may put on the costume of a gentle Horatian nudging or a rough, acerbic Juvenalian wit. Jesus could play kindly with the gentile woman (whose retort that even the dogs – Gentiles – were able to eat the crumbs under the table seemed to strike a comic note with the Messiah) even as Elijah might castigate and mock the prophets of Baal with coarse banter (is your god relieving himself?). Satire may put on masks to deceive, dress in drag to embarrass, or cast its ironic voice as a ventriloquist, but it involves highly exaggerated and improbable situations in which human behaviors and attitudes are held up to ridicule.

In the early 16th century in France, "farce" – the term used for "stuffing" (spicy sausages), from the Latin *farcire* – was employed metaphorically for comic interludes "stuffed" into the texts of religious plays. Silly bits, then naughty bits.

Satire *usually* denotes some comic form of ridicule with a corrective purpose.[1] At its best, satire aims at both shaming with laughter and restoring with love. The good satirist hopes to ameliorate society's ills, not simply vent his spleen. Many satirists hope that change is possible, and that their bit of teasing and taunting will tilt the victim away from his or her vice.

The satirist wishes to see the world made right, to reconcile truth and practice. In his *Companion to Satire*, editor Ruben Quintero defines the satirist's responsibility as frequently that of a watchdog; and no one expects a watchdog to do the double-duty of alarming others that the barn is on fire and of putting out the blaze. Satirists try to rouse us to put out the fire. They encourage our need for the stability of truth by unmasking imposture, exposing fraudulence, shattering deceptive illusion, and shaking us from our complacency and indifference.[2]

Two basic criteria underlie satire. The first, and most necessary, is that it acknowledges some standard, a reasonable norm against which audiences or readers can measure what is good and right. Thus, it must address some folly, vice, or hypocrisy in individuals or institutions that begs to be corrected, or at least addressed. It thus works, as Chesterton was wont to point out, as a standard against which to contrast the actual behavior. We can call a man fat because there is a Greek standard of the human form. One must be able to compare a golden mean against which the target is merely dross. It thus edges to the side of the continuum for reform, rather than slipping into ridicule.

Second, satire is usually leavened with a sense of humor or wit. It is touched with a madness of mirth. Even as one looks at a madman and knows he is touched, so one looks at satire and knows it has touched the fool with its own brand of humor. The face of folly can be shown to be not only foolish but funny.

One of the best and most overlooked biblical satires is that of the Hebrew prophet Isaiah in the 5th century BC. Here is a man who could boldly compare the unrighteousness of God's people to a filthy menstrual rag.[3] Isaiah did not suffer fools or folly, idols or idolatry, but mocked with wit. Isaiah did confess to unclean lips, which may be the professional tool of the satirist. In a call to recognize the only true God, Isaiah ridiculed the origin of false gods.

> All those who make no-god idols don't amount to a thing, and what they work so hard at making is nothing. Their little puppet-gods see nothing and know nothing – they're total embarrassments! Who would bother making gods that can't do anything, that can't "god"? The woodworker draws up plans for his no-god, traces it on a block of wood. He shapes it with chisels and planes into human shape – a beautiful woman, a handsome man, ready to be placed in a chapel. He first cuts down a cedar, or maybe picks out a pine or oak, and lets it grow strong in the forest, nourished by the rain. Then it can serve a double purpose: Part he uses as firewood for keeping warm and baking bread; from the other part he makes a god that he worships – carves it into a god shape and prays before it. With half he makes a fire to warm himself and barbecue his supper. He eats his fill and sits back satisfied with his stomach full and his feet warmed by the fire: "Ah, this is the life." And he still has half left for a god,

made to his personal design – a handy, convenient no-god to worship whenever so inclined. Whenever the need strikes him he prays to it, "Save me. You're my god."

Pretty stupid, wouldn't you say? Don't they have eyes in their heads? Are their brains working at all? Doesn't it occur to them to say, "Half of this tree I used for firewood: I baked bread, roasted meat, and enjoyed a good meal. And now I've used the rest to make an abominable no-god. Here I am praying to a stick of wood!" This lover of emptiness, of nothing, is so out of touch with reality, so far gone, that he can't even look at what he's doing, can't even look at the no-god stick of wood in his hand and say, "This is crazy."[4]

For Isaiah, the Lord makes fools of such diviners and idolaters. How stupid are they? Well, the ox knows his master and the ass his owner's manger, but Israel doesn't have a clue.

Isaiah reveals that fools will be exposed and the scoundrels rendered as worthless and wicked. When King Sennacherib's field commander refused to speak in Aramaic because he wanted to frighten the people on the wall, he threatened that those men on the wall will have to "eat their own dung and drink their own urine" (36:12). But the people remained silent in the face of the threats and deceptive cajoling of the Assyrian commander.

Hezekiah put on sackcloth; for the king of Assyria had "ridiculed the living God." His blasphemy (i.e. ridicule) would bring about his own demise back in his country. To this enormous army God prophesied that the Daughter of Jerusalem would despise and mock him, tossing her head as he ran away. The insults and blasphemies, carried by eyes lifted in pride, would bring their own destruction. Because their insolence reached God's ears, He was going to put a hook in their noses and bits in their mouths, showing the sign of their impending captivity. (And the ultimate irony occurred when Sennacherib returned to worship in the temple of his god, Nisroch: his own sons pushed a giant female idol onto him and crushed him.) The triumph over ridicule and mocking is God's judgment, delivered with a tincture of irony.[5]

However, it is not too long until the virgin Daughter of Babylon, once queen of the kingdoms, hears a similar condemnation. She is told to take off her veil, lift up her skirts, bare her legs and expose her private parts for shame (Isaiah 47:2). While she was wantonly lounging in her security, and trusting in her sorceries, calamity would fall upon her. Her astrologers, stargazers, and magic spells could not save her from what is coming (47:13). Enemies will "lick the dust at your feet" (49:23).

To his own children of Jacob, God laughed, as they blamed their misdeeds on their ersatz gods: "My idols did it; my wooden image and metal god ordained those things" (48:5), like children who blame "nobody" for the mischief. The wicked are like mute dogs with mighty appetites (remember that the Jews thanked God that He did not make them as

Gentiles, women, or dogs) that can never have enough. They call each other to get more wine and drink their fill of beer, believing that tomorrow will be even better than today. "Who are you mocking?" asks Isaiah. "At whom do you sneer and stick out your tongue. You are so stupid that you burn with lust among the oaks, and under every spreading chestnut tree, sacrificing your children to Molech in ravines and under the overhanging crags. Look what you're doing: pouring out drink portions to stone idols, making beds on high and lofty hills." They hid taboo pagan symbols behind doors. They opened up the sacred bed wide and pulled in the nakedness of others (57: 4–8).

Finally, Isaiah describes those who provoke God to His very face by eating the flesh of pigs and rats; such people "are smoke in my nostrils" (65:5; 66:17).

Isaiah viewed the consequences of mocking as being mocked (66:3–4). The people were so flippant, with pointing figures and malicious talk, that his message to them was that their hearts would be calloused and their ears dull and eyes closed so that they would not realize their own miserable condition. Yet Isaiah himself, the one prophet with unclean lips, reminds his people that while he has suffered, even offering his cheeks to those who pulled out his beard and not hiding his face from mocking and spitting, he would not be disgraced, for the sovereign Lord would vindicate him (50:6). No shame, no gain, for the Lord would help and restore the poor prophet and comfort Zion, with joy and gladness. "Don't fear the reproach of men or be terrified by their insults," Isaiah preached, "for the moth will eat them up like a garment; the worm will devour them like wool" (51:7–8). They will refute every tongue that accuses them (54:17). And even eunuchs will be fruitful.

While the ending offers the people of God a blessing rather than a curse, with the promise of being called by a new name, the last word pummels those rebellious, obstinate ones. For these, "their worm will not die, nor will their fire be quenched, and they will be loathsome to all mankind" (66:24). Not a pretty ending, but a great satire.

Luis Buñuel – comically notorious for proclaiming, "I am an atheist still, thank God!" – could not escape the discreet charm of God. His cinema slaps the face of a dead or dull theology that does not wrestle with its questions.[6] His early films deal with individuals struggling with Christian faith and practice, trying to live out their calling in a corrupt and fallen world: *Viridiana* (1961) with its impossibility and hypocrisy of charity; *Nazarín* (winner of the Grand Prize at Cannes in 1959) with its grim story of failed priest and a pineapple of grace;[7] and the high-minded, high-sitting, eating and defecating *Simon of the Desert* (1965) on his high stone pillar, sitting on a column of his own excrement.[8] His scripts overflow with fanatics for Buñuel to showcase, colored by his usual blend of humor, absurdity, and surrealism. When a character tries to live a pure Christian life outside the Church, an absurdity for Buñuel, the ending is pure farce. When St. Simon resists temptation repeatedly, he is undone by being transported to a modern city with its loud, annoying music.

Buñuel quipped that "one can be relatively Christian, but the absolutely pure being, the innocent, is condemned to defeat. He is beaten in advance." His insight is so absolutely and comically true, so that there has been only one Anointed One, who was both innocent and condemned to death. Of Buñuel's two adolescent sentiments, "Profound eroticism sublimated at first in a religious faith, and persistent consciousness of death," it would be this second theme that infused his religious satires.[9]

Buñuel and his collaborators bucked the trend to shoot a religious film, because the cinematic community regarded God as dead. Politics was the important topic. Shot around May, 1968, during the student and worker riots in France, *The Milky Way* (1969) follows two beggars, Pierre and Jean (Peter and John), walking to the shrine of Santiago de Compostela, Spain. As they hitchhike along the Autobahn, their spiritual journey tweaks the noses of Roman Catholic dogma, playing loosely with six principal heresies regarding the incarnation, the Trinity, transubstantiation, the immaculate conception, free will and omnipotence, and theodicy, or the origins and problem of evil. Its protagonists guided by a star to a field of stars, *The Milky Way* provides a *tour de force* for Buñuel's favorite themes to emerge: the hypocritical denial of flesh and desire, the problem of evil, and the impotence of rationality. Episodic and anecdotal, the picaresque film wrestles with dogma and battles against any repression of thought.

In a prologue edited out of the final film, Buñuel wrote:

> Everything in this film concerning the Catholic religion and the heresies it has provoked, especially from the dogmatic point of view, is rigorously exact, except for error on our part. The texts and citations are taken from the Scriptures, modern and ancient works on theology and ecclesiastical history. ... [T]hroughout the film, apparitions, miracles, and accounts of miracles will be treated with the utmost seriousness, in accordance with the traditional representations given by the Church, without any spirit of deformation.[10]

Passionate about the study of Christianity (when he spoke of the Virgin Mary, tears would come into his eyes), Buñuel slyly subverts his own dogmatic pronouncement. In the film, his Christ is alive. In contrast to clichéd representations of Jesus, Buñuel adamantly made sure that He laughs. His mother stops Him from shaving because she says it looks better.

Buñuel was obsessed about heresy, or heterodoxy, and took two pilgrims across a continuum of time and space, with a wild freedom to be in Palestine or Spain. It was the heyday of the counterculture youth movement and the rippling effects of Vatican II, and Buñuel revives the history of Catholicism for the modern era.[11] As heresy was inextricably linked to mystery, the filmmakers chose six major mysteries within the Christian faith, such as the doctrine of the Trinity. Our sense of logic is challenged by the film's question: is God One or Three?

A Jansenist nobleman challenges a Molinist Jesuit ("I thought Jesuits only come out at night, like rats") to a duel with swords and words over free will and predestination. The great debate at the time (May 1968) was between Marxism and Catholicism, with the former collapsing on account of its heresies and the Church being enhanced and even nourished by its debates. In one memorably surreal scene, a beggar imagines Red Brigade revolutionaries lining up to shoot the pope (played, ironically, by Buñuel himself). His satire with all the contradictions within the dogma of the faith calls forth a deeper faith. The pilgrim who scorned and mocked the Virgin Mary encounters her, and she gives him a rosary. His heart is struck, and like Buñuel, he weeps.

The adventuring pilgrims meet the son of a devil who predicts they will encounter a prostitute who will give them two sons, to be called "You are not my people" and "No more compassion," clear references to the story of the Hebrew prophet Hosea and his relation to the prostitute Gomer. Other more comic bits interrupt the narrative with slapstick gags, like Mary stopping Jesus from shaving.[12] In Donald Crafton's analysis of the tension between the narrative and the gag, with the chase and the pie symbolizing the two options, Buñuel goes for the pie almost every time.

Buñuel's satirical (and wickedly ironic) tone has a subversive motive: it wants to raise questions about what we believe and address concerns about how religion can oppress. He is a liberation theologian *sans* God, who wants to shine the light of the sun on all aspects of darkness. In his prologue, the Mad Hatter suggests that this is only a picaresque tale, a series of anecdotes based on actual historical heresies.

An episodic structure of dreams and riddles and odd encounters keeps the narrative disjointed and compelling. One has to watch closely lest one miss a stone in the path, a symbol on the screen. In the first episode, a mad priest brings up the Lateran Council of 1215, where the issue of transubstantiation was debated. If God is everywhere, is he also in pancakes and is that like the eucharist? Numerous allusions and references to the Gospels and Church fathers interrupt the non-linear, even surreal, structure.

The rites of Bishop Priscillian (a Manichean) emphasize the dualism of two separate and opposing natures: spirit and flesh. His followers try to destroy evil not only by claiming to be self-denying ascetics, but also by indulging in sensuality. They argue that they can liberate the soul from the body by following the injunction "to humiliate the body, to subject it unceasingly to the pleasures of the flesh." The issue of theodicy, regarding the origin of evil, and the debate over the nature of Christ as God and human is served up in a restaurant. An exhumed bishop offers the opportunity to discuss the Trinity, and, as mentioned earlier, a Jansenist and

Figure 14.1 In his satire upon Christian theology, Luis Buñuel showed his remarkable understanding of doctrines such as the Trinity, with Father, Son, and Holy Spirit dove. *The Milky Way*, Greenwich Film Productions, 1969. Author's screenshot.

Jesuit duel over the concept of grace versus free will. Finally, at a Spanish inn, the immaculate conception is presented.

According to scholar Virginia Higginbotham, the "heresies forming the outline of *The Milky Way* are, for Buñuel, a rich source of the incongruity, absurdity, and humor which appeal to his surrealist sensibility."[13] Buñuel's use of paradox, in which the mysterious, sinister stranger who joins them is not the devil, but God the Father, is akin to Jesus' parable of God as an unjust judge or a thief in the night. The juxtaposition throws one's hermeneutics out of the window. The stranger is accompanied by a dwarf (the Son) who releases a dove, suggesting the presence of the Trinity throughout the pilgrimage (see Figure 14.1). When one of the characters asks if Christ laughed or coughed, Buñuel cuts to an insert of Jesus running up to catch up with the disciples, late for the feast at Cana, breathlessly asking, "What time is it?" Questioned whether Jesus is God or man, Buñuel depicts Christ laughing, "a mood in which no other artist has ever dared portrayed him."[14]

The ending of the film brings two blind men to Jesus, and as He cures them, He tells them, as He does in the Gospels, not to divulge what he has done. As they rejoice, one says, "Lord, a bird just flew over. I heard its wings beating." As they continue their journey, they come to a ditch, and instinctively make a gesture with their canes. Have they been miraculously healed, are they pretending to be healed, or are they still not used to the new freedom they've been given and stuck with old habits?

Like Flannery O'Connor's grotesque characters haunted by Christ, it seems that Buñuel too cannot rid himself of this Nazarene. The end of his autobiography reveals that he pulled one last joke: when gathering his atheist friends to his side, he called in a priest and "to the horror of my friends I make my confession, ask for absolution for my sins, and receive extreme unction. After which I turn over on my side and expire."[15]

The film was something of a climactic joyride for Buñuel, a "last spin, a final and plausibly anarchic assault on man's capacity to forget his humanity when face to face with what he judges to be immortal."[16] Yet the filmmaker who defies God so openly seems to be open to the idea that "if God exists, how I hate Him." More intense than his disbelief in God is his antipathy to modernity. "My hatred of science and technology will perhaps bring me to the absurdity of a belief in God." Thus, while the film may be an ammunition dump for unbelievers and an amusing Pandora's jar for agnostics, it works as an unprecedented satiric primer for all Christians. What comes through more clearly than anything is the corruption not only of religion, but of the human beings who hold on to it. In orthodox circles, it is called the doctrine of original sin.

In his other films, Buñuel sketches character studies and social satires of what he saw as anachronistic and reactionary religious beliefs.[17] Educated among the Jesuits, Buñuel mocked the bourgeois Church for its fond idealization of flawed priests in *Nazarín*: "what interests me is that he sticks to his ideas, that they are unacceptable to society and that, after his adventures with prostitutes, thieves, etc. they lead him to irrevocable condemnation by the forces of society."[18]

A woman hiding in Nazarín's apartment while recovering from a wound looks at a traditional tragic painting of Jesus on the wall and the face begins to laugh. The failed priest is offered a fruit, a pineapple, a symbol of welcome, which suggests that he also needs charity and that he is not God. As in *Viridiana*, human effort is seen as fruitless. This futility, with the intimation of an eternal need for divine help, is suggested in that film: when Jorge saves a little dog tied to a cart, an identical cart with a replacement dog takes its place. Social injustice remains part of the human experience.

At the end, the priest has learned how to take charity, rather than preach about it. It is a necessary moment of solidarity with the rest of the human race, and with all sinners.

Speaking with Mark Monahan, director Guillermo del Toro reflected upon the power of *Nazarín*:

> The film has a harsh truth, which is that you cannot expect charity, or dogma, or theory, to work in the real world. So he's very much anti-institution. He shows you that the government is a moron; that the police are useless, the army is useless; and the church is equally

Figure 14.2 Seeking to live out the way of Christ, Nazarín (Francisco Rabal) is rejected by many, but offered the pineapple of hospitality near the end of his journey. *Nazarín*, Producciones Barbachano Ponce, 1959. Author's screenshot.

useless. The film has one of the best moments of screenplay I've ever seen: when he's in prison, and the criminal says, "I'm from the bad side, you're from the good side. We're the same." It's great because it's a brutal moment of realization for Nazarín: from then on, all the way to the end of the movie, he is truly horrified about his nature, and then finally, humbly accepts the pineapple that's offered to him, but he first rejects it.[19]

Buñuel works effectively as a satirist, however Juvenalian and biting, almost as if he had memorized Jeremiah 17:9, discovering that the heart is deceitful above all things.[20]

Less profound, but curiously relevant, in *Believe Me* (2014), co-directors Michael Allen and Will Bakke's script spins a story of college seniors who set up a fake Christian charity for donating wells in Africa to earn quick money for their college tuition. It offers the squeezing pinch of a gentle satire on the Christian culture they scheme to dupe.

When the conmen are asked to be keynote speakers for a series of evangelical meetings, they take the bait, assured they can hoodwink the faithful. Working from the premise of what if somebody really wanted to take advantage of gullible Christians, the directors tinkered with what it might look like. With a punchy and pertinent tagline for the age, "it's only a sin if you get caught," the film plays with wrongdoing and conscience. How can you tell if faith is genuine?[21]

As satiric comedies, the emphasis of such works is not primarily upon the laugh, but upon the reformation of the target. Something is amiss and needs to be amended. The use of wit and humor is focused upon the stupidity, folly, and vice of the characters, seeking to correct or reform. Yet, without the laughter, the text is mere preaching.

Notes

1 One finds that when temporal correction seems unlikely, with Israel's enemies beyond redemption, then they may be sent on to a higher court for reform.
2 Ruben Quintero (ed.), *A Companion to Satire: Ancient and Modern* (Cambridge, 2007).
3 Isaiah 30:22.
4 Isaiah 44:9–20.
5 The difficulty in dividing the good satirical prophets from the bad, sacrilegious, mocking prophets cannot always be resolved by the end results during their lifetimes; for good prophets die and do not see the fulfillment of their visions. They are often frustrated in their calling, wondering "how long" it will be until God does what He said. And, as the Psalmist complains, it seems the wicked do prosper. See Terry Lindvall, *God Mocks: A History of Religious Satire from the Hebrew Prophets to Stephen Colbert* (New York University Press, 2015).
6 Carolos A. Valle, "Luis Buñuel and the Discreet Charm of Theology," *Media Development* **1** (1993), 13–14, 20.
7 Joan Mellen (ed.), *The World of Luis Buñuel: Essays in Criticism* (Oxford University Press, 1978): "If Christ were to return, they'd crucify Him again. It is possible to be *relatively* Christian, but the absolutely pure, the absolutely innocent man – he's bound to fail. … I am sure that if Christ came back, the Church, the powerful churchmen, would crucify Him again" (7–8). Renata Adler, "*Nazarín*: Buñuel's Relentless *Nazarín*," *New York Times* (June 21, 1968), acknowledges how one is assaulted by "Buñuel's recurring themes, poverty, meanness, religion, sexual pathology" in this satire of misery.
8 Freddy Buache, *The Cinema of Luis Buñuel* (trans. Peter Graham) (Tantivy Press, 1973), identifies the meaning of the film as "rich people give the instrument of worship to the man who desires to devote himself utterly to glorifying God, which absolves them from making this sacrifice themselves, eases their consciences, and leaves them the time to deal with worldly affairs" (152). Essentially the Christian religion plays nice with the ruling class. St. Simon Stylites is an Olympic champion in asceticism, withdrawing from the world to spend 37 years on top of a 66-foot pillar, but ends up as a beatnik in Greenwich Village. Novelist Henry Miller suggested that "they should take Buñuel and crucify him, or at least burn him at the stake. He deserves the greatest reward that man can bestow *against* man."
9 J. F. Aranda, *Luis Buñuel: A Critical Biography* (Da Capo, 1976), 13.
10 Mellen, *World of Luis Buñuel*, 309.
11 Elizabeth Scarlett has penned a brilliant extended analysis of the film in her *Religion and Spanish Film* (University of Michigan Press, 2014), 45–62.
12 Oswaldo Capriles, "*The Milky Way*," in Mellen, *World of Luis Buñuel*, 306–314.

13 Virginia Higginbotham, *Luis Buñuel* (Twayne Publishers, 1979), 158.

14 Ibid., 162.

15 Luis Buñuel, *My Last Sigh: The Autobiography of Luis Buñuel* (Knopf, 1983), 256.

16 Derek Malcolm, "*The Milky Way*," *Sight & Sound* 39:1 (Winter 1969–1970), 314–317.

17 Luis Buñuel, *Three Screenplays: Viridiana, The Exterminating Angel, Simon of the Desert* (Orion Press, 1969).

18 Mellen, *World of Luis Buñuel*, 8. See Ado Kyrou, *Luis Buñuel: An Introduction* (trans. Adrienne Foulke) (Simon & Schuster, 1963).

19 Mark Monahan, "Interview with Guillermo del Toro," *Telegraph* (September 13, 2004).

20 Kyrou, *Buñuel: An Introduction*; Buache, *Cinema of Luis Buñuel*.

21 Ironically, the lead actor, Alex Russell, seemingly a non-believer, played the happy hypocrite.

15   Dionysian/Transgressive Comedy

Combining low comedy with farce and the breaking of cultural and religious taboos, transgressive comedy showcases characters throughout the history of God's people stretching the boundaries of good taste and common sense.[1] Such comedy becomes carnivalesque in opening up the merrymaking license of the overturning of hierarchies.[2] One such biblical narrative occurs in the erection of the golden calf of Exodus.

Moses had gone up the mountain to receive the commandments and the people grew restless. Left in charge, Aaron gathered all the gold earrings from the grumbling Israelites and shaped a molten calf, a cult image for the people to worship. Not quite as potent as the bull idolized by the Egyptians, the calf became an idol around which the Hebrew people sat down to eat and drink and then got up to party. Their excesses so angered Moses that he smashed the commandments he had brought down from Sinai. Aaron, sounding like John Belushi, with comic chagrin excused himself by claiming that "we just threw the gold in the fire and out jumped the calf." Moses was not persuaded.[3]

The animal comedy we are discussing here is closer to *Animal House* than *The Three Little Pigs*.[4] It is Dionysian, wild, earthy, visceral, magical, and often gross-out, with plenty of wine, revelry, and sexual hi-jinx. In *The Comic Hero*, author Robert Torrance identifies it with the Old Comedy of Greece, where "primordial values and elemental needs … continually threaten to smash the prevailing social order to smithereens."[5] It is impulsive and intoxicating, being contrasted by Nietzsche in his *Birth of Tragedy* with an Apollonian artistic impulse that is rational and orderly, closely aligned to reason and the power of the mind. The chaotic comedy of Dionysus breaks boundaries and goes haywire. Closely aligned to slapstick, it extends the mayhem to forbidden topics and subjects. It shouts yes to the lower body stratum of blood, spit, mucus, urine, sweat, semen, menstrual emissions, belches, farts, and shit. It is Rabelaisian in its celebration of the body in all its natural extensions and excretions. And to a proper, decorous people, respectable and moral, it is excessively and outrageously offensive.

Many of the most popular transgressive animal comedies are Dionysian, full of wild, almost pagan, energy, where the spectators act like the crazed Pentheus, who hides and spies on the partying maenads in their frenzied ecstasy. They will, of course, tear him to shreds, as will wild animal comedies. As voyeurs, spectators participate in the rituals set before them, even when they are pornographic and violent. Dionysian comedy hooks up slapstick with sexual and impulsive forces, seemingly much more Hellenistic than Hebraic. But not so fast.

The hoary old prophet Ezekiel warned us of such iniquity when he mocked the lewd abominations of Jerusalem (Oholibah) and Samaria (Oholah) as two horny women who "spread their legs to every passer-by" (16:25). Oholah lusted after desirable young Assyrian men clothed in purple. After she dies in her harlotry, her more corrupt sister Oholibah engages in pornography, lusting after men portrayed on the wall, images of the Chaldeans colored in vermilion, whose members were like the members of donkeys and whose ejaculations were like the ejaculations of horses (23:20). While not your typical Sunday morning lectionary reading or sermon topic, the scene that Ezekiel scripted offers opportunity for the laughter of derision. Folly stands as a comic signpost warning trespassing fools: "Abandon hope all ye who enter."

Recklessly uninhibited and unbridled, frenzied, and even orgiastic, the Dionysian spirit mocks those who believe they have life under control. The zany tricksters turn over the apple carts and bring down the haughty. It invades film narratives with a ritual madness and a fertility of imagination.

Dionysian comedy rejects authority, involves basic animalistic behaviors, with an excessive amount of eating and drinking and sexual misconduct, a tendency toward chaotic and destructive behavior, and a hint of the demonic.[6] It is Israel goes wild. It is wholly transgressive and exults in its wickedness.

How do religious people make sense of transgressive or seemingly blasphemous portrayals in film? What happens when the protagonist/hero is a thief, prostitute, adulterer, or murderer? While one may quickly acknowledge that the genealogy of Jesus in the Gospel of Matthew includes such notorious characters (from Jacob and Rahab to King David), the moral ambiguity of their lives and ours creates a dissonance. It seems more disturbing when we are laughing with those same sinners, because our laughter indicates we are in the same sinking boat with them.

The Dionysian comedy raises questions of the kind of schemata (mental set or conceptual framework) one adopts in viewing and presumably enjoying moral and spiritual waywardness. Does one morally disengage or add contextual backstory or justify and sanitize the characters? Does one simply accept the story as *via negativa*, an exemplary parable for us to learn what not to do, or might we even identify with the transgressive actions? Watching a comedy about adultery with someone who has been cheated upon and jilted makes one much more sensitive to the complications of the transgressive comedy.

The transgressive category of obscenity derives etymologically from the Latin *obscenus*, which conveys dealing with filth, what is deemed not fitting for public discourse.[7] The primary domains of the obscene are topics of sexuality, excretion, bodily functions, and religion. However, a taboo in one age or culture may not be so in another, and treating some topics solemnly may itself be an invitation to see incongruity. In reference to sex, C. S. Lewis found that too many people take it too seriously. "For I can hardly help regarding it as one of God's jokes," mused Lewis, "that a passion so soaring, so apparently transcendent, as Eros, should be linked in incongruous symbiosis with a bodily appetite which, like any other appetite, tactlessly reveals its connections with such mundane factors as weather, health, diet, circulation, and digestion."[8] Critic Alex Wainer points out that the animal comedies of Judd Apatow (e.g. *The 40-Year-Old Virgin* and *Knocked Up*) employ vulgarity to reaffirm traditional values of morality, of slacker boys trying to put away childish things and become men.[9]

Director Emilio Portes unleashes the demonic with *Pastorela* (2011), his uneven dark comedy on the annual Christmas nativity play, the 2012 winner of the Ariel Award. The film is a magical Mexican mystery tour that devours goodness and indicts the Church for its corporate culture, its lack of faith, and its hypocrisy. In the preparation for the traditional Christmas play, where alms are being gathered for the poor, strains of "Joy to the World" and a warning that the devil will try to thwart the birth of the Christ child open the film.

A heavy, brooding, and grumpy police agent, Jesús Juárez or Chucho (Joaquín Cosío), wants the coveted role of the devil, which he has played for many years; however, the new priest arrives at the parish and wishes to recast the play. Chucho's response parallels the infernal servant expelled because of his pride, with his vanity expressed in his red costume and tail: "I was born to be that devil!" This character's role in the tradition is to be both the most dramatic and funniest character.

Policeman Chucho claims that Father Ben had always selected him for the coveted role, but now the old padre has comically died *in flagrante delicto* with a young nun. The new director, Father Edmundo Posado, is a corpulent exorcist whose primary concern is the raising of money for the parish.

Chucho is demoted to be a shepherd. Juárez becomes possessed with his obsession to own the part, developing demonic powers (first in telekinetically moving a beer for his angry thirst). The alarm clock ticks from 3:33 a.m. to 6:66. Hell hath no fury like an amateur actor scorned. An imminent apocalyptic battle looms in the devil-may-care unleashing of transgressive power, as red-eyed cops and Santas become agents in a spiritual battle. When prisoners in the local jail riot, crying out "better free in

Figure 15.1 After Chucho (Joaquín Cosio) has been denied his customary role as the devil in the annual nativity play, he will do anything to snatch it back. *Pastorela*, Equipment & Film Design, 2011. Author's screenshot.

Hell than servants in Paradise" and "long live the underworld Lucifer," an actual demonic principality is released.[10]

One has difficulty discerning the goodness of the protagonist, as he whacks the little doughy guy who becomes the substitute devil and is accused of murdering the deputy attorney-general. When the substitute devil is locked in a trunk, the priest takes over the role himself. Chucho assumes the role of the Archangel Michael, and all hell breaks loose, in a ludicrous, over-the-top shoot out.

Exorcisms take on the quality of a Three Stooges enactment, with doctors trying to give an enema to a man in a devil's costume. Juárez's fellow cops try to stop men in red suits, evil runs rampant on the streets, congested with Santa Clauses and mobs of devils (some costumed and some real) plaguing the world. The wild, Rabelaisian dark comedy of medieval pageantry is played out with abandon, as ludicrous comedy combines with horror to open up the floodgates to hell. Juárez has donned the costume of a giant angel, and now expelled from the nativity play, he summons the forces of hell. He is a fallen angel. When a character in the play is to have his head chopped off, Juárez slices and lops it onto the lap of a visiting bishop in the front row of the audience, who applauds the "great special effects." In the film's final battle of good versus evil, outlandish deaths occur with the final vanquishing of the devil's forces with a sword of light.

While uneven and even ragged at its climax, where at the maximum security prison, Chucho forms a heavy metal rock band playing "Devil in

My Skin," the film attacks the devotion that many have to the external activities of the Church, such as its nativity play. Christmas is not really about the Christ child. Everyone is a transgressor and everyone suffers the righteous judgment of their obsession.

The Netherlands Film Festival's equivalent to the Academy Award Oscar is known as the Golden Calf. The somewhat lapsed Roman Catholic director Kevin Smith created Mooby, a cartoon representation of an anthropomorphic Golden Calf. This graven image, mocking Mickey Mouse, Ronald McDonald, and Barney, indicts the money-obsessed culture of Disney, McDonald's, and America itself. In his irreverent and sophomoric treatment of the Roman Catholic Church, *Dogma* (1999), Smith's character Loki (Matt Damon), the angel of death, connects Moogy with the money-based obsessions of the Golden Calf of Aaron. With his fellow fallen angel Bartleby (Ben Affleck), he tries to exploit a loophole in Church dogma which will allow them to sneak into heaven and gain a plenary indulgence.[11] God had cast them out of His presence by sending them to a place worse than hell, Wisconsin. (Critic Roger Ebert opined that the film took "Catholic theology absolutely literally," which made one doubt his catechism training.)[12]

As a comedic fantasy, it is more Dionysian excess than satiric catechism. Its one or two satiric shots (e.g. George Carlin as the oblivious hippy-dippy Cardinal Glick unveiling his "thumbs-up" Buddy Christ statue for the "Catholicism WOW!" campaign) are overwhelmed by an excess of animal and demonic activity. The two fallen and conniving angels land in Wisconsin and need to pass through an arch (one assumes golden) in New Jersey. If they do, their sins will be forgiven; they can lose their wings, and be "transubstantiated" into pure human beings. The premise is so outlandish and its theology of sin (and the topics of indulgences and angelology) so muddled that one cannot take its silliness without a complete emptying of the mind.

A seraph named Metatron (Alan Rickman) announces to an infertile abortion worker named Bethany (Linda Fiorentino) that she must begin a holy crusade. Bethany confesses she thinks God is dead, to which her Jewish friend sighs that is the "sign of a true Catholic." (God, it seems, came down to play skeeball and, having been ambushed by three hell-raising hockey players, the Stygian triplets, was knocked unconscious; he is stuck in a self-imposed limbo in the comatose body of a homeless man.) She asks Metatron what God is like; he tells her, "God? Lonely. But funny. He's got a great sense of humor. Take sex for example. There's nothing funnier than the ridiculous faces you people make mid-coitus."

When Bethany responds: "Sex is a joke in heaven?" Metatron quips, "The way I understand it, it's mostly a joke down here, too."

Serendipity, a muse from Greek mythology, boasts that she inspired most of the Bible as well as 19 of Hollywood's 20 most successful, top-grossing products (except *Home Alone*: "someone sold his soul to

Figure 15.2 Kevin Smith's satire on Catholic teaching and practice offers Cardinal Glick's (George Carlin) updated modern version of "Buddy Christ." *Dogma*, View Askew Productions, 1999. Author's screenshot.

the devil for that one"). She espouses a mushy theology that "it doesn't matter what you have faith in, just that you have faith." A foul-mouthed Rufus (Chris Rock) claims to have been the "thirteenth apostle," but was left out because he is black, and that Jesus owed him 12 bucks after he got tabbed with the bill from the Last Supper. Rufus tells Jay and Silent Bob that the dead spend most of their time watching the living, especially in the shower. Jay can't wait to die. Characters are preoccupied with sex and profane it with constant references to getting laid. The duo hang around abortion clinics to meet loose women. However, God, it seems, has been playing a joke on them all. When "She" (Alanis Morissette) appears, it is a playfully pantomime charade. When Bethany asks "Why are we here?" God pokes Bethany's nose: "Nweep!"

The transgressive film, from the Christian perspective, contains Smith's simplistic message of "it doesn't matter what you have faith in, just that you have faith." Jesus is no more than an enlightened teacher. In contrast, the rebellious angel Bartleby knows more than all the others:

These humans have besmirched everything bestowed upon them. They were given Paradise; they threw it away. They were given this planet; they destroyed it. They were favored best above all His endeavors; and some of them don't even believe He exists. And in spite of it all, He has shown them infinite fucking patience at every turn.[13]

The film remains audacious, sophomoric, and hokey, with its scatology and banal references to masturbation, John Hughes' movies, and a Fecalator (which conveniently throws dung at its target). It is too silly and ill-informed to be an effective satire, as it reduces the human to tiring profanity, unbridled sex talk, and excretion. Yet Smith sneaks in his simple theme with one of his characters confessing "I have issues with anyone who treats faith as a burden instead of a blessing."

For the religious film, the Dionysian comedy functions in two contrasting ways. First, it implies judgment upon licentious behaviors. But second, it calls into question the unyielding Apollonian approach to life that modernity and rationality demand. A world of spirit, both divine and demonic, exists, and the Dionysian takes that spiritual war seriously. It knows that the Law cannot save. Human goodness is limited. Flesh was even created good, but has been perverted. Thus *carne* gives us both carnival and the incarnation. It releases one from the shackles of mere morality into the transcending presence of God.

Such transgressive comedies that expose the id and unleash basic human urges can be found back in the Middle Ages of Europe, where it is rooted in what Russian Orthodox literary critic Mikhail Bakhtin called the carnival comedy. Here was an ambivalent derision and celebration of the social order, of the marketplace revelry of *mardi gras* where ordinary people (the vulgar masses) laughed in communal merrymaking. The earth to them was both a "fertile womb as well as a tomb."[14] It was a time to tear down *and* to build up, renew, and revive. For Bakhtin, this was one of the major differences of the "people's festive laughter from the pure satire of modern times. The satirist whose laughter is negative places himself above the object of his mockery, he is opposed to it." But here, the people also laugh at themselves. "They too are incomplete; they also die and are renewed."[15] The coarseness of the comedy reminds one that one is made of dust and will return to dust, but it also whispers of the dust being gathered and revived.

Dionysian comedies are more revelatory than redemptive. In hinting at the animalism and demonism of the human, they show us more about fallen nature than about salvation. Where *Dogma* bores upon repeated viewings, *Pastorela* continues to disturb, in its excess, its cheery nihilism, and its celebration of life. But both films reaffirm what Lewis discovered about the coarse joke. What we discover is an

> animal which finds its own animality either objectionable or funny. Unless there had been a quarrel between the spirit and the organism I do not see how this could be: it is the very mark of the two not being "at home" together. But it is very difficult to imagine such a state of affairs as original – to suppose a creature which from the very first was half shocked and half tickled to death at the mere fact of being the creature it is. I do not perceive that dogs see anything funny about being dogs: I suspect that angels see nothing funny about being angels.[16]

The transgressive comedy stands as a warning signpost; it is not meant to be an exemplary narrative, but a revelatory one. It shows us not only the folly in the mirror, but suggests an ideal toward which we can hope. It is one's "duty," observed Chesterton in an essay on "Spiritualism," "to use silly metaphors on serious questions." One should be able to test one's theology with a defense employing the grotesque and vulgar.

> It is the test of a good religion whether you can joke about it. ... Unless a thing is dignified, it cannot be undignified. Why is it funny that a man should sit down in the street? There is only one possible or intelligent reason: that man is the image of God. It is not funny that anything else should fall down; only that a man should fall down. No one sees anything funny in a tree falling down. ... No man stops in the road and roars with laughter at the sight of the snow coming down. ... The fall of thunderbolts is treated with some gravity. The fall of roofs and high buildings is taken seriously. It is only when a man tumbles down that we laugh. Why do we laugh? Because it is a grave religious matter: it is the Fall of Man.[17]

The Fall is simply another way to describe men and women going wild, of pursuing their own goals and desires. For what is funnier than the idea of someone – either man, woman, or angel – thinking they could orchestrate the nativity or catch God on a technicality? The transgressions, seen from the perspective of grace, are nets to catch us in our pride and remind us that God can make straight the crooked paths of life and living.

Notes

1 Terry Lindvall, *God Mocks: A History of Religious Satire from the Hebrew Prophets to Stephen Colbert* (New York University Press, 2015).
2 Martha Bayless, "Carnivalesque," in *Encyclopedia of Humor Studies* (ed. Salvatore Attardo) (Sage Publications, 2014), 109–112.
3 As in most drunken revelry, there was a hangover. As Moses ground up the golden calf into powder, he forced the fraternity of libertines to drink it. They would not recover from their orgy of beef at the Golden Corral.
4 William Paul, "Bill Murray, King of Animal Comedy: Reaganite Comedy in a Kinder, Gentler Nation," *Film Criticism* 13:1 (Fall 1988), 4–19. Inklings C. S. Lewis and Charles Williams once conspired to write a series of stories on animals in the Bible, from the creature's point of view. Thus Balaam's ass, Jonah's whale, Peter's crowing rooster, the two she-bears that Elisha called out to maul the teenagers, all beg to be the central characters of their tales. But one does not expect these British intellectuals to deal with much gross-out comedy even with their animals.
5 Robert M. Torrance, *The Comic Hero* (Harvard University Press, 1978).
6 Michael V. Tueth, *Reeling with Laughter: American Film Comedies from Anarchy to Mockumentary* (Scarecrow, 2012).
7 Mike Lloyd, "Obscenity," in Attardo, *Encyclopedia of Humor Studies*, 547–549.
8 C. S. Lewis, *The Four Loves* (Harcourt, Brace & Company, 1988), 100.

9 Alex Wainer, "Freaks, Geeks, and Mensches," *Prison Fellowship* (December 5, 2007).

10 The devil and cinema have been intimately connected throughout film history. In 1952, famed Italian neorealist film director Roberto Rossellini released his supernatural comedy, *The Machine that Killed Bad People*. At a small Italian village where corruption and bullying frequently occurred, a small disheveled man appears claiming to be St. Andrew. He approaches a good humble man who is the town photographer and shows him how he can rid the town of its evil citizens by photographing photographs. Every shot taken results in another death, with the victim in the same surreal comic pose of the picture. Each is frozen and embalmed in their vanity or vice. However, the question arises of who is really the bad person, when all of us are bad. The morally principled photographer finally questions whether the blessed St. Andrew would really support all this killing. He discovers that the saint is bogus and is actually the devil, horned and smoky, spreading his corruption through a gullible saint. He deceives the upright men into judging others and executing them with his technological apparatus. Two sly theses of the film are united: first, death comes through the camera and second, behind the camera is the devil. Ten years before the film's release, British don C. S. Lewis had been connected with the devil Screwtape on the cover of *Time* magazine, and it was Lewis who presciently surmised that there is "death in the camera" (C. S. Lewis, *On Stories* (Harcourt Brace Jovanovich, 1982), 16).

11 In messing with a nun's head, Loki compares God to "The Walrus and the Carpenter" from Lewis Carroll's *Through the Looking Glass*. This constitutes a witty indictment of the art of hermeneutics, in interpreting sacred texts in an allegorical manner, where the walrus is Buddha or Lord Ganesha and the Carpenter is Jesus Christ. For the fallen angel, both religions dupe oysters into following them and then proceed to shuck and devour them.

12 Steven D. Greydanus, "Dogma in *Dogma*: A Theological Guide," online at http://decentfilms.com/articles/dogma-article (accessed October 21, 2015); Todd McCarthy, "Review: *Dogma*," *Variety* (May 24, 1999).

13 Janet Maslin, "*Dogma*: There's Devilment Afoot," *New York Times* (October 4, 1999).

14 Ellen Bishop, "Bakhtin, Carnival and Comedy: The New Grotesque in *Monty Python and the Holy Grail*," *Film Criticism* 15:1 (1990), 49–64.

15 Mikhail Bakhtin, *Rabelais and His World* (ed. Helen Iswolsky) (Indiana University Press, 1984), 12.

16 C. S. Lewis, *Miracles* (Macmillan, 1947); see Terry Lindvall, "Taboo Humor," in *Surprised by Laughter: The Comic World of C. S. Lewis* (Thomas Nelson, 2012), 295–301.

17 G. K. Chesterton, "Spiritualism," in *All Things Considered* (Methuen, 1927), 202–203. In 1871, a critic for *Saturday Review* argued that comic perception is not compatible with the highest Christian virtues. "A humorist may be a thoroughly excellent and amiable person; but he is hardly likely to be a saint. We cannot imagine the loftiest spiritual nature having the full appreciation of a joke. We have known some very good men who liked puns and small witticisms; but we have always found them rather shocked even by the innocent varieties of humor. The humorist, in fact, has just that tendency, to look at the seamy side of things, and to delight in bringing high emotions to the test of some vulgar or grotesque association from which the man of saintly nature characteristically shrinks." Cited in Robert Bernard Martin, *The Triumph of Wit: A Study of Victorian Comic Theory* (Oxford University Press, 1974), 9. It was against this prejudice that Chesterton thought and wrote.

16   Mockumentary

The fictional film is easily differentiated from its non-fiction, or documentary, counterpart, which takes on reality as its object of study and does no – or as little as possible – recreation of factual material on its way to telling its story. The people and places do, or at least did, exist. Most of what is presented is based on the photography of live-shot events.

This is different from a particular genre of fiction film called the docu-drama. Sometimes called "biopics," these films are characterized by recreating and in large part fictionalizing actual events, situations, locations, and individuals in order to tell the story of some true event or biography of some interesting person. *I Am a Fugitive from a Chain Gang* (Mervyn LeRoy, 1932) told the real-life story of Robert Burns, a fugitive from a Georgia chain gang who happened to have written an autobiography called *I Am a Fugitive from a Georgia Chain Gang*. The role of Burns was played by the then top Warner Bros. movie idol Paul Muni and "somewhere in America" took the role of Georgia.

The docu-drama has an honored role in film history. Many award-winning films happen to be biopics that fictionalize history and historical figures. *Argo* (Ben Affleck, 2012) told the tale of the rescue of some of the American hostages during the Iranian Revolution in 1978. *Lawrence of Arabia* (David Lean, 1962) was a biography of the Englishman T. E. Lawrence, who joined the leaders of the Arab revolt against Ottoman incursions. These were not comedies. Most docu-dramas are that: dramas.

So these two types of film-making for many years had the corner on covering actual events. The documentary was non-fiction and the docu-drama was the fiction technique. It would be simpler for all concerned if they had left it that way. However, the continuum that holds fiction at one end and non-fiction at the other provides a slippery scale to wrangle. Within the documentary genre there is serious contention between those that would allow some recreation of events and situations and those who adamantly contend for what is sometimes called "pure cinema" – the camera as window on reality. Erol Morris' *The Thin Blue Line* (1988) tested that boundary as it was mostly constructed of recreated scenes and situations. We'll note here that Morris' film was effective in illustrating the unjust conviction of an innocent man in the murder of a policeman in Texas – especially effective in that the film was in large part responsible for overturning that man's conviction.

All this is to say that those who produce and otherwise attend to documentaries are very protective of the genre. Such filmmakers as Morris (*Gates of Heaven, The Thin Blue Line, Fog of War*), Ken Burns (*History of Baseball, The Brooklyn Bridge, The Civil War*), and the Maysles brothers (*Gimme Shelter, Gray Gardens*) have developed films which tend to use certain techniques that are closely associated with documentary film-making. One such technique is the so-called "Ken Burns" effect in some editing programs which cause still photographs to move up or down or side to side to avoid the static quality inherent in still photographs.

Of the tools and techniques most used by documentary filmmakers, several stand out. One technique is the use of the shaky camera. *Cinéma vérité*, or cinema of life, is a persistent style that tends to eschew the steadiness of the tripod and relies on the skill of the cameraman to hold the camera as steady as possible, though it is almost impossible to avoid some shaking of the image that is recorded. Yet it is this shaking that implies that the recording is done with a sense of immediacy.

Another tool of the documentarian is the on-camera interview. This is where a person talks either directly to the camera or, as is the case most of the time, talks to an interviewer who sits or stands to one side of the camera.

A technique that is an offshoot of the previous two is the extended take. This is when the camera opens up on a scene and nothing seems to be happening at the beginning of a scene or it holds the image past where one would normally cut. These extended moments are most effective in showing ill-preparation at the start of a segment or showing embarrassment by those who are in the frame and want the camera to cut away. Embarrassment, shame: these emotions tend to arise from the presence of the documentary filmmaker while he or she is recording real life. And embarrassment and shame are effective in comedy as well.

Another form of fiction film that uses documentary style is the found footage film. These films purport to be the actual footage of some real people involved in real situations that are complete fiction, yet they use the various styles and techniques associated with documentaries to create a sense of realism – verisimilitude that will connect the viewer to the action on the screen. Most found footage films tend to be dramas – many are in the horror genre, such as *The Blair Witch Project* (Daniel Myrick and Eduardo Sánchez, 1999) and *Quarantine* (John Erick Dowdle, 2008). The term often used with these films is "subjective camera" – that is, the camera is a character who records with an unblinking eye the events of the film.

So, just as the docu-drama represents the fictionalized recreation of real events and people, and documentaries represent the mostly serious and dramatic recording of real events and people, there appeared to be a need for the comic use of the documentary. This is where we get the mockumentary. Closely aligned to both parody and satire, the mockumentary lampoons the documentary film. Presented in the form of *cinéma vérité*, it improvises and creates historical facsimiles, a pretense of authentic documents. The Book of Esther parodies the Persian hegemony in that, it flouts male/female relations and the ironies of power structures.

With the simulated appearance of actuality, the "discourse is characterized by the appropriation of codes and conventions from the full continuum of nonfiction and fact-fiction forms."[1] Its key characteristics are its playfulness, reflexivity, and subversiveness. Its less reverential approach foregrounds how and why cinematic texts are put together, showcasing production practices, textual strategies, and a wide range of audience expectations and interpretations that characterize documents. All this announces to its audience that we are to consider how *constructed* the media are.

The mockumentary emerged as a unique format for comedy, as the sub-genre suggests that it is documenting reality when it is really mocking it through a fictional form. It involves a presentation that seems genuine, but combines parody of the form and not a little satire. Authors Craig Hight and Jane Roscoe label its agenda a "parody of the assumptions and expectations associated with factual discourse."[2] As such it deliberately tells a story that critiques a political or social condition. In its choicest form, it produces films like *This Is Spinal Tap* (Rob Reiner, 1984) and *Waiting for Guffman* (Christopher Guest, 1996). While a modern format, it finds a parallel in a parabolic story told in Judges 9. The biblical account mocks a historical event with its own constructed story, even if we stretch this category a bit with poetic license.

After Gideon's victory, the people want to make him king. He refuses and tells them that the Lord should rule over them and he goes home. But one of his many sons, Abimelech, wants to be king. After his father dies, he gathers his relatives at Shechem (the place where Abraham first received the promise of God and Jacob warned the Israelites not to forget their Lord), and poses two options: "Which is better for you, that 70 men, all the sons of Jerub-Baal, rule over you or that one man rule over you?" Remember, he says, I am your bone and your flesh. Good idea, say his mother's relatives, and they give him 70 pieces of silver. He hires worthless and reckless fellows that go to his father's house and massacre 70 brothers, the sons of Jerub-Baal. Then the maternal side of the family gather for a crowning of Abimelech by the oak of the pillar in Shechem.

The youngest son of Gideon, Jotham, had hidden himself. Then he constructs a story that mocks the wicked actions of Abimelech.

The trees gathered to find a king and they say to the olive tree, "Reign over us." The olive tree laughs and asks, Why should I leave my fatness with which God and men are honored and stand over trees?" Then they go to the fig tree to be their king. He asks, "Why should I leave my sweetness and my good fruit and go wave over the trees?" Then they try to persuade the vine and it rejects them merrily: "Why should I leave my new wine, which cheers God and men, and go to wave over the trees?"

So, desperately, the trees say to the bramble, "You come and reign over us." Aha, warns the bramble, "if in truth you are anointing me as king over you, come and take refuge in my shade, but if not, may fire come out from the bramble and consume the cedars of Lebanon." If anyone ever wanted a quick, hot fire, one only needed to ignite the thorny brambles.

The comically ominous parable comes true as after three years the men of Shechem deal treacherously with Abimelech. Even after Abimelech captures their city (after they had held a festival where they ate, drank, and cursed Abimelech) and comes to burn their leaders in a tower, one woman drops a millstone on Abimelech's head and crushes his skull. So God repays the wickedness of both Abimelech and his treacherous allies from Shechem.

Several elements go into making a mockumentary. First is the combination of comedy techniques, including parody, satire, and a spontaneous light touch in telling a story. Second, it demands an intelligent audience, who understand both the subject matter and its context. Just as Jotham's parable imitates the judgment of God upon His wayward people, it throws into the mix familiarity with Gideon's actions being like the olive tree, the fig tree, and the vine. He chose to simply enjoy the life God had given. Third, while affectionate and playful, the spoofing of Abimelech's usurpation includes a sharp critique of his actions. Even though Jotham passionately blasts his nemesis, he employs a mischievous, witty satire on the stupidity of the trees. Interviews with the other plants give the mock narrative a playful bite.

While film mockumentaries demonstrate a factual verisimilitude, the bramble parable captures the spirit of the parodic narrative, one that exposes and indicts the vanity of real life. Jotham's story offers a wild subversion of a factual event.

These techniques and styles easily recognized by the documentary audience have been incorporated into fictional film-making over the years. Woody Allen's mockumentary *Zelig* (1983) purports to tell the story of Leonard Zelig, the human chameleon. Allen incorporates actual historical footage of real people and events and intercuts them with scenes of the fictional Zelig and those who were associated with him, making this one of the earliest mockumentaries. Mockumentary, as a term, is derived from combining the styles of the documentary with fiction (the "mock" is used to mean "fake" as in mock turtle soup – no turtles were harmed in the making of this chapter).

Another mockumentarian of note is Christopher Guest, who co-wrote and starred in the film *This Is Spinal Tap*, which came out one year after Allen's *Zelig*. *Spinal Tap* was directed by Rob Reiner, who also played an on-camera director of the "documentary" of a heavy metal band called Spinal Tap as its band members were reuniting. It was played straight – that is, no winking to the camera (and audience) that this was fake. It was played so seriously that the band formed for the film actually went on tour as a promotion for the mockumentary.

Guest followed up this film with his own directorial effort, *Waiting for Guffman* (1996), which chronicled the events of a community theater troop in the fictional Blaine, Missouri. He followed that with *Best in Show* (2000) and *A Mighty Wind* (2003), the former being a send-up of the Westminster Dog Competition and the latter a reunion tour of (fictional) folk artists who had their heyday in the 1960s.

One thing that Guest is adamant about is that he rejects the term "mockumentary," considering that it implies that he is mocking – making fun of – the objects of his film-making. However, the term has stuck to these totally fake documentaries.

There are certain criteria for inclusion in the mockumentary genre or technical style, depending upon how you view genre designations. The director can be on screen or off screen or even be fictionalized (where the on-screen director is just an actor and the actual director of the film is never seen). The structure of the entire mockumentary film is fictional. That is, the situations, events, characters, dialogue, and action are all fictionalized. This is why such films like Morgan Spurlock's *Super-Size Me* (2004) and *What Would Jesus Buy?* (Rob VanAlkemade, 2007), though comedic at times, are just documentaries. The latter features a fictional character designated as Reverend Billy and his Church of Stop Shopping Choir; the events they go to are real events, and, although the final scenes occurring at Disney World are set up, at most the director has contrived certain situations and events to make his point about the commercialization of Christmas and the idolatry of the Christian religion. *What Would Jesus Buy?* is more in the vein of Larry Charles' *Borat* (2006) and *Brüno* (2009), which both feature a fictional character who interacts with real people in real situations (many of which were staged, just as in Spurlock's documentaries). Even in its similarity to the documentary, the film playfully critiques commercialization, with its warning of a "Shopocalypse." *Mother Jones* found the Christmas hymns and carols "silly and sarcastic but surprisingly critical."[3]

As a style both the mockumentary and the found footage film are hard to pull off. But as a style, when done well, both can be effective either as comedy, with the former, or as horror, with the latter. Two films that do an effective job of the mockumentary are *The Making of "... And God*

Spoke" (Arthur Borman, 1993) and *The Proper Care and Feeding of an American Messiah* (Chris Hansen, 2006).

In 1993 when audiences were just getting used to this new style of comedic film-making that had not yet garnered the name mockumentary, a film was made that purported to chronicle the creation of a film based on the Bible to be called *"… And God Spoke."* This is 11 years after the release of *This Is Spinal Tap* and one year before *Waiting for Guffman*. The story of the film follows the creation of this biblical epic by a producing–directing team of Marvin Handleman (Steven Rappaport) and Clive Walton (Michael Riley). Their credits include such extreme low-budget films as *Dial S for Sexy*, *Nude Ninjas*, and *Alpha-Deatha-De-Capa*. They introduce themselves and speak of the movie business as a great adventure. Marv is focused on the cost of things while Clive is the cineaste – constantly pontificating on the nature of film. Based upon their credits, it is implied that they really don't know what they are doing.

The various crew, such as screenwriter, cinematographer, and casting director, among others, are introduced and they appear not to be the best that money can hire. It's worth noting that the first assistant director role is played by Michael Hitchcock, who a year later would begin to work with Guest on his mockumentaries, starting with the first one, *Waiting for Guffman*.

The film is structured as to follow the hiring of the cast, which include the following recognizable actors: Lou Ferrigno (famous for playing *The Incredible Hulk* on television), Eve Plumb ("Jan Brady" from *The Brady Bunch*), Soupy Sales (a bad-pun comic who starred in *The Soupy Sales Show*), and Andy Dick (a comic actor famous for the television show *Newsradio*). Lou Ferrigno would play Cain against Andy Dick's Abel. Plumb is cast in the role of Noah's wife, while Soupy Sales plays Moses.

The first day of shooting begins with a "tradition" that the director and producer indicate they perform before any shooting starts: they hold hands and pray. This prayer is a twisting of the Lord's Prayer from Matthew 6:9–13. But in the director's version, it's "Hallowed be our film," with various other aspects of their film to replace words in the Scripture. The camera seeks out numerous crew and cast who look uncomfortable. This could be a reaction to blaspheming against Scripture in the cavalier way that Clive the director takes it. It also feels out of place for a film set.

Another way of looking at this moment and the prayer is as an example of how disconnected Marv and Clive are from the source material. They seem to be trying to validate the words of Christ, but instead reveal themselves to be just cherry-picking verses and concepts that serve their purposes. This happens throughout the filming of *"… And God Spoke."*

The first day of the film then switches to the shooting: just one take of one shot of one scene. This is why their executive producer with their backing studio Greenfield Productions lament that the film is one and a half weeks behind schedule and they've been shooting for two weeks. Early on it is made clear that the filmmakers don't know what's in the Bible – the book that is supposed to be the source for the film within the film. When they get ready to shoot the scene of Jesus walking on the water, they cannot agree on how many disciples Jesus had. Only eight show up to get into the boat, while the director shouts out "Anybody have a Bible?" They agree on ten to be the number of disciples because, as they say, this needs to be theologically correct.

Jesus is presented as a method actor, who answers only to his character name. When the first assistant director is calling the actor's name to show up for the scene, he is ignored until the first assistant director curses "Jesus Christ!" and that causes the actor to acknowledge him. This is funny because the film is littered with numerous expletives and blasphemes such as "fuck," "shit," "Christ," and "Jesus" – these being sprinkled around the film to create a sense of what actually happens on a set. Even a religious set.

A number of missteps common to film-making occur. The actors are upset about their pay. The artistic director creates a way-over-budget version of Noah's Ark but cannot get it through the studio doors. The pyrotechnic team try to make a spectacular burning bush for Moses to interact with, but end up creating a small wisp of smoke that could only indicate that God and Moses stepped behind the bush to share a cigarette.

They learn that the "suits" – that is, the production house funding their film up to 15 million dollars – are coming to view the rough cut. They are so disheartened that they pull the plug midway through the production. This causes a rift between Marv and Clive. When Moses shows up for his Ten Commandments scene, he is holding a six-pack of Coke-a-Cola with them. The director explodes and demands the soda be removed. Marv insists that this is the only way they can finish the film: product placement. Marv ends up firing Clive and continuing on as the director.

Clive seeks out a possible investor: his uncle. He is only given some salami for his effort – primo salami, but not what Clive needed. Clive and Marv adopt a truce of sorts and screen the film before possible investors. At the end of the screening, it turns out everyone has left. Finally Marv agrees to take out a home equity loan and finance the rest of the film. After they recruit an editor (who will work cheaply because Marv and Clive gave him his first break in the business) to edit the film, they secure a theater to screen it. Marv also gets a number of critics to attend the first showing.

The film is shown to disastrous reviews. Michael Medved (an actual film critic) comes on screen to declare this to be the worst film ever made. The film is picketed by a group who are presumed to be Christians, led by a pastor who denounces the film as blasphemy. The failure of their film is so epic that they cannot afford to pay cast and crew.

Figure 16.1 Moses (Soupy Sales, playing himself) comes down from the mountain with the Ten Commandments engraved on stone tablets – which he seems to be able to turn at a certain angle in order to improve his tan. *The Making of "... And God Spoke"*, Brookwood Entertainment, 1993. Author's screenshot.

All looks to be lost until about a year later (according to a graphic) when the film has turned out to be a cult classic. For eight weeks straight the film has been selling out to crowds who dress like Bible characters in the film and even purport to have memorized every line.

Marv and Clive sit in front of the screen inside the theater and answer questions. Everyone thinks that this is the funniest film ever made. The implication is that the film has gone the way of midnight matinees across the nation, much as the film *The Rocky Horror Picture Show* (Jim Sharman, 1975) had done. When asked how they came up with the idea, Marv and Clive seem honestly befuddled.

Marv: How did we get the idea for the movie? Good question. Well, Clive and I were sitting around. And we just were trying to figure out what our next film-making adventure would be. And we thought, gosh, there's just so much humor in the Bible. It was definitely a struggle.

Clive: There were times when, you know, to be honest with you, we didn't know what we had. And, uh, lo and behold, by God, we had a comedy. Or we had a comedy by God.

The film ends with a notation that "... *And God Spoke*" made 42 million dollars and the filmmakers were working on their next epic, *The Iliad*.

How do we consider this film? It works as a cautionary tale in some respects. Like all mockumentaries, the fictional mirror is held up to an audience who are always talking about faithful adaptations of Scripture. Is this ultimately what the audience wants: a parody of the Bible, rather than an exploration of the depth of Scripture? In many respects, Marv and Clive represent contemporary filmmakers and audience members who either don't know or don't care that they don't know the details of Scripture. Look at Clive, who settles on ten as the perfect number for the disciples.

Also, there is a sense of asking where the limits to artistic license are. That is, how far away from the source material can people get without alienating their audience? One scene shows the producer noting that the Bible is the most popular book ever. That means all the people who own a bible would be attending the film – an error that many other film producers have made with their investment in biblical films such as Darren Aronofsky's *Noah* and Ridley Scott's *Exodus: Gods and Kings* (both released in 2014).

Could it be that *The Making of "... And God Spoke"* serves to do what Christopher Guest doesn't want to be accused of doing? Maybe this film does want to make fun of its subject matter. But more than that, it is poking a big stick at those who think the Bible is easy to adapt. It's just a bunch of well-known stories. Why should that be so hard? It also presents a parable illustrating that the audience can be easily fooled and that the best thing one can do with Scripture is to admit that one cannot adapt it faithfully.

But it most likely could be that the film illustrates how little the modern American, raised on Hollywood reality, really knows what is in the Bible. At one point, when Clive the director is looking for verification of how many disciples Jesus had, he asks the cast and crew "Does anyone have a Bible?" No one does. Therefore, this film becomes the Bible for the moviegoer – the only version of Scripture the audience will see. And the audience, ultimately, sees what it wants to see. A parody.

The key words in the title of Chris Hansen's film *The Proper Care and Feeding of an American Messiah* are "an American Messiah." The main character in the film is Brian. He is initially shown playing "Bible" with his brother, Aaron, on the front porch. This game consists of Brian dressed as Jesus – white robe, long brown hair and beard, and rollerblades – trying to heal the leper, played by Aaron – similarly dressed, but not exactly the same.

Brian (Dustin Olsen), it seems through the single camera interviews that fill out much of the film, is a messiah. He quickly corrects the unseen filmmaker (who asks questions and otherwise prompts the cast) by saying that he is not "*the* messiah." He is just a messiah – one who is waiting for God to reveal to him his purpose. When prompted, Brian elaborates that the purpose is meant for him and may or may not be connected to his current stomach and bowel distress.

Aaron (Joseph Frost), Brian's dim-witted brother – who wears continually changing T-shirts that have some connection to Christianity or Jesus – provides much of the comedic relief as he so clearly idolizes his brother. Brian's wife, Cecilia (Heather Henry), seems only to be concerned that Brian is able to pay the cable bill and keep her in *Jerry Springer* five times a day. The third of the team is Brian's sister, Miriam (Ellen Dolan). Miriam is seen hiding money in a coffee can.

Throughout the film, we are introduced to Brian's method for seeking out his special purpose as a messiah. He becomes convinced that his purpose is to tell people what to do – more specifically, to tell people what is wrong with them. This illustrates a typically American version of what religion spends most of its time doing: telling everyone what they are doing wrong. He tells a woman with a short skirt to dress more modestly; he tells a body-builder to stop using steroids and he gets punched for it. But mostly, he sits around the house while his sister goes to work to make money to support the family.

His one effort to make some money is to go down to a local lake and set up a baptism stand – much like a kid's lemonade stand. He will baptize anyone for a dollar-eighteen. Much less than what they presume others would baptize for. When the narrator questions Brian on how he came up with the dollar-eighteen price, he said other churches would charge a dollar-twenty-five … probably. When Aaron chimes in with how they could charge 99 cents, Brian quickly puts that down by saying "We're not giving God away."

This exchange at the baptism stand indicates two things: the idea that a baptism would be monetized; and at the same time, a baptism would have value. Maybe a little over a dollar, but it still would have value. This reflects what mainline churches often get caught up in: monetizing grace. Who would blame the poor guy for wanting to get in on the scam?

Throughout the film, Brian deals with stomach-aches and bowel problems. This seems to be an ongoing thorn in the flesh for this messiah. Perhaps this reflects on the constant prayer of the apostle Paul, who in II Corinthians 12:7–9 said:

> To keep me from becoming conceited because of these surpassingly great revelations, there was given me a thorn in my flesh, a messenger of Satan, to torment me. Three times I pleaded with the Lord to take it away from me. But he said to me, "My grace is sufficient for you, for my power is made perfect in weakness."

Or it could be an allusion to I Samuel 5:6 where God afflicted the people of Ashdod with hemorrhoids. Yet, Brian just creates another way to monetize his ailment. He begins to sell "Aunt Acids" to passers-by. This is not successful. He determines that he must get his message out and that way he can discern his special purpose in life. This will have to be a rally. He determines that he must secure the civic auditorium and hold his rally to introduce to the region that he is their regional messiah. He never really gives us a definition of what he means by messiah. It becomes clear that he doesn't actually know what he means. He just is reflecting on what he believes God told him to do.

This is similar to how we are striving after a purpose in life. As odd as Brian and his tactics are, he is still seeking a very common and worthwhile goal. He is trying to discern his purpose in life. To get money for the requisite T-shirts and rental of the hall, he must get money together. Since the baptism gig didn't provide enough money – only five dollars, but that came from Miriam, who placed the bill under the bench for them to find – the three of them set out to go door-to-door selling home cleansing. That is, Brian will let out a vibration that will cleanse the home of bad feelings.

The only door to open to Miriam, Aaron, and Brian is one that is overrun with three unseen demons. The owner of the home (Tony Hale) offers to pay 35 dollars to get the home cleansed. After he offers his exorcising guests some lemonade, he even taunts the invisible trespassers that their time in the house will soon be over. The names of his trespassers are recognizable demonic names – except for the female; its name is Amy and he's okay with her staying. Brian and his team leave without drinking their lemonade.

This sequence echoes in an odd way the actions of Christ when summoned to expel the demons from the man in the cemetery. At Christ's command, the demons revealed their name to be "Legion, for we are many." The scene is somewhat sad in that Brian found a man who truly needed the messiah. But Brian, who is just *a* messiah, can only send a weak vibe before declaring that they are done. Here was a demon-possessed man, but the wrong messiah came to the door. Such is the life of Brian.

The T-shirts are next to be ordered for the rally. Brian wanted the shirt to say "Suffer the Children to Come Unto Me" over an open hand. This proves to be way too expensive. Ultimately they get it down to four words over an open hand that says "Will Suffer the Children."

When the shirts finally arrive, it turns out that they say "The Children Will Suffer" wrapped around a closed fist. Brian is incensed that Aaron approved the printing when the printer called earlier in the week. Aaron serves as a dim-witted punching-bag for Brian's rants. He takes it with what appears to be genuine humility. A gentle soul – dim, but gentle.

The venue calls and demands upfront payment for renting the hall for the rally. They don't have the money. Miriam chooses this time to pack up, take her coffee can filled with money, and head to the bus station to get a ride to California.

When three days pass, they finally notice that Miriam is gone. They rush to the bus station to find that she has been waiting to buy a ticket for three days. When Brian finally admits that he depends on her, she offers to give him the money for the rally. This mirrors the days in the grave for

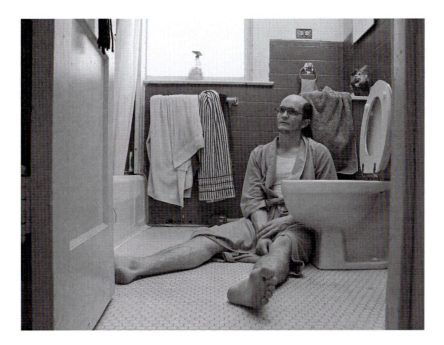

Figure 16.2 When his plans for becoming the American Messiah begin to collapse around him, Brian (Dustin Olson) retreats to his sanctuary for meditation. *The Proper Care and Feeding of an American Messiah*, Theoretical Entertainment, 2006. Image provided with kind permission of writer/director Christopher J. Hansen.

Jesus. Here, as in those two incidents in Scripture, the messiah team of Brian, Aaron, and Miriam is resurrected.

Brian buys a badge and gun to give to Aaron to make him the official security guard. When Miriam sounds alarmed, Brian assures her that the gun isn't loaded. Miriam, in honor of the rally, has sewn a special robe for Brian to wear. Once at the center, they worry about how many people will have seen their dubious TV commercial for the rally or will respond to the fliers they handed out.

When backstage jitters arise, Brian has a fear that he isn't hearing anything from God about his special purpose. When the filmmaker prompts him to elaborate, Brian adds that he thought God would give him the words to say before he goes out in front of the audience. But right then, he has nothing. Then Aaron gives him some wisdom:

Aaron: Maybe God is waiting till the last moment. Like you sometimes wait to the last moment to do stuff. Important stuff.
Brian: Like when?
Aaron: Like when you have to go to the potty.
Brian: That's true.

When he goes out onto the stage, Brian sees that only three people are there, and they appear to be asleep. As Aaron counts the people in the audience by lazily pointing his gun, it accidentally goes off and the bullet hits Brian.

At the hospital, the doctor notes that Brian could've died. Even though they all think he's talking about the bullet, the doc corrects them. The bullet just nicked his bowel and dislodged a mass that Brian subsequently expelled. It's that mass – which has been irritating him all through the film – that could've killed Brian. So, Aaron's firing of the gun saved the messiah.

As Brian is wheeled outside, he notices that there is a bunch of happy people carrying signs and cheering the messiah. Only, they mean Aaron is the messiah. As one of the demonstrators says, Aaron saved Brian so that means Aaron's special purpose was to save the messiah and that makes Aaron the messiah. Also, the crowd reinterprets the mislabeled T-shirts. Its slogan reads "The Children Will Suffer" without Aaron the messiah.

Brian doesn't accept the demotion. Aaron delights in it.

All film-making is intentional. That is, whatever is selected as the form of the film, the genre, the style, and the purpose are all part of the film because the filmmakers intended for them to be as they are. Even if there are mistakes or serendipitous moments, these are allowed to be in the final version of the film. Each of these filmmakers chose the mockumentary style for specific reasons. In both of these films, the simplicity of Scripture is at stake. "*… And God Spoke*" gives us the efforts of a group of filmmakers who don't know anything about the Bible other than that it is a popular book and has some stories that they vaguely remember. In *An American Messiah*, Hansen the director gives us an earnest search by an incompetent who by luck or pure happenstance discovers God's grace in his search for an ultimate messiah-worthy purpose.

As we consider the reasons anyone would choose to do a mockumentary we can see that it is much the same for those who choose to shoot a documentary. Both see the form as revealing a sense of what is real, what is true, what is bad, or what is good. Both count on an audience that would be prompted by such stylistic and formalist cues as shaky cameras, earnest speeches delivered to the audience and, long and embarrassing pauses that reveal the weakness of character. In the end, each film offers a glance at people who found a measure of success in their efforts. Brian finds his purpose as Aaron's John the Baptist. Marv and Clive find their worst film project becomes an unexpected cult favorite.

Yet each film, in its own way, also speaks about God's grace. As the filmmakers Marv and Clive of "*… And God Spoke*" sincerely seek to make a Bible film they find that they fail in front of a window ever open on all that is good and all that is rotten in their film-making process. As Brian and his "A-posse-les" of two seek to find his messianic purpose, they find a window on the good and the bad of whatever they do. The mockumentary form is effective in this way: it allows the fiction film-maker to explore a subject without mocking it, but instead offers a way to celebrate it in all its successes and failures and in both cases to see how God's film of their lives will work its way out.

Notes

1 Craig Hight, "Mockumentary," in *Encyclopedia of Humor Studies* (ed. Salvatore Attardo) (Sage Publications, 2014), 515–516.
2 Jane Roscoe and Craig Hight, *Faking It: Mock-Documentary and the Subversion of Factuality* (Manchester University Press, 2001), 47.
3 Gary Moskowitz, "*What Would Jesus Buy?*" *Mother Jones* (November 22, 2007).

Conclusion

Comedy, Eucharist, and Wedding Feast

The incognito God travels the road to Emmaus and meets up with two baffled disciples, Cleopas and an unnamed friend who are trying to make sense of all the events that have happened in Jerusalem. The man Jesus, whom they thought would redeem Israel, died, but then some of their women astounded them, saying that He was alive. As the two men wrestle with the meaning of it all, a stranger walks up.

The story in the Gospel of Luke offers rich comedy. The men are unable to recognize that it is Jesus who joined them and asked what they were conversing about. Astounded, they ask, are you the only one visiting Jerusalem unaware of everything that has been happening? And Jesus answers with one of the most understated comic bits: "What things?" He asked, assuredly with a wink and a smile. They still don't get it and burst out with all the facts they know. What really amazes these two oblivious chauvinists is that the women reported an empty tomb, and when others checked it out, "It was exactly as the women had said!"

Jesus shakes His head and looks at these foolish fellows; then He unwinds the history of Moses and the prophets that led up to this day. Coming to a village, Jesus pretends to be going on and they urge Him to linger, as it is getting late. Reclining at table, Jesus takes the bread, blesses it, and gives it to them. Suddenly, they get the comedy. Their eyes are opened and they recognize Him – then He vanishes from their sight. "Wow," they say, "Were not our hearts burning when he spoke to us?" And they run back to Jerusalem and relate their joy to the others. Then Jesus Himself appears, and when the startled disciples can't believe, Jesus shows His hands and feet and then says, "Have you anything to eat?" No one realized that Jesus would show up, but He does and He continues the feast, one, we believe, not only with fish, but with much laughter. It is in eating that He joins us on our journeys.

Few films follow the theme of "it was a dark and stormy night" into comedy as much as Danish director Gabriel Axel *Babette's Feast* (1987). Viewing the film as a divine comedy is not as farfetched as it might seem at first bite. The Academy Award-winning film has been duly analyzed as a transcendental and sacramental film, but its place in the canon of comedies seems more suspect.

Adapted from a short story by Isak Dinesen, *Babette's Feast* offers a truly marvelous ending for a comedy, with the biblical imagery of a feast, a celebration of a community of cranky old people transformed by wine and food, and a gaggle of "gags" that invite us to look at it as the apotheosis of divine film comedies. Even Koheleth, the depressing author of Ecclesiastes' futility of life, recognizes both that there is a time to laugh and that "bread is made for laughter, and wine gladdens life" (Ecclesiastes 10:19). Eating and drinking together are grounds for comedy.

Even the story's origin has a comic touch of irony. Dinesen had a bet with a friend that she couldn't get published in the *Saturday Evening* Post and quickly composed this short story. She had been advised "write about food [because] Americans are obsessed with food." Ironically while the *Post* rejected it, it was unexpectedly picked up by the *Ladies Home Journal*.

The setting of a cold and grey Jutland fits the introduction of the pious 19th-century sect of an ascetic Lutheran pastor. He preaches biblical ideals such as "For mercy and truth have met together and righteousness and bliss have kissed one another," but the piety of his leadership seems to emphasize truth and righteousness.

His two elderly maiden daughters, Martine (Birgitte Federspiel) and Filippa (Bodil Kjer), have served their devout father and his austere sect with fidelity and self-sacrifice since they were young and beautiful. They are even named after Protestant Reformers, Martin Luther and Philip Melanchthon. In their beginnings, these two beauties are the flowering fruit trees which young men have to come to church to see and woo.

The stern discipline of reading the Scriptures, congregational prayer, and the singing of lugubrious hymns – "O Jerusalem" – calls for strict obedience in the bleak and severe climate. The aging sisters dutifully practice the charity established by their father, preparing an insipid menu of dried codfish and brown ale and bread soup for the needy. The purity of their intentions is constrained by their own poverty. They give what they have and they have not much. Yet the comedy requires their bland, ascetic diet to set up the pleasures of the palate that will come with grace and abundance. A feast of the Lord will descend upon them, showing, as Mary Lea Bandy described it, "God's proof is in the culinary artist's pudding."[1]

The first half of the film reveals how these two denied themselves what the world had to offer. The temptations of romance and fame were rejected for the calling of their father, to carry on good works in his name.

The first temptation comes for the exquisitely beautiful Martine (Birgitte Federspiel, who had played Inger in Carl Dreyer's transcendental *Ordet*). A somewhat dissolute and callow military officer of the hussars,

Lorens Lowenhielm (Jarl Kulle), comes home to visit his aunt, a member of the minister's congregation, in the remote Danish coast town, where he is trying to pull his life together. He attends the small congregational meeting and upon viewing Martine is completely smitten. As he pursues her, she struggles with her response, and upon realizing the need of her father, chooses to reject his overtures and continue with the family vocation. His vision of Martine, a vision of a gentle angel and of a higher, purer life, propels him to success.

This once irresponsible captain resolves to change his life, disciplining himself to do something worthy. He shapes up and becomes an honored general, but wonders whether his devotion to a career and the emperor was even worth it. Before attending the feast, he ends up spouting out verses from Ecclesiastes, with "vanity, vanity, all is vanity" as he espies his weary, wrinkled frame in a mirror.

Filippa's suitor is the exuberant but melancholy impresario, the Roman Catholic Papin, who has escaped Paris to reassess his life in this quiet village. When he attends the same church, he is overwhelmed by the musical artistry of Filippa, stunned that he found such an artist in this isolated site. In his praise for her talent, he exclaims, "Almighty God, Thy power is without end, and Thy mercy reacheth unto the clouds! And here is a prima donna of the opera who will lay Paris at her feet."

As he receives permission to train her, he cleverly, but also imprudently, uses Mozart's witty, seductive duet from *Don Giovanni*, where the seducer attempts to win over Zerlina. The musical courtship is exquisite and yet sadly comic, as the couple sing of love, even make love, in the words of *opera buffa*. However, as the lyrics become sublimely erotic, Filippa is unnerved by her own stirrings. "I'm fearful of my joy – maestro," she confesses and chooses to stay with her father and sister. The irrepressible Papin laughs over her message of rejection and prophesies, "In Paradise, I shall know your voice again – how you will enchant the angels."

By now, both daughters have given up, either through fear or duty, what aesthetic delights the earth may have offered them.

Critic and filmmaker Paul Schrader once defined three characteristics of a transcendental style in films. He first identified an adherence to the everyday, in which ordinary people, objects, and events are shown to be illumined with spirituality. Second, he pointed to disparity, to the conflicts of the self and of the world. Third, he set these two elements into a narrative that provided stasis, a stopping of the kinetic activity and busyness of life to allow the viewer to pause and see and reflect and decide. The film up to this point has incorporated such moments, with simple images of a grocer watching from his window, still shots of a cold starry night, the quiet decisions of the two sisters to deny themselves the glittering gifts of the world in favor of obedience to a vocation to serve. The film quietly transcends the material world of Jutland.

Then comes the dark and stormy night: an orphan of the storm of the political upheaval in Paris arrives in the midst of pounding rain to knock on the door of the two elderly sisters. Babette (Stéphane Audran) is a refugee who barely escaped from the French political rioters who killed her husband and son. If tragedy is the inevitable in our lives, then comedy is the unexpected. In the cold shadow of the minister, Babette perspires in sensual colors, even altering the spare and gray look of the spinster sisters into more radiant white sacrifices. French actress Audran is deliciously cast as Babette, with her voluptuous, profuse luminosity and her golden-red hues awakening the bleak landscape with a promise of abundance.

Babette's knocking and arrival is such an unexpected blessing, one that will not be revealed until the end. In Roland Bainton's *Behold the Christ: A Portrayal in Words and Pictures*, he tells a humorous story in connection with Holman Hunt's painting of *The Light of the World*, hanging in Keble College, Oxford. Bainton explained that his daughter showed this picture to one of her little boys when he was three or four and she said: "'Now this is Jesus knocking at the door of your heart. What will you say to him?' He answered, 'By the hair of my chinny-chin-chin, you can't come in.' He had learned one response to a knock and came out with it."[2] The knock on their door perplexes the poor sisters, as Babette begs to live with them and serve them. As they receive this least of refugees, they do not realize they receive Christ. They do not realize what unique gifts she brings, namely her culinary arts from serving as the world renowned chef of the Café Anglais. The sisters teach her how to cut slices of ale bread and soak a fish. Babette allows her own kenosis, an emptying of her talents and herself to serve others.[3]

The lovely papist quietly begins to transform the lives and diet of her hosts. With the grocer, she barters with Gallic shrewdness, noting that the last bacon he had given her was rancid. She receives respect wherever she goes. Then an unlikely "miracle" occurs: Babette wins the French lottery. She asks Martine and Filippa if she may prepare a meal for the 100th anniversary of their father's birth. Reluctantly the sisters acquiesce and Babette prepares for one of the most sublime and sensuous meals ever to be shot on film.

When Babette arrived, she carried a note from Papin, who requested that the ladies help her. He shared with Filippa that "in Paradise I shall hear your voice again. There you will sing without fears or scruples ... there you will be the great artist that God meant you to be. Ah! How you will enchant the angels." And then in a postscript, he jotted down, "Babette can cook."

Babette can cook! One of the small running witty quips of the script is the lesson of Jesus on the generosity of God: "If your son asks for bread, will you give him a stone?" Our requests to God are too small; our expectations too meager. Babette comes to show how God showers abundance

Figure 17.1 Into the ascetic Lutheran community comes Babette (Stéphane Audran), giving all her gifts and resources to serve them a sumptuous taste of the abundance of God's grace and love. *Babette's Feast*, Panorama Film A/S, 1987. Author's screenshot.

upon His people. She negotiates the purchase of great delicacies, with cases of wine, quail, cheeses, fruit, meats, and turtle.

Like Peter's vision on the rooftop at Joppa, Martine has a nightmare of allowing a non-kosher meal to be used for a French "witches' Sabbath" at their humble abode, being murdered with French food. She apologizes to the small congregation that planned to gather and honor the memory of the deceased minister. The congregation has dwindled down to a querulous bunch of cantankerous senior citizens, holding old grudges and harboring old sins They agree not "to say a word about food or drink, but to purify their tongues of all delight or disgust of the senses, keeping and preserving them for the higher things of praise and thanksgiving."

As the guests arrive to celebrate the evening, one sister removes her father's portrait so he won't see what is going on. The followers remind each other not to say a single word about food and drink and mournfully sing "O Jerusalem." Bitterness and resentment have clouded the relations among these elderly saints. They may remind each other that "sins will be forgiven," but none remember the taste of such mercies. One woman who cheated on her late husband asks her lover, whom she treats with a mixture of attraction and disdain, "Will God forgive me?" Some feel like damning the church itself and only dull, perfunctory hallelujahs are recited.

But grace comes with this eucharist. Comedy comes with the unexpected gift of the feeding of the twelve who sit with each other at a gorgeous table set with crystal, china, fresh table linens, and shining silver cutlery. Then comes the banquet, the eu-*charis*-t as anticipation of the Messiah's wedding feast, inviting all sour stoics to be and to make merry.

Babette has slaved over her art and produces a culinary masterpiece. For the sectarian children who clamor for bread, she has laid out a feast. She awakes in them a yearning for life, here and hereafter. She awakes in them contradictory desires, exposing the incongruity of their ascetic holy traditions and the abundant gifts offered them.

The menu, offered at a local restaurant in Norfolk, Virginia when the film premiered at the local art cinema house, the NARO, consisted of *blinis Demidoff*, turtle soup, *cailles en sarcophage*, endive salad, cheeses, cake with candied fruit and sauce of liqueurs, grapes, figs, caviar, truffles, and all manner of sensual delights. The banquet became a love affair.

The disciples keep their oath of silence, but slowly are seduced by Babette's art. Soon their spiritual yearnings are complemented by bodily appetites. Wine and bread cannot be distinguished from the presence of God. As they hold their tongues, General Lorens, who served as an attaché in Paris, finds the meal quite extraordinary. He remembers a sumptuous meal that he had once enjoyed at the Café Anglais in Paris, where the chef was, remarkably, a woman.

As a connoisseur he recognizes the exceptional quality of the feast. "But surely," he exclaims taking a sip of the wine, "this is a Veuve Clicquot 1860!" With each drink and bite, he tastes the savory miracle of the drink and food and toasts its wonder. It serves as a running joke whenever he ejaculates the epiphany of an *anagnorisis*, the comic moment of awareness, over each delicacy: "But this *is cailles en sarcophage*!" The joke snowballs as his dour fellow celebrants have no idea of what he is speaking.

However, "righteousness and bliss lurk in the turtle soup." Grace hides in the wine. Even though a prim old lady tastes the champagne and supposes it must be some kind of lemonade, another prissy woman takes a drink of water, scrunches her face and puts down the glass, only to now choose the red wine with a broad smile. As clusters of grapes are brought out, one remembers the report of Joshua and Caleb when they brought such clusters back from the Promised Land.

The stubbornly austere participants in this holy supper begin to be transformed, first by telling stories and jokes about the minister. In one he had promised to deliver a sermon to a congregation across the river in wintertime. When the fjord froze, the minister walked on water. Truly a miracle, they declared, and then drank more wine. The comic hilarity of the experience escalates as the faithful vainly try to deny the pleasure of their eating and drinking together. The glories of this gustatory celebration are intoxicating. "Mercy and truth, dear brethren, have met together" and "righteousness and bliss have kissed one another."

Here is where the second transformation occurs. As they sup and partake of these earthly pleasures together, they not only get tipsy, but begin to confess their sins to one another and to forgive one another. Old resentments are made right; ancient barriers are broken down; old squabbling enmities erased; loves rekindled; fellowship renewed through a meal, and a glorious redemption of lost and broken communion overwhelms the table, as if Jesus Himself reminded all, "Do this in memory of me." As Alyosha dreams in *The Brothers Karamazov*, Jesus is at the wedding feast Himself and invites all to share in the feast.

At the end of the meal, the General recites one of the minister's old sermons:

> We have all of us been told that grace is to be found in the universe. But in our human foolishness and shortsightedness we imagine divine grace to be finite. For this reason we tremble. We tremble before making our choice in life, and having made it again tremble in fear of having chosen wrong. But the moment comes when our eyes are opened, and we see and realize that grace is infinite. Grace, my friends, demands nothing from us but that we shall await it with confidence and acknowledge it in gratitude. Grace, brothers, makes no conditions and singles out none of us in particular; grace takes us all to its bosom and proclaims general amnesty. See! That which we have chosen is given us, and that which we have refused is also, and at the same time, granted us. Aye, that which we have rejected is poured upon us abundantly. For mercy and truth have met together and righteousness and bliss have kissed one another!

The confession of debts and transgressions fills the little band with gladness. All receive the grace and the *agape* meal with gratitude and laughing. Babette herself rests in the exhaustion of giving all one has, of leaving this world with nothing, but having created one's art to the glory of God. At the end of the meal, the entire astonished group goes outside and circles a well, joining hands and singing an old song that now sounds new, "O Jerusalem," lustily and robustly. And the old man lifts up his hands and with a final punctuation to all, gleefully shouts "hallelujah!" After discovering that Babette has given all and will stay with them, the film ends with snow falling, and one candle in the window quietly extinguishing itself. The film deservedly won the Academy Award for Best Foreign Film in 1988.

The underlying theme of the patriarch that "mercy and truth shall lay down together and righteousness and bliss shall kiss one another" should prepare those invited to the feast for an eruption of joy. One might add the Psalmist's call "O taste and see the Lord is good." It is no wonder that Pope Francis confessed that *Babette's Feast* is his favorite movie.[4] It is a sacramental comedy that transcends and lifts a new body and spirit into the New Jerusalem. How fitting that a simple story in the *Ladies Home Journal* should evoke such awe and delight. It is but a preview of the coming attraction of the Marriage Feast of the Lamb, a time of great praising, rejoicing and laughing.

Poet W. H. Auden suggested that Christian societies should be able to produce comedies of "much greater breadth and depth" than classical ones. The Greeks divided people into two categories: those who had heroic virtues and those lesser beings fit for comedy, the fools. Christianity, with its sense of equality, says that all men and women are fools. None are righteous. All fall short of the glory of God and all fall down on their faces and butts. The higher, and more virtuous, a man may be, the further he will fall and the more laughter he will elicit.

The fertile intersection of Christian faith, humor, and film comedies radiates what theologian Peter Leithart distinguishes as "the Christian novelty."[5] In spite of the dismal official report of a humorless history, laughter sneaks into the woof and fabric of human experiences, including religious ones. Comedy resides in the biblical narratives, in the tricks and romances of its peculiar characters. Laughter is the triumph over death, over sin, and over the centripetal self.

The sub-genres of film comedy provide a means of rediscovering that victory. With parallels in biblical stories, cinematic sub-genres, from slapstick to satire, approximate spiritual insights and moral lessons. They testify to the goodness of all creation, the nature of sin in human beings, and the need and hope for redemption and transformation. They become divine comedies, not only in the aesthetic sense of having happy endings, but in the sense that they recognize something beyond human aspiration, failure, and finitude. Their themes are sacred in the sense that human activities like getting married are as sacred as monastic devotion. Eating and drinking are spiritual acts as well as ordinary ones. In them, the joy of heaven is made incarnate in the humor of earth.

Notes

1 Mary Lea Bandy, "Babettes Gaestebud," in *the Hidden God: Film and Faith* (ed. Antonio Monda and Mary Lea Bandy) (Museum of Modern Art, 2003), 177–182.
2 Roland H. Bainton, *Behold the Christ: A Portrayal in Words and Pictures* (Harper & Row, 1974), 28.
3 Philippians 2:4–11.
4 Mark Oppenheimer, "Pope Francis Has a Few Words in Support of Leisure," *New York Times* (April 26, 2013).
5 Peter J. Leithart, "The Christian Novelty," *Touchstone* (June 1, 2010).

Epilogue

In Preston Sturges' classic satire on Hollywood itself, *Sullivan's Travels* (1941), John Lloyd Sullivan (Joel McCrea) has decided that he has directed too many fluff escapist films and wants to make a socially significant "message" film about the troubles of the poor and needy. When Sullivan demands the opportunity to make a picture that comments on modern conditions – "stark realism. The problems that confront the average man!" – the studio vacillates, repeatedly asking that it might have "a little sex in it."

He resolutely seeks to preach his cinematic sermon, to hold a mirror up to life, capturing the dignity of man on this "true canvas of the suffering of humanity" (but with a little sex in it). Sturges seems to be responding to other "preachment" sermons of the time (e.g. Frank Capra's *Meet John Doe*, 1941), which had abandoned fun in favor of the message.

Instead of churning out lightweight films like *Ants in Your Pants* of 1939 that make money for the studio, Sullivan wants to direct *Brother, Where Art Thou?* (a title the Coen brothers did finally appropriate in 2000 as a comic spiritual journey!); he naïvely believes that he can learn how the common man suffers by dressing up as a hobo and taking to the road hitchhiking. His butler tries to warn him that "rich people and theorists – who are usually rich people" don't fully understand poverty. It is not the lack of riches, but is a "positive plague, virulent in itself, contagious as cholera, with filth, criminality, vice and despair as only a few of its symptoms." He offers an exemplary parable about two men who went out on such a lark and haven't been heard from since.

Nevertheless, with only a dime in his pocket, Sullivan begins his travels, his spiritual journey to empathize with his fellow man. At first, the studio executives want to make it a publicity stunt, but Sullivan escapes and stumbles into real trouble.

An aspiring and disillusioned actress, the Girl (Veronica Lake), helps the tramp Sullivan like a Good Samaritan, feeding him bacon and eggs and mocking his privileged fantasies. They eat in soup kitchens and sleep in homeless shelters, gaining a brief taste of being destitute. However, when he tries to help the poor by handing out five-dollar bills, Sullivan is unexpectedly robbed, knocked unconscious, and thrown onto a freight train, and in a very rude awakening ends up in a southern prison labor camp after assaulting a railroad worker.

Released one Sunday evening from a sweat box, barely able to stand, he is helped by a fellow prisoner to the monthly movie showing. They march, their legs in shackles, into a black church, where an articulate and caring black preacher welcomes the chain gang into his evening service (the Secretary of the NAACP, Walter White, praised the depiction of the pastor for its remarkable dignity). The pastor had cheerfully informed his congregation that they are going to have a "little entertainment" this evening. "And once again, brothers and sisters," he instructs them, "we are going to share our pleasure with some neighbors less fortunate than ourselves." The remark is explosive coming from a poor, oppressed back-woods church, yet has no irony in it, rather the bracing honesty of humility and strength. He continues:

> Won't you please clear the first three pews so they may have seats? And when they get here, I'm going to ask you once more neither by word nor by action nor look to make our guests feel unwelcome or act high-toned; for we is all equal in the sight of God. … Let him who is without sin cast the first stone. And the chains be struck from them and the lame shall leap and the blind shall see and GLORY IN THE COMING OF THE LORD! Now let's give our guests a little welcome.

With a full resonance, he leads a rousing hymn, "When Israel Was in Egypt's Land." The fresh, healthy congregation joins in the call and response chorus, as Charles Wesley would describe it, lustily: "Let my people go. Go down Moses, way down in Egypt's land." As the pastor's booming voice belts out "Then to Egypt came," the prisoners stumble in, taking off their hats, shuffling, bent over, broken. And the congregation reaffirms "Let my people go" even as the guards hold their rifles.

The movie projector starts. Sullivan sits in his pew humorless; he has forgotten how to laugh. Only when the Disney cartoon, *Playful Pluto*, is projected onto the makeshift screen, does he find himself joining all others, black and white, young and old, in hilarious laughter. He can't believe his unbridled paroxysms of delight.

Turning to a fellow prisoner, Sullivan asks, "Hey, am I laughing?" He laughs, and breaks into slap-happy hilarity. The last shot is of the church from outside, with its lights shining and the music of the organ and laughter breaking the darkness.

At the end, Sullivan sees the value of comedy, from a cartoon shown in a black church. He confesses that "there is a lot to be said for making people laugh. Did you know that that's all some people have? It isn't much, but it's better than nothing in this cockeyed caravan."

Figure 18.1 It is in the rural black church that comedy film director John Lloyd Sullivan (Joel McCrea) rediscovers the rapturous and significant gift of laughter to the world. *Sullivan's Travels*, Paramount Pictures, 1941. Author's screenshot.

We find it remarkably relevant that Sullivan's eyes were opened to the value of humor in a comic film in the midst of a church. In his movement from naïveté to desperation, he discovered what G. K. Chesterton once quipped, that "life is serious all the time, but living cannot be. You may have the solemnity you wish in your neckties, but in anything important (such as sex, death, and religion), you must have mirth or you will have madness."[1]

Learning, even religious learning, is liberated with an infusion of good laughter. Humor offers benefits in the realm of pedagogy, even as the Talmud testifies. Jokes, according to Rabbi Daniel Feldman, are abundant in the holy writings, showing that the sages not only joked, but their jokes were memorialized in the Talmud itself, offering jokes with a "*hechsher*," a kosher approval. Before beginning his lecture, one Rabbah "would open with a *milta dibidichuta*, a humorous remark. As a result, his students, notably described as '*rabanan*' (which would counter the notion that such a method is only necessary or appropriate for children) had their 'hearts opened' to learning."[2]

To laugh is to see. Like Sullivan sitting in the church watching the Disney cartoon, we finally get it. We understand that it is not just about making serious protests and preaching solemn sermons. It is about laughing in religious community, being joyful among those who are destitute, oppressed and poor in spirit.

The various sub-genres of film comedy offer such lessons. They counter the theology of Umberto Eco's villainous monk, Jorge, who poisoned the apocryphal second volume of Aristotle's *Poetics* that suggested that God laughed. For the angry and solemn cleric, laughter connoted weakness, corruption, pride, and the weakness of the flesh. It was the devil's tool. C. S. Lewis' devil held the opposite opinion, and discouraged laughter because it promoted such undesirable tendencies as "charity, courage, contentment, and many other evils."[3]

As theologian Jolyon Mitchell recognized that films "can act as points of transcendence or even channels of revelation," it is crucial to attend to what the comic films tell us.[4] While the laughter of slapstick, romantic and screwball comedies ushers in recognition of humanity's imperfection and celebrates humility, the darker categories of satire and transgressive comedy attack the folly of earthly authority and power. They offer opportunities to hone our senses of humor, to recognize the smallness of being human (as in Steve Martin's summon to "get little") and not to take ourselves less gravely. There's too much solemnity about religious matters, Lewis said in an interview with the Billy Graham Association.

A distinguished friend and former colleague, Professor John Morreall of the College of William and Mary, ferreted out the presence, or lack, of laughter in the Bible.[5] Challenging the work of scholars like Hershey Friedman, Conrad Hyers, and Elton Trueblood who found abundant examples of irony, sarcasm, wordplay, and humorous images and situations, Morreall identified what he saw as mostly negative characteristics of humor.[6] He closed his article asking "if Jesus intended to amuse his listeners with [comic lines], why did Christians not notice that for almost 2,000 years?" One response is that fresh evidence points to the fact that Christians did notice the humor from the beginning; so much so that caveats were issued against excessive laughter.[7]

Morreall is echoing the very reason why theologian Paul Tillich asked, "Is our lack of joy due to the fact that we are Christians, or to the fact we are not sufficiently Christian?" He later declares that most Christians are "surrounded by an air of heaviness, of oppressive sternness, of lack of humor and irony about themselves."[8] It is this danger that compelled us to write this book and ask what might be some final benefits to this cross-fertilization of biblical narratives, film comedies, and laughter.

One of Solomon's proverbs serves an aperitif as he connects laughter to our general well-being. A happy heart makes a joyous face. The wise man recognized a correlation between what we put on our faces and what we practice in our hearts. Humor offers physiological benefits, splashing one with humidity, even as Mark Twain's old man "laughed loud and joyously, shook up the details of his anatomy from head to foot, and ended by saying that such a laugh was money in a man's pocket, because it cut down the doctor's bills like everything."[9] A cheerful heart is good medicine (of course, Proverbs 31 also advises that when one's life is miserable, one take strong drink – all this before discussing the ideal woman).

The laughter and wisdom coming from this experience also work as an antidote to pride, to taking ourselves too solemnly. They usher us into the world of others, of strange characters in sacred texts as well as comic fictions, and both direct us outside of ourselves. They are centrifugal rather than centripetal, throwing us into a world to see comedy rather than mucking about in the morass of our own petty concerns. An immersion into this playful cross-fertilization of biblical narratives, film sub-genres, and comedy, combining such unlike categories, gives that vantage point from which we can look at ourselves. As Peter Berger saw it, this redeemed human act of laughter offers a sign of transcendence. When Scriptures and film comedy hold up the mirror to vain lookers, it can shake their spectators awake. Laughter enables one to live in light of eternity, recognizing that the sting of death is not the final act. The *Divine Comedy* takes one through infernos and purgatories, only to find a guide like Beatrice ready to usher us into paradise. And here, the Christian hears all the laughter of the heavens ringing in her ears. Such a fuller perspective does not deny the pain of tears, but affirms something greater than tears, laughter. As some martyrs were able to laugh and jest at death, so we receive a perspective that transcends all our fears and sins.

The promise of "filling our mouths with laughter" may be more aptly set in the next world, but these comedies showcase a preview of coming hilarity and festivity. To understand through God's perspective, "a full mouth" connotes complete understanding, which is not possible in this world. Once history has culminated in its divine ending, one can look back and laugh, seeing the divine plan.

Mixing humor, biblical narratives, and film sub-genres also provides triangulated perspectives. One can see in the foolish things of the world divine jokes and incongruities that confound the wise. One sees in weakness a confounding of the strong.[10] Reading biblical narratives alongside viewing comedy films opens up both, juggling our perspectives to see the humor in a situation and the presence of God in a Christmas movie about a little boy, burglars, and the Old Man next door.

Finally, we are not claiming that this laughter will cure diseases, save souls, or stop wars. Laughter, like every other good gift, is tainted by the Fall and our own selfishness and malice. It needs redeeming just as our appetites do. We are claiming, however, that it will prepare us for being posed for surprises in God's universe. It will make us more like the saint of sunshine, G. K. Chesterton, and lighten our journey of faith.

At the 68th annual Al Smith Dinner in New York City in 2013, Cardinal Timothy Dolan, Archbishop of New York, proclaimed that a "sense of humor comes from faith, faith that everything is in God's providential hands, a faith that frees us up to laugh." He explained in his benediction that his "pleasant task is simply to thank God – thank God as we leave laughing, placing our guests, our honoree, our speaker, our board, our children that we love and help, the city that we love, our country we cherish, our families to which we're now going to return safely into His providential hands."

Thus we echo the prologue of Sturges' *Sullivan's Travels* as our epilogue. "To the memory of those who made us laugh: the motley mountebanks, the clowns, the buffoons, in all times and nations, whose efforts have lightened our burden a little, this picture is affectionately dedicated." We celebrate those divine film comedies that have made us think and explore our faith and send us *ad fontes*, back to the fountain of our laughter and love. We hope to join Kierkegaard's man who stood before the gods and critics with his one request – to have the laugh on his side – and in response, heard only divine laughter. As King Lear reminded us in the twilight of his tragedy, "so we'll live and pray, and sing, and tell old tales, and laugh at gilded butterflies ... and take upon us the mystery of things, as if we were God's spies." And yet we are spies, if we truly see beyond, of a divine comedy.

Notes

1 G. K. Chesterton, *Lunacy and Letters* (ed. Dorothy Collins) (Sheed and Ward, 1958), 97.
2 Rabbi Daniel Feldman, "Does God Have a Sense of Humor?" *Jewish Action* (Summer 2013), online at www.ou.org/jewish_action/05/2013/does-god-have-a-sense-of-humor/ (accessed October 10, 2015).
3 C. S. Lewis, "Epistle 11," in *The Screwtape Letters* (Macmillan, 1974), 50.
4 Jolyon Mitchell, "Theology and Film," in *The Modern Theologians: An Introduction to Modern Theology since 1918* (ed. David Ford, with Rachel Muers) (Blackwell, 2005), 736–759.
5 John Morreall, "Sarcasm, Irony, Wordplay, and Humor in the Hebrew Bible," *HUMOR: International Journal of Humor Research* 14 (2001), 293–301; John Morreall, "Biblical Humor," in *Encyclopedia of Humor Studies* (ed. Salvatore Attardo) (Sage Publications, 2014), 80–83.
6 T. D. Friedman, "Humor in the Hebrew Bible," *HUMOR: International Journal of Humor Research* 13 (2001), 257–285; Elton Trueblood, *The Humor of Christ* (Harper & Row, 1975); Conrad Hyers, *And God Created Laughter: The Bible as Divine Comedy* (John Knox Press, 1987); Conrad Hyers, *The Comic Vision and the Christian Faith* (Pilgrim Press, 1981), 11.
7 See Terry Lindvall, *God Mocks: A History of Religious Satire from the Hebrew Prophets to Stephen Colbert* (New York University Press, 2015).
8 Paul Tillich, *The New Being* (Charles Scribner's Sons, 1955), 142–143.
9 Julia Wilkins and Amy Janel Eisenbraun, "Humor Theories and the Physiological Benefits of Laughter," *Holistic Nursing Practice* 23 (November/December 2009), 349–354; Mark Twain, *The Adventures of Tom Sawyer* (Modern Library, 1940), 208.
10 I Corinthians 1:27–28.

Index